365 MEDITATIONS FOR WOMEN

Jean Beaven Abernethy
Carol Goll Burris
Alice Joyce Davidson
Mari González
Martha Whitmore Hickman
Mary Ruth Howes
Ruth C. Ikerman
Vera Chapman Mace
Barbara Owen
Dorothy Sickal
Phyllis Tickle
Käaren Witte

Abingdon Press
Nashville

365 MEDITATIONS FOR WOMEN

This book is printed on acid-free paper.

Library of Congress Cataloging-in-Publication Data

365 meditations for women / Phyllis Tickle . . . [et al.].
    p. cm.
ISBN 0-687-41886-0 (alk. paper)
    1. Women—Prayer-books and devotions—English. 2. Devotional calendars. I. Tickle, Phyllis.
BV4844.A14
1989
242'.643—dc19   89-194
                                                                         CIP

MANUFACTURED BY THE PARTHENON PRESS AT
NASHVILLE, TENNESSEE, UNITED STATES OF AMERICA

Foreword

What is *365 Meditations for Women*? It is a book of meditations for each day of the year. It is a collection of personal spiritual writings by twelve different women, each of whom has contributed one month's worth of meditations. Thus this book is not only a journey through the year but also a series of encounters with twelve women and their individual ways of relating to God and to life.

The meditations in this book follow no set pattern. Some writers incorporate phrases or selections from Scripture; some end each meditation with a prayer; one includes a poem for each day. But in their various styles, these writers share common themes: a strong sense of values, belief in God as the source and meaning of life, and recognition of the value inherent in daily meditation.

Because the writers tend to begin and end their segments, you will have a real sense of the beginning and end of each month. The contributors themselves represent various age groups and life-styles. Among them are women who are single, married, widowed, and divorced; women who work primarily outside the home, inside the home, or who are retired; daughters, mothers, grandmothers, and great-grandmothers; residents of the East Coast, the West Coast, and the heartland; natives of China and England.

It is our hope that the discipline of daily meditation and the thoughts that will be triggered by these particular pages will make every day more meaningful for you.

About the writers:

Jean Beaven Abernethy has written three books and before her retirement was a lecturer in family relations and child development at Douglass College of Rutgers University.

She served as editor of and was a contributor to the original *Meditations for Women,* which was published by

Abingdon Press in 1947. She lives in Stanford, California.

Carol Goll Burris is a freelance writer and public speaker. Her writing has appeared in *Vital Christianity, Ligourian,* and *The United Methodist Reporter,* among others. Her writing has been influenced by her myasthenia gravis, a neuromuscular disease. She lives in Woodburn, Indiana.

Alice Joyce Davidson counts among her published writings *Because I Love You, Loving One Another,* the Alice in Bibleland series, and *Christmas Wrapped in Love.* A good deal of her writing is done in poetic form. She lives in Cincinnati, Ohio.

Mari González has collaborated on two books and has been a newspaper reporter, a managing editor, a UPI stringer, and a radio news director. She writes youth curricula and meditations as well as inspirational material for magazine publication. She lives in Teton, Idaho.

Martha Whitmore Hickman has written books for children and adults, including *Lost and Found, When James Allen Whitaker's Grandfather Came to Stay,* and *When Can Daddy Come Home?* She has taught creative writing classes and has worked with children in a variety of settings. She lives in Nashville, Tennessee.

Mary Ruth Howes is senior editor at Guideposts Books in New York. She has written devotional material and has been an editor in the field of religious publishing for many years. She grew up in China, the daughter of missionary parents. She now lives in Jersey City, New Jersey.

Ruth C. Ikerman, a freelance writer, has written fifteen devotional books for Abingdon Press and articles for a variety of publications and has reviewed books in the field of family relations for the *Los Angeles Times.* She has served for many years as a volunteer worker in her church. She lives in Redlands, California.

Vera Chapman Mace has cowritten many books on the subject of marriage. A native of England, she organized the first training course for marriage counselors. With her husband, David, she founded the Association of Couples in Marriage Enrichment (ACME). She lives in Black Mountain, North Carolina.

Barbara Owen has written books for children and adults, as well as magazine stories and articles. Both a writer and a writing teacher, she is a frequent lecturer at schools, libraries, and writers' conferences. She lives in Annapolis, Maryland.

Dorothy E. Sickal is a minister, speaker, and writer. She is a coauthor with her daughter, Gloria Gaither, and her granddaughters of *Hands Across the Seasons*. She lives in Alexandria, Indiana.

Phyllis A. Tickle is director of St. Luke's Press in Memphis and senior editor of fiction at Peachtree Publishers in Atlanta. She is the author of *Final Sanity, What the Heart Already Knows,* and *The Tickle Papers*. She lives in Lucy, Tennessee.

Käaren Witte is a journalist and the author of *Flying Solo* and *Great Leaps in a Single Bound*. She has traveled extensively in the Middle East, has been a singles' director, and is former editor of *Solo Magazine*. She lives in Tulsa, Oklahoma.

Contents

Slowly Awakening

PHYLLIS TICKLE

JANUARY 1   **THE HOLY NAME OF OUR LORD
JESUS CHRIST**

The year begins today, and I like beginnings. We all do. I like also the quietness of unmarked calendars and the gentleness of a holiday that wants little of me as a helpmeet—that allows me to interrupt routine and rest in pleasure without having to be its source for those around me. There are not many such days in my year and no other holidays, so I will hoard this one and distill its thoughts into memories that will sustain the winter . . .

. . . which, of course, is what Mary did on this day so many centuries ago when she and Joseph took the young child into the temple for the rites of circumcision and naming. "But Mary kept all of these things in her heart and pondered them," Luke says. "And," he adds, "when they had performed all things according to the law of the Lord, they returned into Galilee, to their own city of Nazareth. And the child grew and waxed strong in spirit, filled with wisdom: and the grace of God was upon him" (Luke 2:51-52, paraphrased).

. . . which has probably always been so for us, because what women ponder, their children and the future tend to become . . .

. . . which is why this day, of all days in the year, most calls

me to prayer, most demands of me the deepest reverence for
the work of being "woman."

TO BLOOM

The window in front of my kitchen desk faces north into
the clean light of new snow and open fields. Between me and
the cold beyond the window runs a broad sill that my
husband Sam fashioned years ago of redwood and on which
sit nine unmatched pots of African violets. They are lush now
with blooms, as if each were personally frantic to outdo its
fellows on the sill. The rivalry of their color is so keen, in fact,
that it makes the frozen winter beyond the window seem at
times to be only a backdrop for their preening.

Watching them, enjoying them, even caring for them this
morning, I know it is their determined assertion of
themselves that makes me keep and treasure them. Were any
one of them to turn suddenly and be less sure of its urgency
for blooming in this winter room, then the whole would
shrink by that much. The sill would become only a sill, and
the snow beyond only a winter.

Cautioned constantly by our times and by other faiths to
scorn ambition and deplore the self, I look at the violets and I
am taught another way. "O, Lord, give me the courageous-
ness to bloom."

JANUARY 3 **A PROMISE**

I finished rereading *Adam Bede* last night for the
who-knows-how manyth time now. Always, upon setting it
down, I am amazed anew at the strength of Eliot's insistence
that family is our greatest burden in life. Her thesis is that
God gives us as our nearest associates those who are most like
us and, therefore, most repugnant to us. I wouldn't argue
with that position at all; nor would I argue with her corollary

that in the church community God traditionally has restored us by giving us as our nearest those who share with us the same aims and affections of the soul. But I would add an update from where I sit, 125 years later, on this cold, cold morning.

In a world so unlike that of George Eliot and Adam Bede, in the raucous life of modern culture that denies most of us any significant or extended family, in an urbanization that requires that we share physical space with disparate human beings who are as unlike us in every way as they are unlike each other, but who are always in the way of our careers and/or our comfort—in today's social structure, in other words, I am isolated, alone in a land without mirrors to reflect me. It is this that drives today's Christian toward the communion of the saints. It is the promise of spiritual similarities that draws contemporary believers into Christian community, and it is that same promise that each of us, once there, must fulfill for our fellows who have been likewise drawn.

To the extent that I ever make resolutions, mine this year is to pray that I may fulfill my part of that pact, that I may give as well as receive within that holy communion.

JANUARY 4   **BACK TO CLASS**

Sam junior regards school as a mixed blessing, to say the least, a point that is much on my mind at the moment. Today is the first day of classes after the Christmas break, and the morning began with the absolute chaos of first-day-back emotions.

Now Sam junior is a very bright kid who spends his holidays, when he's not at work, in reading and in building everything the imagination can contrive. Thus his remark this morning that "school sure does get in the way of learning anything important" was not without some real basis in fact. His father, however, chose to mutter some wisdom about random education always being easier to swallow than formal education. Because it was first-day and feelings were high, Sam junior refused to let it alone. Instead he asserted with enthusiasm that while it might be random, his reading and building and experimenting would provide him all he needed to know quite nicely, and thank you very much.

Sam senior never even missed a bite of cereal over that one. "There are things you need to know and there are things we need for you to know. Don't ever confuse the two. So let's haul it out of here and get going" . . . which is one reason for authority that I sometimes tend to forget . . . that, and how much we rob ourselves and the kingdom when we do forget.

JANUARY 5   **EVE OF THE EPIPHANY**

The scriptures appointed in the Episcopal lectionary for reading today are among my favorite: Hebrews 11:32–12:2. Or, to be more accurate, I should say that the verses appointed for today are the concluding ones (for it is the Eve of Epiphany) of a whole, favorite section of Holy Writ: Hebrews 11:1–12:2, the "Roll Call of the Heroes."

Broken into four sections, the Roll Call has provided the assigned lectionary readings ever since Holy Name on New Year's Day. But, as is true for so many of us, it is the last words of the selection that most move me: "Wherefore seeing we also are compassed by so great a cloud of witnesses, let us lay aside every weight, and the sin which doth so easily beset us, and let us run with patience the race that is set before us" (Hebrews 12:1).

Tonight at midnight Christmas liturgically ends with the coming of the Three Kings—with the revelation of the promise to the Gentiles and their adoration of it in incarnate form. On such a day, surrounded by such words, my heart sings, sure that for now at least I can run with gratitude as well as with patience.

JANUARY 6   **THE FEAST OF THE EPIPHANY**

"Epiphany" as a word and as a holy day always makes me think of Robert Hayden. Some years ago he and I were both teaching at a writers' conference at Vanderbilt University. Although I had long admired his poetry, we had never met before, and I was looking forward to the opportunity.

The Vanderbilt campus lends itself more to walking than to any other mode of transportation, and I was walking away from the opening session on Sunday afternoon when I heard footsteps behind me on the asphalt path. I turned and, from his pictures, recognized Robert Hayden. What the pictures had not told me was that he was almost blind. Not being sure how else to begin, I simply said, "Mr. Hayden, I'm Phyllis Tickle. May I walk with you?" He smiled, and we began the first of the many walks we would take together that week.

Our last walk, however, was the one that mattered. Classes were done and I was in the campus bookstore, shopping, as I always do, for some pen or pencil to take home with me as a talisman. "Do you do paper also?" he voice said from behind me.

I grinned, sheepish over having been caught at what is basically a juvenile trick. "No," I said, "just pens and pencils."

"I do paper as well," he said, gesturing toward the loose sheets and two pads in his basket. He looked as uncomfortable with his admission as I felt with mine.

We paid our bills, left the store, and headed across campus one last time. We were almost to the campus gates when he stopped in the middle of the path and laid his hand on my arm to stop me as well. "You do know," he said, with all the earnestness of his huge body and full voice, "you do understand that I always thought I could be a better poet if only I could find the right tools to buy . . . that that's why I do it?" I nodded, stunned by his candor and humility. "Is it that way with you?" he probed, and I nodded again, too near to tears now to use my voice. "Strange," he said, beginning to walk again, but more slowly. "Strange and sad . . . that

15

we spend so much of our allotted time thinking that tools will make the difference. They won't, you know. It's not about tools." Ten months later he was dead.

That moment became "epiphany" for me, its perfect definition . . . the arresting frame of insight, the quiet clink of the round die into the round bore, the sharp rush that says, "Of course," while the rest of the outside world goes on unaware. When it comes to us, it is simple, final, surgically clean; only we are different.

It was so on that last walk, it has been so in all the years since, and I believe it to have been so in Bethlehem of Judea in the days of Herod the king.

JANUARY 7   **THE DAYBOOK**

Now that the children have been back in school long enough for me to have gotten the holiday detritus raked out and the house more or less clean, there was time this morning for me to perform the annual ritual of the daybook. With all the private flourishes and anticipation that attend a true ritual, I sit down in early January each year and transcribe from loose slips of paper and notes all the talks I have agreed to make during the coming year, all the deadlines I have agreed to meet, all the conferences and professional shows I have been asked to attend. Anything that reduces random messages to a system always gives me enormous satisfaction; certainly this one in particular does.

But the daybook has another use as well. One day is all we ever have, any of us. One moment, really, is all that is granted; and the kingdom of God is bought with the "now" and not with "tomorrow." So the daybook gives me somewhere to store tomorrow, somewhere other than in my consciousness or in this moment's purposes.

As I finish my transposing and close the daybook, I pray for the grace to leave tomorrow inside its pages and for the wisdom to spend well the protected now.

JANUARY 8   **A LESSON**

Rebecca, who is thirteen and just beginning to understand the pilgrimage, killed a ladybug last night. She was fumbling for the light switch in her bathroom when she unknowingly stepped on the thing, but it was not until this morning that she realized what she had done. Like her father, who taught her most of what she knows, Rebecca is a grower and tender, especially of plants and especially in the winter when she feels that they most need her ministrations. As a result, her bathroom is a kind of intensive care unit for every cutting, weak bulb, and struggling philodendron we have. Rebecca's concern during the winter routinely includes the maintenance of a large number of ladybugs whose duty it is to help her keep the patients free of mites, spiders, and aphids. It was therefore a fellow-healer whom she killed inadvertently in the dark and whose carcass she discovered this morning when she bent over to pick up her bathmat.

It is typical of Rebecca that she was at first annoyed with herself and then, by the time she left for school a little while ago, philosophical. "I'll tell you one thing," she said to me as she headed out the door. "It was a heck of a lot easier living when I thought I was like that ladybug and God was like me . . . just so much bigger that he didn't see us until he found us lying around dead where he'd stepped on us."

"How do you figure that?" I asked her, because I couldn't remember this part of being at the front end of things.

"Fate's easier than faith to live with, sweetheart!" she said, somewhat tartly, somewhat wearily, leaving me here with the shell of a crushed ladybug on my desk and a laughter in my heart that will warm me all this day and probably for many more.

JANUARY 9   **A SENSE OF PLACE**

Every literary critic and college English teacher will assert that Southern writers are informed more by locale than by any other theme or influence. The professional term for this phenomenon is "a sense of place," and I bought into it years ago in undergraduate courses and long before I had any notion of ever becoming that other professional thing, "a Southern writer." Yet now that I have more or less done just that, I am still persuaded of the accuracy of the critical rhetoric on this point as well as of the potency of the force to which it refers. This is especially true for me on January 9 each year.

The Episcopal lectionary for January 9 includes in its propers Psalm 122, the one we all learned as children and loved to recite:

> I was glad when they said unto me, "Let us go into the house of the Lord."
> Our feet shall stand within thy gates, O Jerusalem.
> Jerusalem is builded as a city that is compact together:
> ....
> Pray for the peace of Jerusalem: they shall prosper that love thee.
> Peace be within thy walls, and prosperity within thy palaces.
> For my brethren and companions' sake, I will now say, Peace be within thee.

If there is anything at all that we—Southerner and Northerner and Westerner alike—should have learned from these spiritual forebears of ours, from the psalmist and his singers, it is certainly that "sense of place" informed their lives even more constantly than it has ever informed any of ours, and under even greater adversity—except that "sense of place" for them lay more in their faith than in any particular piece of ground or in any nation or body politic.

Such an expansion doesn't seem to me to be a bad one to emulate. When place becomes a metaphor and our faith becomes a basis for our citizenship, then Christian hearts too can be glad and sing to each other across the barriers of politics and geography and station, can sing of a kingdom compact together, within whose walls there is peace and within whose palaces there is prosperity.

JANUARY 10   **ABOUT MONEY**

We had a Vestry meeting last night, the first of the new year. As usual, it was about the parish budget . . . or it was until I unwittingly broke it up.

We had been at it for almost an hour when one of the men muttered, "I just don't understand about money!"

"I do," I said. "It's more intimate than sex." Dead silence followed, then the relief of laughter . . . partly embarrassed, partly relaxed, because now we would quit and go home.

But I had meant what I said (although I had not meant to say it in just that way). Any writer will tell you that the average American will discuss his or her entire love life, both real and imagined, with a perfect stranger, but that that same American will never willingly reveal his or her fiscal situation. In America, we are our money. It is truer to us than a mirror, at least for looking at ourselves. When our pockets are empty and our bank accounts gone, we feel a loss of personhood, the demise of our last and only power.

One of the suggested propers for today is the story of Jesus' feeding the multitude with a boy's lunch of five loaves and two fishes (John 6:1-14). Saint John says Jesus had to do it that way because the disciples lacked the money to do it any other way. It's good this morning to recall that we too have that kind of Father-given bank account to draw on, but oh, what a mirror to have to look into for viewing one's self.

JANUARY 11   **SOUP**

We are having soup for supper tonight . . . not because it's cold outside, which it is, and not because I love to make soup, which I do. We are having soup tonight because I am a writer by trade and not much of a cook.

I sat down early this morning at my desk and began casting about through my stack of notebooks, looking for an essay I had begun sketching out weeks ago and am just now ready to finish. Scrawled in one of those notebooks and with no date or place to aid my memory, I had written, "A really good soup, redolent with sesame oil and garlic; thick, savory, beautiful, with perfect potatoes and colored with sweet carrots and parsley. The odor pulled us toward it, the taste so full and comfortable that we sank into the goodness of life, eating a reward greater than any other the day had given. Even before it was done or the table cleared, we couldn't remember how the tureen looked or which one was used—its color or shape or age—so compelling and possessive of our senses were the contents."

And below that and apparently at some later date, I had added: "I would like to be a good tureen, a vessel unmemorable, lost to view in the comfort of its contents."

Since, as I say, there is neither date nor place to help me, I cannot gauge the age or guess the cause of my observation, but it still seems to me valid . . . which is why we are having soup for supper tonight.

JANUARY 12   **FAITH THROUGH ILLUSION**

The big family bookcase, the one that runs the length of one whole wall and reaches almost to the ceiling, is downstairs in Sam junior's room because his is the biggest room in the house and because he is the most viciously assertive among us about the place of books in a well-ordered life. He is not, however, a very well-ordered housekeeper, which is why I was plowing, dustrag in hand, through his room this morning. In doing the bookcase I discovered that he had somewhere or other, probably in the attic, discovered my old *Illustrated Bible Stories* book from fifty years ago.

Its illustrations, of course, are somewhat questionable by our modern standards, but they fascinated me when I was a youngster, and they must have been fascinating him because the book fell open readily and there, stuck in the stories from Numbers, was his favorite book mark. And there also was one of the illustrations that had most commanded my own attention years ago.

The picture is an engraving in black and white of Moses holding up the brass snake in the wilderness (Numbers 21:5-9). All around him the children of Israel are struggling to escape from a plague of enormous vipers of the most impressive ferocity. The Israelites in the picture who have their hands outstretched to the brass snake on Moses' cross are well and unbitten. Those who cannot look to the upheld snake because they cannot take their eyes off the invading vipers are being mercilessly bitten and killed.

As I looked at the picture again after all these years and remembered how its story had troubled me as a child, I wondered anxiously about what it might be saying to my own son. It has taken me a lifetime of following faith through illusion to understand the message of that wilderness cross with its fiery metal snake, and I was, as I have been briefly with each of our children, sad that there is no escaping the pilgrimage. Each of us must make his or her own, and those of us who are nearer the end can only pray for those who are beginning, which is why I left my dusting and came upstairs just now.

JANUARY 13   **HILARY, BISHOP OF POITIERS, D. 367**

The most obvious difference, at least for us, between being part of a small and relatively rural parish and part of an urban one is that the small rural church is liturgically much more active. This is due, in no small part I suspect, to the fact that it is less active in social ministry. Lacking, in

general, the destitute to house and feed, any sizeable
number of the sick to visit, or any populace to provide with
child-care or social programs, the country church still sees
its mission, its structures, and its pastors as being focused
on prayer, worship, and praise. Like the city mouse and the
country mouse, neither is better, nor is either more
substantially involved in the work of the kingdom, at least
not in any way that I would presume to judge. They are just
different.

But since we are country mice now, we follow country
ways, and that means a parish life full of assemblies and
services. It means daily offices each morning and midweek
Eucharists. It means daybreak mass on Fridays and the
careful keeping of the church year. And it means that in our
kitchen window the calendar, which comes each January
from the parish office, reminds me that today is the feast day
of Hilary of Poitiers.

Hilary, according to the family's book of Christian saints
and heroes, was the Bishop of Poitiers whom the Emperor
Constantius ordered to support the unitarianism of Arius
and to oppose the trinitarianism of Athanasius. Persuaded of
the truth of the trinitarian God, Hilary chose exile rather
than heresy. It was while in exile that Hilary first heard his
unitarian opponents using songs and musical slogans to
promote their point of view and to make their doctrine
accessible to the average man. Fascinated by the efficacy of
their methods, Hilary began to mimic them. The results, in
his hands, were the first hymns of the Christian faith
. . . which makes him not a bad man to remember as I go
humming through my day, filling my winter house with
spiritual commercials:

> Great is Thy faithfulness! Great is Thy faithfulness!
> Morning by morning new mercies I see;
> All I have needed Thy hand hath provided;
> Great is Thy faithfulness, Lord, unto me.
>   ("Great Is Thy Faithfulness")

JANUARY 14 **"I WILL TRUST IN THEE"**

There were angry words this morning, very angry words. They hung about me everywhere in my bright kitchen, and my morning song was cut short before it could leave my mouth.

It was about cars . . . or cars were the focus about which all the vortex whirled and hissed. One boy had driven the other boy's car without refilling it. Neither had remembered, in their animus, to properly acknowledge the fact that the cars weren't "theirs" but privileges that their father's hard work and largess had made possible. Because one car was in the shop, I was, as usual, going to be the one left stranded all day while each of them went off in "his" car, regardless of whose largess wanted stroking.

Now, an hour later, repentant but still sore of soul, I have opened my Bible to the psalms for the day, 56 and 57. Psalm 56 begins, "Be merciful unto me, O God: for man would swallow me up; he fighting daily oppresseth me." My eye scans on, and it is as if David himself had been at our breakfast table just now. "Every day they wrest my words: all their thoughts are against me for evil" (56:5).

But at the end of each complaint, at the conclusion of every piece of discontent, King David returns to the mandates of his life as a believer. "What time I am afraid, I will trust in thee" (56:3). "Be merciful unto me, O God . . . in the shadow of thy wings will I make my refuge, until these calamities be overpast" (57:1).

As for our family fight? Well, it was never solved, of course. The clock got us, and besides, there really are no solutions because there are no causes. None of us created the problem, created the evil that sat at table with us. It simply happened because of the rules of the game, because of more than one personality in the same space. But I am taught by an ancient king now, by a poet-believer:

In God have I put my trust: I will not be afraid what man can do unto me.

Thy vows are upon me, O God: I will render praise unto thee.

(56:11-12)

JANUARY 15   # MARTIN LUTHER KING'S BIRTHDAY

It would be difficult for any American to turn the year's pages and not stop in anguish before this one. January 15—the only day on our calendars, either sacred or profane, that speaks to the still unresolved tensions among us, to the bitterness that separates compatriots, to the cultural weakness of a citizenry at odds with itself.

For the Christian in America, however, be he or she black or white, to observe January 19 either privately or communally is to give body to the central petition of the faith: "Thy kingdom come. Thy will be done on earth, as it is in heaven. . . . And forgive us our trespasses as we forgive those who have trespassed against us. For Thine is the kingdom." May we pray it well, my sisters, in this and every other year, lest our children and our own souls pay the consequences for our errors and our mutual arrogances.

JANUARY 16   # OUR BEST THINKING

I don't know about your house, but at our house we watch "Wheel of Fortune" every night, or we know the reason why. If we don't catch it in the half-hour after supper, then we change stations and catch it in the half-hour before bedtime. In general, I think, we watch it for the puzzles, but occasionally it garners some real insights as well. One of those occasions occurred last night.

Last night there was a young woman on the show who introduced herself as a student in both the college of business and the school of divinity at a major university. Now, my attention was first caught by the patent incongruity of such a curriculum and by the intriguing question of what in the world one would do with the resulting combination. The more I thought about it and the more the young woman talked, the more obvious it became that she was taking business courses to earn a living and divinity courses to inform herself. What she seemed to think, in fact, was that divinity school is the best way available to learn about people, because divinity school is not about God. It can't be. It's about what men and women have thought and written over the centuries about God. And, she concluded, that's when we do our best thinking as people . . . not a bad notion to bring out of last night and into a new day.

JANUARY 17 **ANTONY, ABBOT IN EGYPT, D. 356**

On this day in A.D. 356 a man named Antony died. Though he would probably be surprised to hear it, he has always bothered me.

Orphaned when still a very young man, so the story goes, Antony inherited a large fortune from his parents. Converted to Christianity, he read the Scriptures voraciously and was so convicted by Christ's words to the rich young ruler, "Go thou and sell all thy goods and feed to the poor," that he did just that. Then, divested of his fortune, Antony retired to the desert and years of isolation and self-denial.

During his desert years Antony was troubled by numerous apparitions, a phantasmagoria that came to plague him and tempt him away from his faith. Renaissance painting is full of canvasses of poor Abbot Antony in the desert fighting his demons and staving off his private devils. Yet he must finally have been successful, like Martin Luther with his ink pot, for Antony emerged from the desert to found monasteries all over Egypt and to serve out his final years as their abbot.

The Episcopal Church, the denomination to which we belong, is not much given to saints and martyrs or to saints' days. That fact notwithstanding, January 17 appears on our liturgical calendar marked as the feast of Antony, abbot in Egypt. It was the honoring and all the vivid images of Renaissance demons that troubled me for years, until one day a priest, quipping about something else entirely, said to me, "Even madness can praise God."

"Like Antony in the desert?" I asked, holding my breath for his answer.

"No," he thought a minute. "No, I think that one's there to keep us unsure."

"Unsure?"

"Unsure," he repeated, "about which one is which and about our own ability to decide the question."

I have felt a lot better about January 17 ever since . . . and a lot worse.

JANUARY 18   **CONFESSION OF SAINT PETER**

On this day, according to The Episcopal Church's calendar, Christians everywhere call to mind again the words of Saint Peter, "Thou art the Christ, the Son of the living God," words of perception and faith that caused our Lord to respond, "Thou art Peter, and upon this rock I will build my church" (Matthew 16:16-17).

On this day also, according to the Episcopal lectionary, we read the words that Saint Peter himself later wrote about the business of pastoring in the name of Christ: "I exhort you . . . feed the flock of God which is among you, taking the oversight thereof, not by constraint, but willingly . . . being examples to the flock" (I Peter 5:2-3).

The children have all gone off to school now, leaving me with the beds and lunch sacks and dirty dishes that come from having shepherded and fed my part of God's flock on its way to another day—from having, if you will, performed the traditional ministries of our sex, which are so easy nowadays to scorn or even to evade. Sometimes I think, as I turn the calendar to Saint Peter, it is good to have a day to remember what we really want and who wants it of us.

JANUARY 19 **HOLINESS AND DOMESTICITY**

I have been thinking about a reading from earlier in the week. It is Mark 1:29-45, the section that says, among other things: "And forthwith, when they were come out of the synagogue, they entered into the house of Simon and Andrew, with James and John. But Simon's wife's mother lay sick of a fever, and anon they tell him of her. And he came and took her by the hand, and lifted her up; and immediately the fever left her, and she ministered unto them."

There are few stories in the Gospels—few private glimpses of daily life—that are dearer to my reading time than this one. The Gospelers must have felt the same way, for three out of the four include Peter's mother-in-law in their writings, and it seems especially significant that hers should be one of the stories opening Mark's Gospel as well as our new year. Its placement at the beginning of things becomes a kind of assertion of sorts, an assertion of the humanness of the Christ and of domesticity as integral to his incarnation.

No part of life flies so completely in the face of our human notions of holiness and saintliness and transcendence as does domesticity, with its diurnal responsibilities, financial anxieties, marital tensions, physical labor. Nothing draws us farther from meditation and more into immediacy than does the world of the home. Nothing. Yet here and throughout Jesus' biography, Holy Writ speaks frequently in domestic metaphors, and often of his domestic concerns. What, I wonder this morning, am I to infer from all this save that in engaging life prayerfully he would have us know that we are engaging the kingdom?

JANUARY 20 **TREASURES**

One of our married daughters has bought a new sideboard

for her dining room. We will drive in tonight after work to see it and to rejoice with her over its acquisition.

When she called last night to invite us all to come see, she was as excited as I have ever heard her be. The new piece was as strong and handsome as any sideboard she had ever seen. In addition, it had all the capacity they would ever need. They had finally found it at a yard sale in midtown. Her younger brother, who was on the other line, interrupted. "You did what?"

"We found it at a garage sale," she repeated. "After all these months of shopping, we found it right there in somebody's yard! And you know what, Mama? It is big and well made, but what we really wanted was how all the years of being waxed and polished and dusted and repaired and loved on have made it different from every other sideboard in the world. It's at least a dozen families more valuable than a new one would have been."

"Weird!" said her brother from the other phone, and he hung up . . . leaving me wondering this morning what he will say when he gets a little older. When he begins to comprehend that old culture, in giving patina, also humanizes, what will he say of the church? And, more significantly, what will his generation of Christians say? And, as with Mary with her sideboard, what have I taught him to say?

JANUARY 21   AGNES, MARTYR AT ROME, D. 304

The Gospel proper appointed for today is the parable of the sower and the seed, as Mark retells the event in chapter 4, verses 1 to 20.

I read the story again just now, remembering as I read how much it used to please me as a child. It was one of the few parables I could understand, because its metaphor was a simple one and very accessible to the child of a gardener-father.

I used to pray earnestly that I too, like the good plants in the good soil, would bear fruit thirty-, sixty- or even a hundredfold for the kingdom. In fact, I prayed that prayer as recently as yesterday, and I will probably pray it again, earnestly, before today is over. As I grow older, though, I am increasingly led to consider another part of Jesus' metaphor, a part the little girl and the young matron did not know to want.

I pray for the roots of Jesus' story as well. When the fruit is all harvested, it is they that, probing and clinging to the soil, still hold the spent stalk straight in the winds of autumn and through the storms of winter—into which, like Sam's garden beyond my icy window, it will eventually enclose itself and sink toward its spring.

JANUARY 22   **ANNIVERSARY OF *ROE V. WADE***

I sit, at the invitation of my bishop, on the diocese's Task Force on Abortion. It has without a doubt been the most shredding but instructive activity of my lay life.

There was no intent on my part to deceive either myself or the bishop when I accepted his invitation. With seven children to my credit, it was reasonable for us both to assume that I would have very clear ideas on the subject. Such, alas, was not the case.

Over a year after the Task Force began its work and well after the bishop and I had both discovered that I was not too sure about the party line, I was wrestling one afternoon with my thoughts in preparation for a forthcoming Task Force meeting. Suddenly I began to cry. In fact, sitting in my own house in my own bedroom, I was doing something very close to sobbing.

Over the years of our family-building, I miscarried frequently. It seemed often as if I lost two babies for every one we brought to term, and each loss was an agony of grief. In all those years, no priest ever offered me the words of the church in consolation.

No service was ever said for the inch-long fetuses I had to dispose of myself. No prayer other than my own ever acknowledged the two little boys, less than half-formed, whom I would have given years of my own life to rear. Anger and rage that I did not know I had boiled out that afternoon, against a largely male church with until recently an all-male clergy and until even more recently only male bishops, against years of grief denied and loss unrecognized. Some of my mourning may have been self-pity; who knows? But most of it was genuine, and all of it was angry.

I was still angry the next day, and I was still fed by its force when our meeting began. Twenty minutes into some inane and highly theoretical discussion, I suddenly interrupted the deliberations and demanded that the three men and one woman sitting there listen to me. It all poured out—the hurt, the rage, the betrayal—and it ended with my turning to the bishop and saying, "How can you sit there and call the thing trapping some poor girl a life when the very same thing was nothing to you or the church when I lost it and cried over it! You wouldn't even acknowledge it when I was flushing it!"

There was an absolute silence. So absolute that even the breathing in the room was lost in it. Then he said, very softly, "Because nobody ever asked me that before. Because only a woman could know that. Because you must help us to understand."

There is another meeting of the Task Force this afternoon. As always, I dread it a little and look forward to it a little. But whatever happens in this or any other of our meetings, I have at least learned one thing well. Private pain, like every other part of life, must be shared if it is to purchase the common good. Otherwise it readily becomes mere self-indulgence.

JANUARY 23   O LITTLE TOWN OF BETHLEHEM

"O Little Town of Bethlehem" seems a long, long time ago today, as I sit at my typewriter and stare out the window at the snow that is as black as the paper in front of me but also bright from the sun that will soon melt it into submission. It is the light, of course, that changes first, that first says that Christmas and early winter have slipped into late winter and will soon slip even farther into Lent and early spring.

I went to the piano just now and tried to bang out my own painful rendition of "O Little Town," but all it got me was a howl of protest from young John, who's home on semester break.

"Maw, for Pete's sakes!" was what it got me, in fact, which is pretty much what it got me last year on this day, and the year before that, too.

On this date in 1893 Phillips Brooks died. He was, at the time of his death, the Episcopal bishop of Massachusetts, a fact that probably mattered a great deal then but very little now. What matters now is the Little Town and the faith that made that one, single, stately song possible. It is that simple sufficiency that I want to reverence every January 23 when I play. And what I pray for is the grace to emulate it throughout the rest of the year.

JANUARY 24   **CROWNS OF GLORY**

The cold months, because they belong liturgically to the business of Incarnation, Christmas, and Epiphany, belong in their readings to Isaiah, that wondrous old man who saw in the physical world around him the imaged shape of the real one toward which the redeemed are moving.

On my typing stand and left over from last night's reading, the book of Isaiah lies open now to some of those promises:

> Thou shalt also be a crown of glory in the hand of the Lord, and a royal diadem in the hand of thy God. Thou shalt no more be termed Forsaken; neither shall thy land any more be termed Desolate: but thou shalt be called Hephzibah, and thy land Beulah: for the Lord delighteth in thee, and thy land

shall be married. For as a young man marrieth a virgin, so shall thy sons marry thee: and as the bridegroom rejoiceth over the bride, so shall thy God rejoice over thee. (62:3-5)

It was Father Andrew Greeley, Roman Catholic priest and novelist, who in writing recently on an entirely different matter in the *New York Times* made me look at those words again. "God himself is frequently depicted in the Bible," Greeley said, "as desiring every woman, and every man too, with a passion that makes sexual desire seem weak."

I do not know—cannot know—what such words must mean to a man, but for me as a woman, an imaged half among the redeemed, Isaiah and Andrew Greeley call me irresistibly to glory this morning, and to thanksgiving.

JANUARY 25   **CONVERSION OF SAINT PAUL**

Today is one of the strangest and most compelling days in the Christian year . . . or perhaps merely the day that recalls one of the strangest and most compelling stories in the Christian tradition. On this day almost two thousand years ago, one Saul of Tarsus became a Christian and, in doing so, underwent the kind of experience that converted him into Paul the apostle.

Paul himself tells us the story of that event in chapter 9 of the Acts of the Apostles. He recounts his fervor for God as he understood God to be and of how it had driven him to the persecution of all Christians. He speaks of his journey to Damascus at the behest of the high priest and of his intention of returning from Damascus with many Christians bound and condemned to their deaths. He speaks graphically of the light that blinded him on that road and of the Voice with which he had conversation. "Saul, Saul, why persecutest thou me?" "Who art thou, Lord?" "I am Jesus whom thou persecutest" (Acts 9:4-5).

And after that Saul was a different person. I always wonder who among us would not have been. Who among us would not have stood up, blinded but ecstatic, and made our way to three days of prayer and to a new name in honor of our new selves.

But it is not Paul I tend to dwell on this day. It is rather all of the rest of us for whom my concern is offered . . . all of us who have had no blinding light and no three days of sightless dark . . . all of us for whom the conversation has had to grow gradually clearer over the years . . . all of us who slowly have come to new identities but for whom there are not yet any new names. It is for all the little saints and mini-heroes that I pray, and for an ordinary faith that will sustain us as effectively as a more dramatic one sustained the man of Tarsus.

JANUARY 26

TIMOTHY AND TITUS, COMPANIONS OF SAINT PAUL

Just as on January 25 the church retells the conversion of Saint Paul, so today it remembers in gratitude those who were faithful companions in his work. In The Episcopal Church there are no propers, however, specifically for this day. Instead we use the "Common for a Missionary" for Timothy and Titus:

From Psalm 96: "O, sing unto the Lord a new song. . . . Declare his glory among the heathen, his wonders among all people."

From Isaiah 52: "How beautiful upon the mountains are the feet of him that bringeth good tidings."

From Luke 10: "Pray ye therefore the Lord of the harvest, that he would send forth labourers into his harvest."

From the opening verses of the Acts of the Apostles: "Ye shall be witnesses unto me both in Jerusalem, and in Judaea, and in Samaria, and unto the uttermost part of the earth."

The last reading, from Acts, ends with "And when he had spoken these things, while they beheld, he was taken up; and a cloud received him out of their sight" (1:9). The lector always stops there, since that is the assigned place, but I usually cheat a little and go another couple of verses: "And while they looked stedfastly toward heaven as he went up, behold, two men stood by them in white apparel; which also said, Ye men of Galilee, why stand ye gazing up into heaven?"

I cheat because I have to get to that last question before I'm content with the day's business and with Timothy and Titus. If ever there were two boys who didn't stand around stargazing, it was those two, and I always like to conclude their day by remembering that.

JANUARY 27   **JOHN CHRYSOSTOM, BISHOP OF CONSTANTINOPLE, D. 407**

Occasionally the Episcopal lectionary will cite readings from the Apocrypha, especially from the book of Wisdom. Today is such a day, inasmuch as today honors another early believer and uses the Common of a Saint for his scriptures.

Specifically, the Common of a Saint calls us to read the first nine verses of the third chapter of Wisdom. Since I read Wisdom infrequently, I have only one translation of it readily at hand, that of the Jerusalem Bible. In whatever translation the words appear, however, they speak to the role of a saint, to the habits and uses of a holy life. In whatever translation they appear, also, it is always verse 7 that arrests my attention. It begins, "When the time comes for his visitation they will shine out," and concludes, "as sparks run through the stubble, so will they" . . . a most wondrous image, I think, for those of us who forget how near to the ground and how ordinary a thing true holiness is, as well as how powerful.

JANUARY 28

THOMAS AQUINAS, PRIEST AND FRIAR

One of the reasons for having a "church year," a liturgical calendar of observations, is that it gives believers a historical perspective. By compacting into twelve months the great events and lives of followers of the faith, it circumvents the caprices of any given age and steadies the swing of the eternal pendulum that is humanity.

This is particularly true today when the church calendar bids us remember Thomas Aquinas, who died on this date in 1274. Aquinas was an intellectual, a professor in Paris and the founder of another university in Naples. With his arguments and his treatises, he persuaded men to God by means of logic. In effect, he gave his life to converting the human intellect, and, as we all know, his work changed not only individual lives but also the church and the whole body of Western thought as well.

In an age when our religion is too often inclined to emotion and too often scornful of reason, it is somehow comforting to have one day a year to remember a Christian who saw things in a rather different light. It also occurs to me, as I am writing this, that we might all do well to use that memory wisely during the rest of the year ahead.

JANUARY 29

SHOPPING

I hate shopping . . . more in the summer, I confess, than in the winter, when at least the cold is exhilarating and the bustle of crowds more comforting. But basically I just hate shopping and do it by catalog whenever possible. Yet some things have to be bought; they can't be "just ordered up," as Sam says . . . things like a new watch, when one's beloved old dilapidated one has finally died, which is why I was shopping this morning.

Torn between spending a lot of money for a permanent

35

piece of jewelry and considerably less for a glitzy digital I could throw away when I had wearied of it, I was down to the last showcase in the store and to the hour of decision. Next to me at the counter and obviously absorbed in watching me was a Catholic priest. He was clearly a man of some standing, and every part of him bespoke breeding and taste. Embarrassed by his frank observation, I turned and half-smiled an "I can't make up my mind" apology. Then thinking to divert his attention from me, I asked, "Which would you pick?"

He did not answer me at first. Instead, his long, immaculate fingers reached out and touched the cross I was wearing around my neck. He felt it a moment, gave the lightest shrug of his shoulders and said, very slowly as if remembering an answer he had learned elsewhere, "We Christians should never allow ourselves to own anything we would not be willing to part with immediately in order to relieve another person's necessity." He smiled, and I thought he was done with his answer and that he had voted for the digital, when he suddenly added, "But which, at the same time, of course, we would not keenly and painfully regret having to part with because of its beauty." I looked up startled. He bowed just slightly, turned, and left the store.

By the time I had recovered enough to try to follow him, he was gone. I was only as far as the sidewalk when I lost sight of him, but I did not go back in to buy either watch. I will do that some other day. My mysterious priest had given me quite enough to carry home from one day's shopping.

JANUARY 30   **WOMEN SAINTS**

Over the years of rearing the four of our seven children who are female, I have grown increasingly zealous about relaying to them the stories of great women, zealous about insisting that they know how Christianity has been transmitted through the faith and the ardor of *both* sexes.

Because of that longstanding habit, I can never leave January without a roll call of the heroines of the faith that it holds within its thirty-one days.

In addition to the Virgin who presented the young child on Holy Name, January is the anniversary month of Genevieve, the fifth-century Parisienne who took the veil at age fifteen but then twice left it long enough to lead her people. Once, when Childeric of the Franks had encircled the city and was starving it into submission, Genevieve singlehandedly led a brigade of boats out, procured food, and sailed back in to rescue the city. Years later, when Attila the Hun was marching against Paris, Genevieve left the convent to lead Paris in a vigil of prayer. Attila's troops were miraculously diverted and passed around Paris on their way to the destruction of Rome. Genevieve herself lived to see the king of the Franks become Christian, and when she died on January 3, her body was interred in the church the king had built for her in the middle of Paris.

January 4 remembers, on the anniversary of her death, Elizabeth Seton, born and reared a Protestant but converted to Catholicism, and the first American to be canonized by the Roman Catholic Church. She gave her life after her widowhood to the poor and to education, founding the teaching order of the Sisters of St. Joseph.

On the eighteenth there is Margaret of Hungary, daughter of King Bela IV, who scorned the throne and spent her years in worship and lowly service.

The nineteenth is the anniversary of Martha, matron of Persia. She made a pilgrimage with her husband and two sons to Rome, then being ruled by Emperor Claudius. As soon as they arrived in the Imperial City, they discovered that the emperor was burning Christians and leaving their ashes unburied. Instead of fleeing, Martha and her family gathered the ashes from the amphitheater and buried them. The Roman governor then executed them by torture, and they were buried by their fellow Christians in the Via Cornelia outside the city. Their graves, however, were finally opened in the fifteenth century and their remains reburied in churches across Europe.

On the twenty-first there is Agnes, who refused marriage to a non-Christian and for her obstinacy was sentenced by the governor to life in a Roman brothel. So great were her purity and faith that no man would violate her, and the governor finally resorted to execution. She was buried on the Via Nomentana where, years later, the Emperor Constantine came in order to baptize his infant daughter near the remains of one who so exemplified his new faith. The Church of Saint Agnes now marks that site.

There is Paula, who died on January 26, 404, in Bethlehem, but who with one of her daughters, Eustochium, spent her years and her fortune in friendship with and support of Saint Jerome. Mother and daughter together founded a hospice in Bethlehem, a monastery, and a convent. It was here that we first hear of all members of the community wearing humble and identical clothing because Paula taught that all people were equal in God's sight.

There is Angela Merici, whom January celebrates on the twenty-seventh. A sixteenth-century Italian nun, she dreamed one night of a ladder extending from her pillow up into heaven and, climbing the ladder, a crowd of young women. A voice spoke to her saying that some day she would lead just such a group in holy work. She never doubted the vision, and in 1535 she established the teaching order we know as the Ursulines. She once wrote, "If any person, because of his state of life, cannot do without wealth and position, let him at least keep his heart empty of the love of them."

And on this, the next to the last day of this month of women, the church around the world stops to memorialize two others of our sex, Martina and Bathildis.

Martina, one of the patron saints of the modern city of Rome, lies buried now in the church of Santi Luca e Martino under a Bernini shrine that Pope Urban VIII commissioned in 1634 as a way of honoring her devotion to Christianity under persecution.

Bathildis, the last woman whom January celebrates, was born English. As a young girl she was captured by pirates and sold into slavery to the Major Domo of King Clovis II of the Franks. So great were her intelligence and beauty that Clovis married her. In time she converted him to her faith, and together they had three sons—all of whom in time became kings in their own right. Widowed, she spent the last fifteen years of her life in prayer in one of the nunneries she had helped to found.

So January also brings us a cloud of female witnesses and a full panoply of all the roles "womanness" can assume, from matron to queen, girl innocent to adventuress. It also celebrates a pattern within those roles of devout, active Christianity, which only prayer can give us the strength and grace to carry on. Let us pray.

JANUARY 31   **THE INTERCOM**

Five years ago, in a moment of irritation, Sam decided to install an intercom system. The irritation came from several prior years of hollering at children without result when their chores, or occasionally their friends, called. In a big farmhouse with three stories and a basement, it is possible to lose a lot of children . . . and, of course, for a lot of children to conveniently lose themselves, which is why we tried the intercom experiment . . . that, and the fact that more and more of their friends were calling. At night it is usually our doctor-father who answers the phone, and it was as a result he who was getting the sore throat.

Right from the first, the kids were opposed to "those tacky things," and I wasn't too thrilled. Years of motherhood had convinced me that the same kid who wasn't answering the paternal bellow was not very likely to answer the electronic squawk that only compounded the bellow. However, things being as things are, Daddy has ideas like most bull terriers have bones, and we got an intercom. Not a plug-into-your-house-current-and-go-with-it intercom—heavens, no! That kind can be picked up by every ham and CBer in range. (We are ten miles into deep country, so I had trouble sharing that concern, but I let it ride.) No, instead we got a string-wire-everywhere, totally private intercom. Because there was considerable skepticism about this project, however, Sam astutely decided to lay the wire without initially investing a lot of effort and interior devastation into its permanent installation.

As predicted, of course, the child not expecting a call had no reason to answer the intercom; the child expecting one was already by the phone waiting; and the girl children among us at that point had absolutely no intention of being available on the first try or two anyway. Three months later, still sucking Sucrets every night, Sam wisely collected the ugly little boxes and dropped them along with miles of wire into his workshop bin of failed projects. The intercom has not been mentioned since except by me.

Stringing the intercom from the base station in the kitchen (the box was on my desk, of course) down to the basement had required some fairly major roof work. Sam had deliberately left the roof wires loosely attached so that he could yank them down easily if the intercom did not work. On the day of defeat, however, the wire that went over the house and into the basement rooms snagged somehow and would not let go. The result was that my kitchen window, the favorite one by my desk, suddenly had a brown cable flapping off the sitting room roof and right in my face. I was not a happy housekeeper. In all fairness, Sam wasn't too happy either, but it was the dead of winter by that time and nobody thought it would be very smart for anybody—father or hearing-impaired sons—to climb up on the roof just to tear down some cable they could clip in ten minutes as soon as the weather turned.

Except that spring came instead, and with it came the trumpet vine . . . the one that felt its way out of the snow just at the end of January and that by March had found the cable and by June had covered it with blooms . . . the one that by October had withered and by Christmas, when the roof was slick again, bore a festoon of brown leaves and black seed pods. That trumpet vine, the one we all know, the one that every woman who ever lived has, metaphorically speaking, at least one of. The vine that is the gift love gave, although love had originally intended something else. The vine that holds the wire in its tendrils and weaves the good and the bad of its beginnings into one strong cord stout enough for all seasons . . . The vine I wanted to share with you before I go because, as I am writing this, I can see it. It is the one below the window there with its first leaf pushing lightly through the snow.

Hope and Faith and New Beginnings

DOROTHY SICKAL

THE PROMISE SIDE

"Therefore, if anyone is in Christ, he is a new Creation; old things have gone, the new has come!" (II Corinthians 5:17-18 NIV).

February is the promise side of spring. The days are a little longer, buds are a bit more visible on the trees, and pebbly brooks gurgle with a louder rhythm.

These are natural examples to remind us of God's renewing grace. A new sunrise inspires hope for better things to come. A clean sheet of paper urges us to write more legibly today. In him we remain a new creation, not just new one day to start getting old the next. The newness is always now.

Then he sets before us an open door. If we need new direction, it is there, or we can take new territory on a path already pointed out. He renews us for his service.

I have a friend who goes to five Bible studies a week. Then she goes home, shuts the door, and cooks spaghetti. All people we encounter need to have either the dirt of the world washed off their feet, so to speak, or to be helped to the Fountain of Living Water. With this always in the back of our minds, we can meet each new opportunity and each person with the mind of Christ.

I must go to the door, the store, my school, or my office

with a caring attitude and an open heart. I must realize that Jesus is in every encounter. I always need a new beginning for this.

Empower me, my ever-present Lord, with whatever it takes to share the joy found only in you. May I think the way you think about each person I meet today. I am aware that hope and faith increase with obedience.

FEBRUARY 2   NUTS

In late summer the hickory nuts were full and fat in their sectioned hulls. Early ripeners fell and left their green caskets in flower-like patterns on the ground. White, gently curved nuts were there for takers.

I lived with my young husband, his little brother, and his parents. The house and farm buildings snuggled at the end of a lane half a mile from the main road. It was a fine place to live because the squirrels and other free creatures had no fear of us as they went about their daily business, just like we did.

This was before specialists had conditioned us to believe that we could not live with our in-laws or even close to them. I did not know I was supposed to hate my mother-in-law, and she was a dear. We were quite happy and agreeable. We lived in a little village within walking distance from the railroad tracks.

Cisterns were the main source of water for the houses of most families in the area. When it rained, women caught roof water in jugs, jars, and other containers and used it to wash their hair and best underwear.

Floyd, my husband's mother (she had named herself Flaxy Floyd when she was five years old), carried out a large copper washboiler with an oval lid and long wooden handle. She set the lid under a tree and shoved the boiler under the downspout. Rains came and went, and the boiler remained there for dippers who needed to wash a pair of hose or whatever.

During the rest of the summer Floyd gathered hickory nuts and stored them in gunnysacks in the woodshed off the kitchen. She was a magic cook, and there could be no flavor richer than her cakes, pies, and rolls studded with hickory nuts, flavored with vanilla, and baked in an old-fashioned wood stove. It is no wonder that so few young people ran away from home in those days.

But she kept losing nuts. It did not seem to matter how many pailfuls of nuts she stored in the bags—they seemed to get no fuller. Nobody knew why the nuts were shrinking in quantity, so the mystery remained.

Ice crystals spread across the water in the washboiler one day, and all the nuts were gone from the trees. Geese honked across the sky. Floyd dumped the water out of the boiler and picked up the lid. With a woody rattle hundreds of hickory nuts tumbled and spread out on the ground. At last the culprit was exposed. A sleek red squirrel on a fence post glared at her, its tail jerking up and down.

Floyd looked at it and scolded, "How silly can you get? You have stored all your treasures in one shallow pile!"

All summer it had worked, gleefully hoarding for the long, cold winter, but it had trusted its treasure to a perishable vessel. It had seemed like a good idea at the time.

Like those who are not eternity-minded, his work and his treasure would be lost. He would never know how much he would miss it until it was too late. He had trusted his survival to a washboiler lid.

Don't store up for yourselves treasures on earth, where moths and rust destroy and thieves can break in and steal, but lay up for yourselves treasures in heaven (Matthew 6:19-20).

FEBRUARY 3   **CHOICES**

Every day of our lives we are confronted with choices. It is possible that each one of them has eternity in it. Our choices determine the direction we take in life.

We, as Christians, have the Holy Spirit to guide us (John 16:13); even so, sometimes we may become careless and make human choices that lead us away from God's will for us or for someone we influence.

To live by "rules" instead of principle may lead us to a dead end. If we trust our emotions or natural desires, we can be caught up in the world's systems and reap only temporal results.

Sometimes people get bored when parents or ministers repeat so often, "Stay unto the Word," but we need to know the nature, character, and purpose of God so the Word will stay in us. It is so very easy to become dull of spiritual hearing and be caught offguard when we have to make surprise decisions. Parents are sometimes forced to make choices for which they have had no previous experience. The Spirit, the Word, the providence always agree. We can check them out.

Let us suppose that a mother has to make a choice between spending the morning of her day off from work in a class of women who are studying sign language for the deaf or staying at home with her young son. Certainly churches are long overdue with this kind of outreach to the hearing-impaired. But her little son needs her, and although it is not often stated, she needs him.

She will probably feel guilty; there are an abundance of people who spend much energy making mothers feel guilty. If she stays home, she will wonder if she is selfish. Only she and God can make this choice. They alone know all the circumstances. There are others who can take this training at this point in time. A mother's first field of mission is in her family, unless God has made it clear otherwise.

Sometimes we have to say *no* so we can say *yes* to something more important. It is hard to say no, because we fear other peoples' opinions. Often we would feel better if we only had God to deal with. He never uses us.

After we have done our best to make a right choice, we should enjoy doing it. God loves to make his children happy.

When my husband said, "Let's go for a ride, I have something I want you to see," I almost answered, "The dinner dishes are still on the table, and the kitchen is a mess!" But I remembered my mother saying so often, "People are always more important than things."

My companion is gone now, and I am so glad we had those precious times together. They are eternal moments I could have missed.

Life is full of big choices, but I am not sure there are any little ones. God is always trying to show us something he wants us to see.

This day I must choose whom I will serve. Lord, don't let me stumble around in fields of indecision and miss the glory.

But what things were gain for me I count but loss for Christ (Philippians 3:7-9).

FEBRUARY 4   **FORGETFULNESS**

Does it seem reasonable that one should ever say that God is forgetful? He is all knowledge, ever-present, and unchangeable. Yet God is forgetful.

When we repent of our sins, are truly sorry we have offended and overridden the will and love of God, we can ask and he will forget our sins. Because Jesus loved us enough to die in our place, we can turn from our wicked ways, and he will forget our unrighteousness.

Joy and gratitude well up in our hearts when we see that we can begin to live all over again because God has forgotten our sins (Hebrews 8:12; 10:17): "For I will be merciful to their unrighteousness and their sins and their iniquities will I remember no more."

When we love the Lord with all our hearts and set out to fulfill our mission as his children, we want to do everything to please him. We become aware of his presence, and our desire is to share the wonderful good news. We think everyone will only have to hear it, and they will love him too.

If things go well with us and we meet up with the right people and do not have much opposition for a while, we may forget where our strength is. We can see what others should do, and we become self-righteous. Soon we learn that we cannot walk alone, and we search the Scriptures all over again to find where our strength really is.

When the enemy can get us to feel so confident that we depend upon our knowledge, or so discouraged with our failures that we have no confidence at all, he will do it.

God is better to us than we are to ourselves. We are often our own worst critics. This is true if we are perfectionists in the first place. Yet it is just as bad to think that God is so forgiving that it does not matter what we do. Faith takes a holiday when we fail to put Christ in the center of our lives so that our vision is clear.

It is easy to do one of two extremes: We think we can do it or we feel we cannot do it at all. We do something right and God blesses our commitment, so we find ourselves thinking, "I must be really spiritual." This is a danger sign. Or we fail after real effort and become discouraged and ashamed. We can hardly stand ourselves.

May I share with you a prayer I have prayed over the years?

God, my strength, help me not to beat myself to death with my failures or gloat over my achievements. I will forgive myself and forget it.

Philippians 3:13-14: "Forgetting those things which are behind, and reaching forward unto those things which are before, I press toward the mark for the prize of the high calling of God in Christ Jesus."

We too need to be forgetful as God is forgetful, and forgive.

FEBRUARY 5   **RELATIONSHIPS**

I often wonder about the conversations that Mary and Elizabeth had while Mary was staying in the home of

Zacharias and Elizabeth before the birth of John, the revelator.

How wonderful that God would reveal to Elizabeth the coming of Jesus and give her the witness of the Holy Spirit so that Mary did not have to *prove* her wonderful message to Elizabeth. She too was to give birth, to one called of God to be the greatest prophet of all time, the introducer of Christ as Savior.

How much they had to share about that great mission. Over and over they must have shared their unearthly experiences and asked each other, "Why me?"

Probably nobody in history has properly given credit to Joseph for his attitude and commitment to this unheard-of event. Of course, it had been foretold by the prophets and sung by the psalmists, but who could actually understand it until it happened?

It was essential that Mary should have the loyalty and support of this godly man. How God is glorified in one of so beautiful character and dedication! For Joseph to ignore the scorn of the people and the letter of the law as he did made his mission outstanding. Mary's commitment was one of submission; his was one of chosen activity, almost blasphemous in the eyes of the community.

After Joseph and Mary settled down in their home, Jesus began at an early age (as was the custom) to learn his father's trade and to study Scripture. How did they tell him he was called of God for a special mission and plan for his life? They probably did not comprehend it fully themselves, but they must have demonstrated great faith before him.

With parents like his, Jesus must have been a wonderful and sincere child. His daily approach to life must have been one of joy and eager curiosity.

I heard a speaker once who said that Jesus was a willful and bratty little boy like everybody else. Everybody else? If so, then proper love, training, and discipline are futile. I had a fine brother who was kind, obedient, and loving; surely Jesus could have done as well as he. I knew the speaker was not qualified to make such a judgment. We do know that when Jesus was twelve years old, he confounded the lawmakers and was astonished that his parents seemed to forget that he "must be about his Father's business."

I think they had a close and precious relationship. I believe it began with day one and continued to the cross and beyond.

We can know that God has a special plan for each life. We can teach our children that, and by grace help them to reach it.

Lord, from this day help me to be responsive to your will and purpose for me, that my relationships may be touched by your love and direction (Luke 1:28-56).

FEBRUARY 6   **I AM PERSUADED**

It is there. Bedded down in the heart of every human being is faith at least as big as a grain of mustard seed.

Faith does not come by shock treatment: Show me a miracle, raise the dead, grow a leg, call down fire, and then I will believe. Prove it, Lord; show me—and a child might add, "I dare you!"

When sight has come, we shall not need faith anymore. *Now,* God would have us exercise that inborn faith so that the glory may come to his name. We choose to trust him, and faith is enlarged by this use.

Parents strain to see that first spark of responsive love in their baby so they can know it has made the choice to return their devotion. An active and meaningful relationship can then develop.

We choose whom we will serve. We weigh all the evidence we can find. We compare the Bible with other religions we see demonstrated. Only the God of Calvary changes people at the core of their beings. Some take on good rules and commandments. They demand allegiance. Some do good works for the wrong reasons, and some do evil that good may come of it.

Only the God of Heaven through Jesus the Savior offers complete change of character through principles that stand in any culture, age, or circumstance. Only by grace can we live as the law demands, and the only force is love!

We are persuaded by the very character of God that he alone will be our Lord. We risk all on the stirring of that little mustard seed of faith in our hearts. It grows and gives all the proof we need. Joy follows commitment and obedience, and faith in who he is controls us.

We don't base our trust upon what God does for us but upon God himself, the Creator of all existence, who permeates every atom of life.

If we will not believe Moses and the prophets, neither will we be persuaded though one rose from the dead (Luke 16:31). When we are persuaded by intellectual reason, our hearts pick up truth and we are on our way. Eternity begins that day for us.

A new Christian is amazed and surprised to learn that God has been there all along, waiting for him or her to respond to his love.

A rich fellowship with other Christians follows because we can only express our love for God to others. We need this power and support to live daily in this crazy, mixed-up world.

"For I know whom I have believed, and am persuaded that he is able to keep that which I have committed unto him against that day" (II Timothy 1:12).

FEBRUARY 7 **TRUTH AND TACT**

A young man in theology class said, "It just seems to me that Jesus could have saved himself a lot of trouble if he had used more tact."

Making no comment upon the audacity of a pipsqueak who would dare to even think of correcting the Lord of

Glory, and knowing that Jesus did not come to "save himself a lot of trouble," let us look at truth and tact.

I am sure there is always a way to be tactfully truthful, but a dear old minister once said, "Some people use tact, but some just tell the truth."

My mother often reminded me to always tell the truth and that way if I were asked to tell the same story next week, I would not have to worry about what I had said.

A few people I have known seemed to associate telling the truth, or being honest, with being critical, negative, or unkind, even unloving. Perhaps this is because we so often deal with material things in a commercial world where getting to the top is often attained by foul means. But I do not think Jesus would find these two words—*tact* and *truth*—incompatible.

In the best sense of the word, *truth* is liberating. It is kind, positive, and complimentary. Truth and tact do not need to be at war, even in this culture where "white lies" are considered harmless. We don't need to pretend; we don't have to sell ourselves in order to make people like Jesus. When we honestly love our Lord Jesus, we need no artificial accomplishments to win others to anything.

A loving concern and an honest spirit are all the tact we need. A good attitude and motive will show through mistakes and poor communications. Both honesty and pure crystal have a ring that is hard to duplicate.

"The truth will make you free. . . . You will be free indeed" (John 8:32, 36 RSV).

Thank you, God, for the freedom of having to pretend nothing. Keep us from being tactless. Is not tact just good manners?

FEBRUARY 8   **IT IS EASY TO HUG A STRANGER**

The boy was only seven, small for his age, and his hands moved nervously. He stood looking up at me just inside the door. His mother has told me how difficult he was; he flew into uncontrollable fits of rage if corrected at all and was downright mean and quarrelsome when playing with other children.

His father had been brought up in a home where being the male parent gave one the privilege of doing whatever one pleased, and everyone else had to fit into one's program, regardless. The boy's father played with him sometimes, but always at his convenience and at what the father wanted to do. If the child was playing with a top when his father wanted to play ball, tops had to go. The situation was one of long development and misunderstanding. Nobody could do much about it in one afternoon.

It is interesting that the ego will make us think that we have answers ready that would take someone else a lifetime to learn. (That dog may bite everyone else, but it won't bite me!) I did not want to fall into that kind of trap with this little boy and think that I could be in control of something I knew so little about. So I decided to devote the time to having as good a relationship with him as was possible.

He looked gentle and quiet. I silently ventured a few opinions about their problems and ached in my heart for all of them. "What do you want to do?" I asked, knowing full well that the poorest way to train up a child is to spend blocks of time entertaining him. Life is a school and the method of learning can be a joy or a prison. Entertainment can become a growing obsession.

"I don't know," he answered dully, as if whatever we did would be boring. He seemed unused to the question.

"We have some choices," I said. "We can make something from this clay; it is nice and soft and just right for molding. We can paint rocks. We can play marbles, but I am terrible at that, or we can go look at the new kittens in the duckhouse."

His eyes were bright and wide. "Let's do them all!" he shouted and started off, not even knowing where he was going.

His mother came to pick him up before either of us was ready for her.

Now, I know that no busy, tired mother can do every day what I did that one time. Life is built upon a series of events. Sometimes we get off balance, and awful things happen. Because I did not know how mean he could be and he did not know how lazy I was, we could hug each other. When we do not like ourselves, we assume that others don't like us either. Strangers begin on the scene. It is like visiting a new church; we can't see the problems or the problem people, so it seems heavenly. But life is not like that. We have to face reality. By God's grace and our repentance, we can sometimes reverse the damages. It is worth a try.

For one afternoon we can see one another's face value and, like strangers, learn a whole new side of others. It takes more grace to forgive failures than to think there are not any.

Parents are always around and sometimes know us too well for our comfort. Even Jesus seemed so commonplace to his relatives and friends that they failed to see his wisdom and love and missed the miracles (Mark 6:4).

FEBRUARY 9   **THOU SHALL HAVE NO OTHER GODS**

Before we learn to know Christ as Savior, personally and by choice, there are so many things between us and God that we must see through. Strange as it may seem, a fly on your nose close to your eyes can keep you from seeing a mountain.

Without my understanding it, my mother taught me not to follow personalities. When I asked, "Why can't I go? Judy is going. All the kids are going," she would answer me, "You don't make choices by what others are doing. You must first ask, 'Is it right? Could it lead to trouble?' Then, 'Would Jesus go with me?' "

Isaiah said, "In the year that King Uzziah died I saw the Lord . . . high and lifted up" (6:1). We often have to get some person or some thing out of the way before we can see the real King. We cannot let our direction and character be shaped by some personality so close to us that we cannot see God.

I never quite understood the words, "Jesus is all I need." I was not so sure I could say that and mean it. Now at last, I see that with Jesus as the closest thing in my life, all other people, things, and situations take their proper places without getting in the way of my proper vision and focus.

Thank you, Lord; come ever closer.

FEBRUARY 10 **SHOES**

"Does she want this on her charge, or will she pay cash for these?" I had tried on a pair of shoes and liked them. My friend carried them to the cash register while I got out my wallet. Then I walked up beside her to finish the transaction. With cash in hand I waited.

Again, the salesclerk repeated to my friend, "Does she want this on her charge card, or will she pay cash?"

When you are nearly eighty years old, many people think you cannot hear, see, or feel as others do. Add to that a wheelchair and you will get a whole new education in communications.

"Why don't you ask me? I am the one buying the shoes," I said.

As we rode home, I struggled with feelings of resentment. I pictured myself walking up to the salesclerk, opening my mouth very wide, and saying to her, "Look inside! I am in here. Don't look at me as if I had moved out." This sort of thing does not help one's self-esteem very much.

A woman who deals with the public told me that one day she found herself conversing with a woman who spoke a foreign language. Struggling to make the woman understand, she found herself shouting at her as if she could not hear.

We often talk down to children, aside to the aged and handicapped, and up to those we feel are superior to us.

After I simmered down and meditated upon the whole thing, the Lord seemed to ask, "How do you think *I* feel?" I was shocked at myself. How many times had I talked around Jesus to others when he is closer than my own heart?

A friend of mine was to have surgery the next day, and as we parted I said, "I will be thinking of you tomorrow."

She softly answered, "While you're at it, pray for me," which of course, is what I meant. I should have taken her hand and said, "Our Jesus, direct and control this whole thing. We accept victory for all concerned and trust in you."

Why must we often take on certain airs to approach our Lord? He can hear straight on. When I was a child I thought preachers had to change their tone of voice and clear their throats to approach God. I found myself doing it too. I thought it sounded holy.

Lord Jesus, I don't want to talk around you or about you when I should be sharing with you. I don't need to find myself; I need to know you. You are closer to me than life, and I am glad!

"Lord, show us the Father and that will be enough" (John 14:8 NIV).

FEBRUARY 11   **YES, YOU CAN GO BACK!**

So often we hear people say, "You just can't go back." In some ways this is true. And it is a good thing we can't. Memory is a wonderful gift, but to try to retain the past by keeping our minds there is to shut off growth and miss today. We can cherish the good things in our past, learn by experience, and anticipate the future, but we only have the *now.*

However, some things we must go back to, such as the wisdom of our mothers. If yours was an unwise mother, you can pray for the wisdom your own children can go back to some day. Wisdom is partly inborn, partly learned. Wisdom is good sense; good sense is truth; truth is integrity. Yes, you can go back to all of them.

You can go back to simplicity—back to balance. You can go back to the Word. Go back to foundations, to the Chief Cornerstone. Go back to repentance. Go back to Calvary; go back to the beautiful Resurrection.

Yes, you can go back! Go back to go forward—to basics, to cardinal doctrines. Some things are eternal.

When things get so complicated you are dizzy, when right is called "square," when adultery is the expected thing, when license is called liberty, when selfishness is labeled "finding yourself," when convictions based on the Word of God are called opinions, and when sin abounds, it is time to go back.

Accepted clichés can lead you astray: Old dogs can't learn new tricks; you can't change a leopard's spots; you can't go back. These are not necessarily true. If you can't go back, you probably won't go forward. Go back to the Solid Rock. Yes, you can go back!

Lord, when our vision gets fuzzy because of warped psychology and misconceptions, give us the will to go back to grace. Praise your name—we can go back (Jeremiah 29:11-14).

FEBRUARY 12   **HEATHEN AND STRANGERS**

The well-known preacher was expounding upon the topic of broken communications and what to do about them. I was listening but I had heard it so often . . .

"Go to that brother, and if he won't hear you bring two or three other good Christians together and share the problem. If he won't be reasonable, take it before the church. If you can't resolve it there, [then the bombshell] treat him like a heathen and a stranger! You cannot win them all; Jesus did not win everyone! You must not waste your life on one person—others need the Lord; so forget it."

It sounded great; we like to give up sometimes and get people off our consciences. But my heart was not ready for that. Must it be either/or?

I went home thinking about the times we had little rifts in the family and were not able to resolve the issues. We had left it with the Lord and waited.

"Treat him like a heathen—like a stranger," the preacher had said. Pretend I never knew him? Close the door upon the relationship?

I am a stubborn person. It is not my nature to give up. There must be some other way. That seems so final. Forget it? How?

As the days passed, that message kept coming to my mind. I was not thinking of any real lost relationships. I simply wanted to understand what God was trying to say, but there was something missing. If the preacher understood it, he had not made it clear to me.

To me, "the mind of Christ" (Philippians 2:5) means to think as Jesus thinks about people, so I asked the ceiling over the sink how Jesus thinks about this person. Would he wash his hands of this whole matter and let him be lost? "Even Jesus never won them all," the preacher had said.

As I placed some plates on the cupboard shelf, an inner voice whispered, "How did Jesus treat the heathen and the stranger?"

Then the veil lifted. He sent missionaries to the heathen and took the stranger in! He is forever the same. He would begin all over again from scratch! He would give up the difference and keep his love in action. I could do that.

I would ask God to send someone to do what I could not. He will have someone else ready. I will keep that person in my heart and wait for the opportunity that will come if I continue to care. I will never cross him out like a lost cause. Jesus never gives up.

Jesus did not win them all, but he never quit trying—even

on the cross. That is the mind of Christ toward the heathen and the stranger. My heart can rest with that. Thank you, Lord.

FEBRUARY 13 **COMPETITION**

One natural human trait that does not seem to be encouraged by our Lord is competition. And it is so much emphasized in social affairs that the world seems to exist by it and for it.

The way of the cross and the way of the world are always in conflict. That in itself seems to be very competitive! The main difference is the motive involved.

"Oh evil man, you make 'justice' a bitter pill for the poor and oppressed. 'Righteousness' and 'fair play' are meaningless fictions to you!" (Amos 5:7, paraphrased).

A young boy said to his grandmother concerning his two older sisters, "I am bigger than they are; I could beat up both of them!"

The world is very competitive: My daddy is stronger than your daddy; my mother is prettier than your mother; my car is newer than your car; I heard that before you did; my grades are higher than anyone else's.

To out-do, out-number, and be superior seems to be the important goal these days. But of whom much is given much is required. Every achievement brings responsibility, in proportion. Power misused is a grievance to God.

A little girl was heard to say during a family ballgame, "But Daddy, if I win somebody else has to lose. Let's play something else." Achieving and excelling may have their place but the children of the kingdom have discovered a greater joy. They know that to share good things brings the joy we are all reaching for.

Winning to make others feel inferior has no place in the pattern of God. God not only gave us the power of choice, he also gave us the *will* to carry it out. We cannot get our instructions from this world's systems. Carnal answers are always in competition with the way of Christ. Nobody has to lose so that others may win. When anyone wins, we all win.

Today, most precious Savior, by your grace let me see the eternal in all the choices that are before me. Give me the will to pursue the more excellent way.

FEBRUARY 14   **VALENTINES**

We were gathered around the table. There was plenty of colored paper—mostly red—and doilies. There was the paste that always fascinates kids, and adhesive tape (the ultimate attraction), pins, and little red and white hearts.

I was telling the children, "When I was a little girl, most valentines were given secretly. A boy who was too shy to let a girl know he liked her could slip a valentine in her reading book or under the front door of her home. A girl could make a really pretty one from lace, scraps of ribbon, and cardboard, write 'I love you' on it, and have some other girl hand it to her favorite boy and hope he would not make faces at her in the hall. It was fun but a little frightening.

"The really bad thing about sending valentines was the awful habit some people had of sending very ugly cartoon valentines to someone they did not like, or to children who were thoughtlessly called names that hurt their feelings. This could make them have bad memories and poor self-esteem for years afterward.

"I am glad people have learned not to do this now. All we have to do is imagine how we would feel to get an ugly valentine with our name under it to know that we would never do that to anyone.

"You can send a valentine to just about anyone: your father and mother, sister, brother, grandparents, friends at school and church, teachers, the janitor, elderly people on your block. Sometimes, when we care about people, we seem to think they should just know it and forget to let them know we appreciate them. Why not make a valentine for that person you love very much but haven't told for a long time?"

I could see little mental wheels turning, and a murmur went around the table. After a busy half hour, little rows of valentines gathered in the center of the table. "Oh!" and "Ah, how pretty!" punctuated the activity.

One quiet little girl pushed her chair back, took a special valentine across the room, and placed it on the bookcase behind the worship center the children arranged every Sunday.

I walked over to her; she seemed so seriously involved. She opened the valentine's centerfold to reveal a big red heart with a lace edge. Red teardrops were falling from it. Underneath the heart in carefully printed letters were four words: I love you, Jesus.

We stood in silence a moment, and I asked, "Has it been a long time since you told Jesus that you love him?"

"Oh yes," she answered, "not since last night!"

"How long has it been?" I asked myself, and we whispered together, "I love you, Jesus."

"Your strong love for each other will prove to the world that you are my disciples" (John 13:35 TLB).

FEBRUARY 15 **BEAUTY IS WORTH THE INVESTMENT**

> Flower seeds
> A bird feeder
> A rock carried home from the lake
> Driftwood
> A frame for a treasured picture
> Cosmetics
> Fine-textured fabric
> Time spent watching a storm gather
> A jar of ruby jam
> Marbles

An apple tree
A dam across a stream
Soft slippers
Fresh paint
A pine chest
Hand-woven blankets
A rustic well
Seeing God's hand in all of life
   Beauty *is* a good investment.

—Hebrews 13:15

FEBRUARY 16 **THE COST OF GIVING**

And love without some action
Praise that costs us nothing
Cannot be praise at all,
And love without some action
Shows gratitude too small.
     ("Little Nell")

David said, "I will not give unto the Lord that which costs me nothing" (II Samuel 24:24, paraphrased).

Is it possible that we are not giving until it costs us something? Our cast-offs may be helpful to others in need, but it is possible that we may be giving them so we will not feel guilty for being so wasteful. We could be giving of our time to obliterate our own boredom.

The joy of giving comes when we deny self. Love thrives on self-denial—not in feeling holy about it, but in adding to someone's wholeness at the cost of self.

My mother always ate the bony pieces of chicken, giving the better parts to her children. I often wondered why she seemed to delight in nibbling around all those bones to get so little chicken. When I became a mother, I understood her better. She loved us so much that it was easy for her to give. Service because of love became natural for her.

The strange thing is that when she grew older, she was still "taking the bony pieces," not just in food but in life. Her life was a living sacrifice; her joy was a result of her way of life. Joy never comes from looking for it.

The witness of her giving service was all around her town and neighborhood. Only God knows what it cost her; only she knew the joy she gained. This is a discovery, not a pursuit.

Some people wonder where the saints get their joy and, like Jerusalem of old (Matthew 23:37), will never see the joy of peace.

FEBRUARY 17   **THE CHALLENGE**

A new Christian is so delighted just to know the weightlessness of sins forgiven and the prospect of life in a whole new kingdom that no thought is given to the responsibility of grace.

"But we are given the responsibility of the ministry of reconciliation" (II Corinthians 5:18, paraphrased). *Reconcile* is a beautiful and fascinating word and a redeeming force in the world.

When the apostle Paul took on the call to a preaching ministry, it only extended his ministry of reconciliation, which is given to each of us as soon as we see the need of sharing the love of Jesus with our families and acquaintances.

Paul had no idea what the cost of discipleship would be. It cost everything, even as it does for each one of us, whatever that may be. For Paul it meant: in much patience, in tribulation, in needs, in distress, in stripes, in imprisonments, in tumult, in labors, in sleeplessness, in fastings, by purity, by kindness, by the Holy Spirit, by sincere love, by the word of truth, by the power of God, by the armor of righteousness, by honor and dishonor, by evil report or good report, as deceivers yet true, as unknown yet well known, as dying yet living, as chastened yet not killed, as sorrowful yet rejoicing, poor yet making many rich, as having nothing yet possessing all things (II Corinthians 6:4-10).

This kind of commitment is expected of every Christian, though the extent of our experiences may never reach that of Paul's.

Sometimes people ask, "Could I die for Christ, as many others have?" The answer is this: We are given grace as we need it. Living grace is victorious for living; dying grace is for dying and will come when we need it.

Grace cannot be stored up for use later. Like the manna from heaven in the Old Testament, we have a daily supply as we need it and as we depend upon Jesus. May we never forget that our study of the Word, times of spiritual growth, and rich fellowship build us up so we can give of ourselves to reach a hungry world that needs Jesus.

This goes far beyond Sunday morning worship services, evening vespers, midweek prayer services, choir practice, women's study sessions, men's softball practice, aerobics classes, singspirations, get-acquainted hours, or youth fellowship and picnics.

Wonderful as these may be, they are means to an end: the ministry of reconciliation. Whatever is required of us as individuals for this ministry of reconciliation, God will give to us as we use it. It is the giving of self that brings the results and expresses our concern.

Paul finishes by saying God will dwell in us and walk among us and be our God, and we shall be his people (II Corinthians 6:16). That should keep us from worrying. To him be the glory.

As the world closes in on the church and we see the "great day of our Lord" approaching, we can take the pledge of loyalty by the same grace Jesus gives us to live by. Faith grows as we obey him.

We can say, "Where he leads me I will follow," and mean it.

FEBRUARY 18   **SEARCH ME**

On a bright Sunday morning we stopped off on our way to services to have a sausage biscuit in a fast-food restaurant. At a table beside a big window sat three little children. They were not talking. They looked as prim and serious as little Quakers in a meeting.

As my daughter picked up our food, I slipped into the booth next to the children. "Are you hungry?" I asked cheerfully.

The boy who looked to be about five years old, answered, "Yes. Our dad is getting our breakfast." The two girls nodded.

"That's great!" I said, "You must have a fine daddy who orders your breakfast for you and you don't have to do a thing."

"Yes," agreed the boy. "And he's mean, too!" Nods, again, from the girls.

Their father came with their tray, and I tried not to stare at him. He was well dressed in a neat Sunday suit and looked as stiff and proper as the children.

As I looked at him, I wondered what he would think if he knew what his children thought of him. I wondered why he felt it was more godly to show his authority than to show his love. God doesn't do that.

It isn't important what I thought of him or what others think about me, I suppose. But it is important what God thinks about each of us. If God thinks well of us, there will surely be others who will appreciate us too.

Search me, O God, and know my heart, I pray. See if there be any wicked way in me (Psalm 139:23-24).

FEBRUARY 19   **HOLY ROOTS**

The importance of keeping ourselves pure is more and more evident as time goes on. Disease, handicap, and sorrow can be the result of someone's sin.

That God will forgive such sin is one of the greatest miracles of all time. But far better it would be if parents would be pure and teach little children why they should live clean, wholesome lives. To say, "The church teaches against it," "the Ten Commandments say *no*," or any of hundreds of other vague answers to vital questions does not impress youngsters much. It leaves children with no vision or incentive to live as they should. The greatest need is for a good example, followed by pleasant teaching day by day.

Influence, both good and bad, has awesome effects upon families. "If the root be holy, so are the branches," declares Paul in Romans 11:16, and in the Old Testament it is stated several times that the sins of the fathers influence the children even to the fourth generation (for example, Deuteronomy 5:9).

Only by God's redeeming power can we be the parents of children who can live lives pleasing to God; we have the wonderful privilege of helping God make and train eternal souls. This thought alone should cause us to lift our heads above the world and be holy roots, pure in heart.

Lord, whatever I can do, I will start now.

FEBRUARY 20 **RULER OVER MUCH**

They had lived in a tiny house on a side street. It seemed just perfect when they moved there. The rooms were small, but they did not have much furniture. They were young and in love.

Now, with two wonderful children—Laura who was eight and David who was five—they began to feel the pinch for space. The parents didn't complain, so the children were not conditioned to complain.

Laura and David had always shared a room between them, and not having known anything else and supported by the love and insight of their parents, they had managed well—Laura's things at one end and David's planes and birds at the other.

The family prayed and looked and at last found just the right place, in a better village with better schools and a good place to go to church.

Now Laura and David could each have a bedroom, with a door to close and a feeling of privacy. They had not noticed how neat that could be until, at last, they had it. They each developed a great sense of maturity and responsibility, and they loved it.

A dear aunt came to see their new home and enjoyed David's delight in his desk by the window, his own bookcase, and a large bed where he could sprawl to his heart's content. As they walked out into the hall, his aunt noticed a large sign on the door: "David's Room."

She asked, "Why do you need that?"

His answer: "Well, everybody has to be boss of something!"

We have to learn for ourselves if we can be trusted, if we can take responsibility. Parents can give guided responsibility to children from infancy. This is as God intended and is least painful for everyone.

The phrase "the terrible twos" suggests that that's the way they are, so that's the way they must be. I helped with the rearing of two daughters and five grandchildren, not as doting grandmother but as second mother. I never knew that any of them was supposed to be terrible when the calendar said "two."

Parents are to train, not to grit their teeth and endure a "stage." This little family faced life squarely, through understanding and communication. They did not make a big problem out of daily growth.

It is not possible to ignore daily training and growing and then, when children become teenagers, to just punch a button and expect them to be responsible, strong adults with godly values and mature judgments.

"You have been faithful over a few things; I will make you ruler over many things" (Matthew 25:21, paraphrased).

FEBRUARY 21   **LOVE IN ALL SIZES**

Love either oozes out and touches others, or it dries up and encrusts the soul.

Once we have tasted the luxury of love in our hearts, there is no desert so barren as a heart expanded by love and then left puckered by its absence.

Love does not count the cost in effort, time, or substance. Love is not for sacrifice or service; it is sacrifice and service. But the one who loves counts it neither. Love delights in serving; it does not measure the cost like those who want value returned. Love strikes no bargains.

When we deny self to better another, we are amazed to find that the things we meant to do for ourselves get done; if not, it usually turns out that they were not very important anyway.

Love smooths out wrinkles, takes off weight, builds muscles, improves the vocabulary, and sharpens awareness. Love greets the day with wonder, blossoms at noontime, closes the curtains of night with peace, and blankets the dark hours with insight.

Love does not measure time, squander opportunities, or destroy nature.

There is no "secular" or "religious" with love. It is all a sacred trust and makes humble tasks wear a crown to lay at our Savior's feet.

Love is not a burden thrust upon us, even when it is in the form of a cross. No one can make us love or keep us from it. It can only be freely given, never forced.

Love is a discovery. It is indispensable and inexhaustible. While all God's promises are conditional, his love is unconditional because it is eternal.

Love cannot be measured in pints or gallons. It adjusts to

each relationship and is different for each recipient—tailor-made for each individual.

Love is pure. Although it transcends every emotion, lust and covetousness take over when self-gratification extends beyond the welfare of another.

No one can have the love that belongs to another. A daughter-in-law cannot take the love that belongs to her husband's mother. Likewise, the mother cannot steal the love meant for her son's wife. There is always enough love to go around.

A sly, grudging relationship diminishes the love one would hoard for self. And though we may damage the relationships of others, we are always the losers and may never realize what caused our loss. Love may bring us pain, but it also heals.

Love is strong yet fragile, and should never be taken for granted, particularly when it's from God.

Love cannot be bought or sold, though many try; yet love that costs us nothing is not love at all. Love given for rewards consists of bargaining, but the rewards of sacrificial love bring surprising rewards we never dreamed possible.

Love is God at work in our lives. At the cost of everything else, Lord, give us love.

FEBRUARY 22   **THE BRICK CHURCH**

Two young ministers, one just out of seminary, the other pastoring a small village church, were riding in the country and came upon a beautiful brick church building. There was a large cemetery enclosed with the church by a stately iron fence. The lawns were well kept, but the church windows were boarded over.

The young ministers had visions of opening the church and winning everyone around the area to Christ. It never occurred to them that many of these people may have been

Christians before they two had even been born. Such is the enthusiasm of youth.

They contacted the proper caretakers and obtained permission to hold some evening meetings for two weeks. If they could enlist six families to help them, there was a possibility of starting a Sunday school and a preaching ministry.

Their young wives were as excited as they were, so with mops, brooms, and furniture polish they went to work. They washed windows, scrubbed, and polished. At last the clean, fresh smell overcame them, and the four of them knelt at the altar and dedicated their lives and labors to God and slept that night in their homes under blankets of peace.

The next day one of the pastors asked his wife to go with him to the little church in the country to pray. They had prayed in their own church in the village many times, but going away from their field of labor and activity seemed to give the pastor new inspiration.

When they got to the church, the young wife went inside to arrange some flowers she had brought, while her husband walked out into the cemetery. It was a quiet, peaceful place. The great pines planted many years before by someone's loving hands whispered eternal things in a gentle breeze. The young man knelt by a stone wall surrounding a family plot and lifted his aspirations to God.

After a while he went into the building where his wife sat turning the pages of a hymnal. "Are you ready to go?" she asked as she turned to her husband. He did not answer, and she rose to meet his puzzled expression.

"I think God is trying to tell me something," he said. "While I was praying, a scripture came to my mind several times."

"Well, what is it?" inquired his wife, staring at him. They opened his Bible and quickly turned to Luke 24:5. "Why seek ye the living among the dead?" they read in awe.

It had seemed the perfect place to pray, but God did not think it was the best time.

The next morning the young pastor laid the telephone directory beside him in the car and visited every family within twenty-five miles of the church. Many attended elsewhere. Some scorned a "preacher." Others promised to come. Children were excited. One man said it was the first time in thirty-two years that a minister had cared enough to come into his home.

Prayer has a vital part in the Christian life, but there are times when the best prayer is work.

In every congregation there are dead rituals, outgrown customs, moth-eaten pianos kept for sentimental reasons, and teachers who have long ago lost their fire and inspiration and who should retire to other ministries.

In our personal lives we need to check our testimonies, our willingness to work. We need to lay aside that weight, and sin that so easily besets us, and run with patience the race that is set before us (Hebrews 12:1).

Lord, keep our congregations alive with your presence. Make us aware when some of the things we have practiced for years are dead and should be relegated with respect to the past. Help us to seek the living Christ, the living Word, and living people who need your grace. Begin with me. Maybe I should have a funeral.

FEBRUARY 23   **HUMILITY**

Job learned that the arrogance of man can only come from ignorance and inexperience. When his advisors came up with all the answers and judged him by things they understood not at all, he was taken off balance for a while. After he had time to review his life and his knowledge of God, he was able to right himself. He had long before discovered the fact that his strength was in God and not himself. He said:

> His wisdom is profound, his power is vast.
> Who has resisted him and come out unscathed?
> He moves mountains without their knowing it.
> (Job 9:4-5, NIV)

It should not surprise us that the person who knows the least about something is often the one who has all the answers. From parenting to governing to pastoring, the same is true.

I know a young man who went to serve as associate pastor to a rather large church. He was fresh out of seminary, with all the books on theology and homiletics and all the statistics about church problems. He was ready to solve all the problems. His first sermon consisted of telling the church what was wrong with its people and its program.

This was a fine group of people, more dedicated to Christ than most congregations of its size. The pastor, an excellent Bible preacher, and the other pastors of various ministries sat lovingly through the whole discourse. The congregation was attentive. The message was completed with a flourish, and the young minister was quite satisfied with himself. A wise person would have been led by the Holy Spirit to give a message that would have fit the people and fed and encouraged them. It was evident this young man's experience did not fit his mouth.

During the rationing of World War II, someone in Washington decided to save large quantities of grain for overseas shipping by ordering "Mashless Thursday" for midwestern farmers, who depended upon the egg market for much of their income. Farmers knew that to withhold laying mash from their hens for even one day could throw them into a molt that would keep them from laying any eggs at all for six weeks or more.

The more we understand about God and the various laws governing his universe, the more we honor and worship him. We learn to trust in who he is and not in what we know. From Proverbs 3:5-6 (NIV) we learn:

Trust in the Lord with all your heart
    and lean not on your own understanding;
in all your ways acknowledge him
    and he will make your paths straight.

Humility before God makes us humble toward our fellows. Humility and good manners belong together. Good manners are not forms of conduct we mimic but are a result of the respect and honor we hold in our hearts toward God and his Word.

Submit your ways to God and be at peace with him;
    in this way prosperity will come to you.
Accept instruction from his mouth
    and lay up his words in your heart.
                      (Job 22:21-22 NIV)

Dear God, please don't embarrass me by showing me all the times I have been arrogant by thinking I knew more than I did. Just give me your grace to be humble of mind for the next time.

FEBRUARY 24   **THE PEACEMAKER**

Peacemakers live above the battleground. They know that people are more important than things; that the possessions and advantages we are conditioned to seek are temporal.

Peacemakers have made peace with the Peacemaker. This makes it easier to open the fist, palms up. Surrender to God is the best weapon for peace.

This does not mean that peacemakers have no need of things or opportunities. It does mean that they have begun to be able to separate the eternal from the perishable in everything. Values turn right-side up.

This is not a peaceful world. Paul said he had fought a good fight. It was a fight of faith, however. It was a fight against the love of money and things that pull us downward.

He advised us to flee these things in order to follow after righteousness, faith, love, patience, meekness (I Timothy 6:10-12).

Peacemakers have discovered a goal higher than economic gain. Values and relationships become more easily sorted out when the heart is at peace.

Let us stand on tiptoe to get a better view into the eternal.

Peacemakers turn battlegrounds into vineyards.

FEBRUARY 25 **BROKENNESS**

"And it came to pass, as he sat at meat with them, he took bread, and blessed it, and brake, and gave to them" (Luke 24:30).

This high point in Christ's relationship with his disciples is sometimes relegated to the *ritual* of Communion and left there. Not that this is a minor thing, but that, as such, it can become dull to our awareness of what God wants us to know.

We know that he said, "This is my body," which should make our hearts melt in adoration and praise at the very thought of *his* brokenness. There are not enough praises to say this properly!

He also teaches that this loaf represents his church; the individual grains molded together and passed through the heat of purifying submission to form the body of Christ. This is the church of the living God.

Individually, and as the church, we must be *broken*. Self is too big, the carnal mind too stubborn, and the preservation of self too strong a force for us to be of much use to God in our natural condition. A broken church is a caring church—molded together in a loaf.

Romans 8:7-8 (Amplified) states it so well: "That is because the mind of the flesh—with its carnal thoughts and purposes—is hostile to God, for it does not submit itself to God's Law, indeed it cannot. So then those who are living the life of the flesh—catering to the appetites and impulses of their carnal nature—cannot please or satisfy God, or be acceptable."

Is it any wonder that a "church" that stops short of the true gospel of Christ is filled with all kinds of self-exalting people who cannot glorify Christ? It is interesting that the Scriptures usually say that he took bread and blessed it, then *broke* it. He does not crush us or mash us or damage us; he breaks our stubborn will so we can be used to win those out there who are hurting because they have no Savior.

Someone has said, "Only the wounded can heal the wounded." I did not know I was not broken until we were called to the ministry. One day I was praying for my unsaved loved ones. In my eagerness I prayed, "God, I would give anything to see my mother, father, and sister saved!" Then the question came to me: Would I give Evelyn? Now, Evelyn was our golden-haired daughter. I had never known what life is all about until she was born. Outside of finding Christ, there was nothing so important to me as our dear little girl. I would give up any personal pleasure or ambition for her good and welfare.

Why did God impress me with this idea? If I had an idol, it was that child; houses, cars, friends, position could all go down the drain, but everything we planned or desired was measured by what was best for her. This is not bad to a point, but Jesus must be first. I had not realized he was not.

At last I said, "Lord, be first in my life—whatever it takes." God knew where my weakness was, but I had to see it too. My heart was completely broken, and I gave my child to God. I laid her upon the altar, for sacrifice or service. Compared to that, all other commitments were easy. Our ministry went forward, my love for people doubled, and I experienced an abandonment of self to God very unnatural for me.

"Where your treasure is, there will your heart be also" (Matthew 6:21) made sense to me at last.

My two children love and serve God. My sons-in-law are

in his service, my five grandchildren are Christians, and the three who are married have husbands in some ministry. I did not cause this; but if I had refused to let God break my selfish will, who knows what my influence would have been?

He broke it, the scripture states, and gave it to *them*. Lord, keep me broken so the crumbs will feed the poor in spirit, for we are all poor in spirit, needing your wisdom to mold us into something with eternal values.

FEBRUARY 26 **HELPMATES**

A young man I know quite well dedicated his life to the ministry of preaching. He went to seminary and came home filled with joy and enthusiasm. I had given him many of my husband's good books, collected over the years, and he was thrilled, hoping at last to read something he wanted to instead of all those things he had been reading because they were required in school.

He married a Christian girl and brought her to see me. We had so much to share, and he was trying to bring me up to date on his growth in the Lord. Every question I asked him, his wife broke into the conversation and tried to answer— things she did not really know anything about. She had done most of the talking up to then, and they would have to leave soon.

At last I said to her, "I asked John, Ruth; please let him speak."

She answered, "Well, we are one now that we are married."

"Which one?" I asked her.

The next time they came, she did not do that. (Maybe it helped his ministry.)

Both helpmates in marriage must keep their identities. Kahlil Gibran said about marriage: ". . . Let there be spaces in your togetherness/and let the winds of the heavens dance between you."

Humorously put:

Helpmates

Marriage is not a thing of bliss,
But neither is it a wilderness.
The beauty, if you find it there,
Is brought about by wind and tear.
The things we seek through selfish lust
May turn on us like subtle rust.
A mate can be just as bad
And two like that are really sad.
Our "self" concern becomes a joke;
Our mate's self-love it will provoke.
He wants the lakes to fish and sail
While she prefers a rummage sale.
Two spoiled children always clash;
Their ordered life turns into hash.
While man should not live alone,
Two stubborn people ruin a home.
So what's the answer, may I ask,
If in peace we want to bask?
A loving person cannot fill
The wants of one self-centered will.

The Solution:

He gives himself to make her whole;
She yields herself to save his soul.
Then together they can walk,
But most of all, they have to talk!

"Giving thanks always for all things unto God . . . in the

name of our Lord Jesus Christ; submitting yourselves one to another in the fear of God" (Ephesians 5:20-21).

FEBRUARY 27 **MINISTERING ANGELS**

"The child Samuel ministered unto the Lord before Eli. And the word of the Lord was precious in those days; therefore there was no open vision" (I Samuel 3:1).

It is evident that God is going to see to it that there are those who will minister to his people.

After the temptations of Jesus, angels came and ministered to him (Matthew 4:11).

God's ministering angels take many forms. When God's people get careless about their ministering, they become lean in their souls and often start complaining. Healthy Christians serve. God's glory is our highest aim, and it comes through service prompted by our love and freely given.

I knew a pastor who ministered to a small congregation who had had no training in looking after a pastor. The parsonage was small and run-down. The only heat in winter was from a little woodstove. The walls were thin and drafty.

The minister and his wife were praying for the price of a load of wood. They went to church early to enjoy the warm building and to pray for the services.

A young man who lived on the other side of town drove his pickup truck past the pastor's home and saw that there was no wood on the woodpile. Although he did not know the pastor at all, he felt an urge to take some wood, which he did.

When the minister's family arrived home after the services, they were amazed to find a large pile of wood. They praised the Lord for answered prayer. The minister later found out that nobody in his congregation had brought the fuel and inquired around until he located his benefactor. They became lifelong friends.

There are many ways to minister to one another, the most thrilling of which is to give of oneself.

There are many records of God using animals to minister to people. Balaam of the Old Testament was blind and deaf to God's will for him. God used his donkey to open his spiritual eyes and obtain his obedience. The donkey suffered much at Balaam's angry hand (Numbers 22:23-30). It must not have been very flattering for Balaam to learn that a donkey knew enough to serve God when he did not.

God used ravens to minister to Elijah when he was praying by the brook Cherith. Every day the raven flew overhead and dropped meat and bread and fed him (I Kings 17:4-6).

When his neighbors ignored his poverty and pain, dogs came and ministered to Lazarus and stayed with him until he was escorted into Abraham's bosom.

A rooster ministered to Peter after he had denied his Master. His loud crowing made Peter remember how he had sinned, and he wept in repentance (Mark 14:72).

Sheep minister to all of us when we see their meek obedience to their master. "The sheep hear his voice, and he calls his own sheep by name and leads them out" (John 10:3 RSV).

When God can even use animals and birds to minister to us, we should look for opportunities to serve our fellow Christians and to bring the living Word to a lost world. We are called to minister, to bear one another's burdens, and to show the love of Christ wherever possible.

Lord, keep me aware of your presence. Don't let dumb animals see God more clearly than I do because I am absorbed in myself. Make me one of your ministering angels in my human form.

FEBRUARY 28 **NEW BIRTH**

Out of the womb of winter
Moves the triumphant spring

And dark days are forgotten
As we embrace the joy it brings.

"This, too, shall pass," it is sure—
So treasure the gifts of life;
If things are bad, endure them;
There will come an end to strife.

In winter we dream of summer;
In summer we cry for cool.
We waste the jewels of springtime
Reaching out of a summer pool.

Peace is the fruit of contentment,
Look back and you miss the now.
The future is God's—don't touch it.
Let spring clear your furrowed brow.

—Genesis 8:22

With Christ in the Gospels

MARY RUTH HOWES

THE FIRST WORD

(Read Mark 1:1-14.)

"The first word of the good tidings of Jesus Christ Son of God. . . . Jesus went into Galilee proclaiming the good news from God" (Mark 1:1, 14 Rieu).

The first word is "good tidings," good news.*

What a marvelous statement that is! The first word, the basis of God's relationship to us, is good news—the good news of his love. God is for us, as Paul put it in Romans 8.

When I was a freshman in college, Dr. Kilby, my English literature teacher, picked me out of his survey class to work for him. My first job was to put footnotes in the biography he had written of the college founder, using the careful records he had made and the files he had kept. I often marveled that he had chosen me, a scared freshman. It was something I could never have anticipated. But as I look back at my life, his choosing me was good news for me—a first word that changed my life. Because he believed in me, I could begin to believe in me. I worked for him for six years and have spent my life in one way or another with Christian literature.

God's coming to us is good news. And that's a great beginning, to a new life.

---

*The Greek word *arche,* "beginning," is also used for the first item in a series.

Thank you, O God, that you "chose us in Christ before the foundation of the world" (Ephesians 1:4 Rieu). I will walk in that good news today.

MARCH 2   **THE GOOD NEWS IS CHANGE**

(Read Mark 1:1-3, 14-15.)

"Jesus went into Galilee proclaiming the good news from God. 'The time has come,' he said, 'and the Kingdom of God is near. Repent and put your trust in the Good News'" (Mark 1:14-15 Rieu).

I have often wondered what the people in Galilee understood as the good news from God. I suspect that like most of us, they thought of good news in terms of more money coming in, a better job, better crops, better relationships—a happier life. Perhaps it was also, for many of them, the coming political kingdom, when God's presence would mean death to their enemies.

If the first word is "good news," the second word is "change." The Greek word translated "repent" means literally to change one's mind, one's way of thinking, and therefore one's way of acting. They had to change their thinking about God and his presence. How have I been thinking about God?

If I'm honest, I must admit that down deep I'm afraid to let God come near. I can't believe that God's coming near to me is good news. But that thinking is what Jesus calls me to change. Because the good news is that God is good news. And that is something I can rely on.

Lord, help me to change my way of thinking about you, and to rely on the good news of your presence.

MARCH 3   **THE WILDERNESS**

(Read Mark 1:9-13.)

"The Spirit drove him out into the desert" (Mark 1:12 Rieu).

Everyone has a wilderness experience at some point in life,

when the good news that God has chosen us seems to have vanished along with all the things that make life enjoyable. We are no longer living where the grass is green and the trees full, but are out in the hot, dry desert.

This is the anniversary of a wilderness experience. On March 3, 1943, our family of four entered Chapei Civil Assembly Center outside of Shanghai, to spend the rest of World War II behind Japanese barbed wire. (It is odd that this date on which my sister, my parents, and I lost our freedom is one we never forget, whereas the date on which the war was over and we were told we were free is not firmly fixed in my memory, though the occasion remains vivid.) For my mother, especially, the next two and a half years were very hard. She became extremely ill, lost forty pounds, and nursed both of us girls through serious illnesses. The fact that we were not able to be repatriated in 1943 caused her a great deal of emotional suffering.

I watched Mother fight the temptation to despair. There were times when she nearly went under. But she knew that she did not live by bread alone (by the end of the war we were down to one very small meal a day) and found help and strength from words from the mouth of God. The biblical accounts of prisoners who found that God was with them in their wilderness days gave her great encouragement. And we too experienced the ministry of angels (Mark 1:13, but that's another story).

O God, help me always to remember how you kept us through our wilderness experience and met our needs. Thank you that you continue to meet my needs today.

MARCH 4   **ANGELS**

(Read Matthew 4:1-11.)
"The Spirit drove him out into the desert. . . . He was with the wild beasts, and the Angels ministered to his wants" (Mark 1:12-13 Rieu).

Not many of us have seen angels, though we read about

them throughout the Bible and sing about them every Christmas.

But perhaps we *have* seen angels, even, like the Hebrews, entertained angels unawares. We get the word "angel" from the Greek word *angelos,* which means "messenger." And God can use anyone, even you and me, as his messengers.

During our two and a half years in internment camp, the angels who ministered to our wants were Germans—our enemies. But they were first of all followers of Jesus Christ and fellow missionaries. Since Germany was allied with Japan, they were not interned but were able to continue living in their homes in Shanghai. Every month they bought two thousand pounds of foodstuff and packed it in two hundred "comfort parcels," which they sent to their fellow missionaries in the various camps. The Japanese allowed us to receive these parcels, but the Germans faced the constant risk of being accused of consorting with the enemy. The parcels supplemented the meager food supplied by the Japanese and helped to keep us alive.

God's angels are all around us—and not just the invisible kind. His messengers meet us every day, offering words of cheer and encouragement, greeting, friendship, help. As I open my eyes to see his messengers, I realize that I am one of them. *I* am called to meet the needs of people in wilderness places, as other "angels" have met mine. It makes me smile to realize that I am an angel!

Lord, how great that you have a sense of humor! I thank you for the many "angels" you have used to meet my needs throughout my life. Help me to be your angel to others today.

MARCH 5   **AMAZEMENT**

(Read Mark 1:21-22.)

"[Jesus'] way of teaching filled them with amazement, for he taught them like one with authority and not like the Doctors of the Law" (Mark 1:22 Rieu).

I once read through the Gospels, marking all the words that showed emotion. I found all the basic emotions mentioned or demonstrated, many of them by Jesus. Mark gave me the clearest picture of an emotional Jesus. He also referred again and again to the amazement, wonder, and awe of the people who met Jesus, heard him speak and teach, saw him do miracles, and followed him up and down the roads of Palestine.

God's coming near to us in Jesus Christ is not only good news, it is amazing news. Jesus didn't fit neatly into any category. He was always confounding expectations. People and leaders alike thought they had God pegged—they knew what he was going to do. Instead, he did something new. He amazed them.

Has anything amazed you lately? Have your expectations been confounded this past year? Could that have been the presence of Jesus? Could God have been working in your life, drawing near you? Confounded expectations don't always bring joy at first. But remember, the good news of God's presence involves changing our way of thinking.

Lord Jesus, you astonished people by your life and words when you lived among us in the flesh. I would like to have that sense of wonder and amazement at your working in my life.

MARCH 6 **AUTHORITY**

(Read Mark 1:21-28.)

"A new doctrine, this! And it has power behind it" (Mark 1:27 Rieu).

Part of the amazement of Jesus' hearers stemmed from the way he taught. He didn't buttress his teaching with lots of quotations. He didn't provide fanciful interpretations of Scripture. He taught from his own knowledge of God, his own knowledge of the Scriptures, his own knowledge of human nature, and his own inner authority.

Jesus' powerful teaching has come to be connected in my

mind with his statement recorded in John 14:6: "I am the way and the truth and the life." To *be* truth—that is to have every aspect of one's life open, in harmony with God. Paul described it as demonstrating the fruit of the Spirit (Galatians 5:22-23).

Many people claim to have God's authority for their teaching. But do their actions prove their words? Jesus' deeds had the same quality of authority to them. Evil was challenged and beaten. People's lives were *changed*—by a word!

O Jesus, as you cast out evil spirits from people's lives while you were on earth, root out the evil in my life so that I may begin to live in truth and in harmony with God.

MARCH 7   **FOLLOWING**

(Read Mark 1:14-20.)

"Jesus said to them [James and John]: 'Come, follow me, and I will make you fishers of men' " (Mark 1:17 Rieu).

When I was a little girl, we were taught to sing a chorus in Sunday school based on this verse: "I will make you fishers of men, / If you follow me." For some reason, I never liked that chorus and rebelled against the idea of being made a "fisher of men." (I've never particularly cared for fishing, either.)

But reading through the Gospels as an adult, I have come to see that Jesus doesn't call me to be a fisherman. He didn't call Nicodemus or Mary of Bethany to become a fisherman. He called people who were already fishermen to a different kind of fishing, using for a metaphor the pursuit that already described them. Mary, a thoughtful, relational person, was called to sit at Jesus' feet. Peter's mother-in-law was called to serve. The Gadarene demoniac was called to tell his family and friends what Jesus had done for him.

So it has dawned on me that I am called to work with words and books. But like the fishermen who dropped their twine nets and left their fishy boats to follow Jesus, I must follow Jesus first and let him make me his book person.

O Lord, I am so grateful you call me to be your person, using the gifts you have given me. Let me be open to receiving new gifts and discovering new areas of service—perhaps even fishing for people!

MARCH 8   **SERVICE**

(Read Mark 1:29-31.)

"Simon's mother-in-law lay in bed there with fever. . . . He went up to her, seized her hand and raised her. The fever left her and she began to wait on them" (Mark 1:30-31 Rieu).

The first woman mentioned in Mark's Gospel (and there are only a few as compared with Luke's Gospel) is an unnamed mother-in-law. Mothers-in-law tend to get a bad press in our day, and sometimes for good reason. Yet the two mothers-in-law mentioned in Scripture get special attention and blessing. Naomi, mother-in-law of the Moabite woman Ruth, so inspired her daughter-in-law's loyalty that Ruth left her homeland to settle in a strange land. In the process Naomi was brought from bitterness to joy, from barrenness to prosperity.

Peter's mother-in-law was sick. Some Bible students have suggested that her fever was an emotional one, caused by the sudden appearance of several extra people to serve a Sabbath lunch to, and perhaps by Peter's taking up with an itinerant rabbi. But whether emotional or physical, a fever is a fever, bringing aches and pains and great discomfort. At Jesus' touch the fever left, her health and strength returned, and she got up to do what needed to be done—put food on the table.

An old cliché says, "Saved to serve." When God calls us to change our way of thinking and acting, when he turns our lives around, he asks us to serve—*where we are*. That is, in our homes, fixing meals, waiting tables, changing sheets and diapers, cleaning house, entertaining guests—as well as in our offices and places of employment. Eventually it may also mean leaving home and family for Jesus' sake, as did Peter and Andrew and all the disciples, and as did a number of women in Jesus' own day (see Luke 8). But we start where we are, with what we have in our hands and homes to offer our Lord.

Thank you, Jesus, for your healing touch. Help me to serve you first in my home, making it a place of refreshment and hospitality.

MARCH 9   **COMPASSION**

(Read Mark 1:32-34, 40-41.)

"Jesus was filled with compassion. He stretched out his hand, touched him and . . . the leprosy left him immediately and he was cleansed" (Mark 1:41-42 Rieu).

The first emotion attributed to Jesus by Mark is compassion. The Greek word used here is sometimes translated "bowels of compassion" or "heart" by the King James Version. The root word is the word for stomach, which for the Greeks was the seat of the emotions! Compassion is far more than pity. It is a deeply felt emotion that leads to action. Here it led Jesus first to touch and then to heal an untouchable leper.

Mark has already demonstrated Jesus' compassion in action, without naming it. On the evening of that Sabbath day in Capernaum, Jesus' compassion had brought healing to the sick and diseased that crowded around Simon's house. Now Mark names the emotion in connection with a hopeless leper—the AIDS victim of his day. For the leper the touch meant as much as the healing that followed. Both actions restored the man to society, and the recommendation to show himself in the temple was to be the proof of that restoration.

Lord, forgive my easy pity that costs me nothing. Change me, so that I feel deeply and act out my compassion, whatever the cost.

STERNNESS

(Read Mark 1:40-41.)

"Jesus dismissed [the leper] promptly, with a stern injunction. 'Be careful not to say a word to anyone,' he said, 'but go show yourself to the priest' " (Mark 1:43-44 Rieu).

Compassion isn't soft. Jesus didn't treat the newly healed man with kid gloves. He "sternly charged" him (RSV) to shut his mouth. The Greek word here is another visceral one, sometimes used of a snort of anger or "indignant comments" (John 14:5 Rieu), other times of a bodily trembling (John 11:33 Rieu).

I don't know the reasons for this prohibition. George Lamsa suggests that the Aramaic phrase behind "tell no man" (Matthew 8:4 KJV) really meant to "tell everyone" *(My Neighbor Jesus)*. On the other hand, why the sternness and controlled anger? Mark suggests that Jesus foresaw the problems of publicity—the resulting crowds made it impossible for him to work inside the towns. Perhaps, too, he was angry at the disease that exiled people from human contact when they needed it most.

I suspect also that Jesus wanted to make sure the man didn't just sit around enjoying celebrity status, being made much of. He was to get back into society and take up his place as worshiper, fulfilling the law's requirements.

Having our lives changed by Jesus Christ does not make us any more special to God than we already are. We are not to bask in the adulation and amazement of the crowd. We are to show our changed lives *in our living*.

O God, I thank you for your sternness that calls me not to sit back and relax but to do the next thing required of me.

PARALYSIS

(Read Mark 2:1-12.)

"[Jesus] was telling them of the Word, when he was

approached by some people bringing him a paralytic carried by four men" (Mark 2:2-3 Rieu).

Some years ago I was worried about a friend of mine who was in a nearly suicidal depression caused by a lifetime of abuse. I didn't know how to reach or help her. At the time I was editing Earl Palmer's commentary on John *(The Intimate Gospel)* and had come to his treatment of John 5, the healing of the man by the pool of Bethesda. Dr. Palmer wrote, "It takes more emotional strength to ask for help than to tell about the impossibility of help. A human being may be so fatigued and emotionally depleted that it is not possible to risk even the 'Yes, I want to be well.' The wonder that breaks upon us in this incident is that Jesus Christ is able to heal just such a person" (p. 61).

Those words were exactly what I needed to stir *my* faith in the One who can heal paralytics and who responds to faith *for* someone else. I mentally lowered my friend to the feet of Jesus for healing.

Some days later, I got a call from my friend, who told me of having been shown personally that God did indeed love her and that she had worth for him. Her life continues to be changed and to grow.

Thank you, O Christ, for your healing love that touches us where and as we are and that allows us to act in faith for the helpless.

MARCH 12   **HOSPITALITY**

(Read Mark 2:13-17.)

"Jesus sat down to a meal in [Levi's] house" (Mark 2:15 Rieu).

For the years of his ministry, Jesus had no permanent home. He stayed in other people's homes and ate other people's meals. He told some would-be followers that though animals had nests and lairs, he had no place to lay his head. Yet Jesus had a strong sense of home—God was his home. Even at twelve, he wanted to be in his Father's house.

But his lack of a place of his own meant that he offered the people he met a chance to show hospitality. And so we keep reading in the Gospels of invitations to meals that Jesus accepted—sometimes with pleasure, sometimes with frustration.

I saw the gift of hospitality worked out in my parents' lives. In spite of never owning a physical house in their forty-seven years of marriage, they were continually opening their home—wherever or whatever it was—to others. Even in internment camp we would have one or another of the single folk up to our cubicle (we shared one seventeen-by-forty-five-foot room with nine other people) to eat with us and share our "homeness."

And today, at the age of ninety, my father still invites people over to share his homemade turkey soup on Sunday after church—often a newcomer, or one or two other single people.

Lord, forgive me for feeling I must wait until my house is in perfect order before I can invite others in. Help me to remember that a home *is created by the spirit of the people who live in it far more than by its physical perfection.*

MARCH 13   **MENDING**

(Read Mark 2:18-22.)

"No one mends an old cloak with a piece of new cloth" (Mark 2:21 Rieu).

I used to watch my mother turn her muslin sheets sides to middle, so that they'd wear evenly. And until she died, whenever she came to visit me she would always ask it I had any mending that needed to be done. She'd be happy sewing and patching and darning.

I don't mend clothes much any more these days. I get the sense that not many people do, unless we paid a lot for them, like a good coat or a wool skirt. Even then we tend not to patch clothes like our mothers did unless it's part of a trend, like prepatched jeans or jackets.

Apart from the meaning of these words—that attempts to improve and repair must fit the situation or the problem will get worse—what I see in this tiny vignette is the sensitivity of a young man to his mother's constant need to mend the torn clothing of her family—clothing ripped by the rough lumber and nails of the carpenter shop. Perhaps he himself had unwisely tried to mend a torn cloak with unshrunken cloth, creating a bitter hole.

It encourages me that Jesus drew his illustrations from a woman's world as well as a man's. He shows us that whatever our worlds, God sees the least details and finds them important—even when we have to scrimp to make do.

Lord, thank you for your sensitivity to us and to our activities, as well as to our reluctance to change. Help me to notice the people around me with as much sensitivity, and to be careful how I try to create change.

MARCH 14   **ANGER**

(Read Mark 3:1-6.)

"After an angry glance round the circle, and grieved at their insensibility, [Jesus] said to the man [with the withered hand]: 'Hold out your hand'" (Mark 3:5 Rieu).

Jesus let his audience know that he was angry, because he knew he was angry. But he didn't let his anger get away from him. He used it to focus on the truth—being permitted to do good on the Sabbath day—and then he became the truth, both for the synagogue worshipers and the impaired man himself. The truth was that the people were insensitive, hard of heart, and a man needed to be made whole. Their concern for the status quo had blinded them to the truth of worship, of God's presence, and to the possibility, even necessity, of change. That insensitivity and blindness caused Jesus deep grief. With emotion he reached out and made the man physically whole.

What makes us angry? A personal slight? When things don't go right for us? Or a wrong done to someone else?

Thank you, O God, for anger. Help me to know and admit when I am angry and also to be honest with myself over the cause of my anger. I want to learn to use my anger in the right way.

MARCH 15   **FEAR!**

(Read Mark 4:35-41.)

" 'Master, do you not care if we are lost?' Jesus rebuked the wind and said to the sea: 'Silence! Be still!' "* (Mark 4:38-39 Rieu).

I got on the wrong commuter van the other day because I didn't ask the right questions, and found myself north rather than south of the Lincoln Tunnel, stranded in a part of Union City-Weehawken I didn't know. I walked several blocks to a busline and just missed a bus headed for Jersey City. I ended up waiting forty-five minutes for another bus.

My initial reaction to being lost or stranded is always a terrible burst of fear and panic, followed by tears and then anger at myself, compounded with frustration over feelings of abandonment and desolation. Whatever my mind told me—that I would get home okay, that I wasn't really lost, and that if worst came to worst I could walk the four or five miles home since I had my sneakers on—made almost no impression on my first feelings.

I wish I could say I specifically turned to Jesus to calm my fears, but I didn't pray consciously. Yet in another sense I did do what Jesus said. I told the waves of fear and panic, "Shut up! Be quiet." And they shut up. When the bus finally came,

---

*The two Greek words can be translated "Stop making noise" (that is, "shut up") and "Be muzzled."

I was laughing and talking with a fellow passenger who had shared the long wait.

With Jesus' help we can command whatever threatens to swamp us: "Shut up! Quiet! Calm down!"

"And the wind dropped and a great calm ensued" (Mark 4:39 Rieu).

MARCH 16   **HUMOR**

(Read Luke 14:1-6.)

" 'Which of you here, if his son* falls into a well, or his ox, will not pull him out on a sabbath day without hesitation?' " (Luke 14:5 JB).

When this tiny parable is put into Aramaic (the language Jesus spoke), the reason for pairing "son" with "ox" is apparent. Jesus is making a play on words.

" 'Which of you here, if his son [bᶜra] falls into a well [bēra], or his ox [be'ira], will not pull him out . . . ?' " (Matthew Black, *An Aramaic Approach to the Gospels and Acts,* p. 126). I can see the gleam in Jesus' eye as he watches the critical lawyers waiting to trip him, knowing that of course they would immediately pull their sons out of any well or ditch.

In his introduction to his translation of the Gospels, E. V. Rieu says that he found Jesus "a master of ready speech and witty repartee." His parables "are full of quiet humour. The crowds must often have laughed." Dorothy Sayers writes in *The Man Born to Be King* that Jesus "said surprising things, in language ranging from the loftiest poetry to the most lucid narrative and the raciest repartee. If we did not know all His retorts by heart . . . we should reckon Him among the greatest wits of all time."

If you enjoy puns, know that Jesus did too.

---

*Some of the oldest Greek manuscripts have the son rather than the donkey (see RSV) falling into the well.

(Read Luke 1:5-13.)

"Her name was Elizabeth . . . and both [Zacharias and Elizabeth] were well advanced in years" (Luke 1:5 Rieu).

Luke is the Gospel of women. He tells more stories about more women than any of the other Gospel writers, and he gives the names of many of them. He begins his Gospel with the names of a couple—an old man and an old woman.

In many parts of the world, including our own, being old, and especially an old woman, means being invisible. In her book *The Desert Blooms* Sarah-Patton Boyle recounts the terrible pain she experienced when, after a full and rewarding life in which she was recognized as a complete person, she came to be treated as a nonentity—because people saw only her gray hair, they considered her of no value. *The Desert Blooms* also tells about her courageous journey out of the resulting depression and despair.

The good news of the gospel is that as women—even gray-haired women—we are not only valued by God, but our names are also recorded in his history, and we may play a pivotal role in the working out of God's purposes.

Thank you, Father, that you count even my gray hairs, that my name is important to you, and that you continue to have a place for me.

MARCH 18   **BARREN**

(Read Luke 1:14-25.)

"His wife Elizabeth in due course conceived" (Luke 1:24 Rieu).

All her life, Elizabeth had wanted a child. To be barren in Jewish culture was to be pitied, disparaged, and considered under God's judgment. Now, in her old age, her dream was coming true. Now, "the Lord had . . . deigned to bring her humiliation to an end" (Luke 1:25 Rieu).

Today our culture is gradually relaxing the demand that every woman have children, or even be married. Nor do we consider childlessness a sign of God's displeasure. But there is another kind of barrenness that we may know and carry in our hearts that is as hard to bear as Elizabeth's was for her. That is the barrenness of creativity, of achievement, of having a work of our own that "will be a joy and a delight" so that "many others will rejoice" (Luke 1:14 Rieu).

Elizabeth's experience lets us know that with God age is no barrier. If there is a dream in our hearts, a creative "child" awaiting birth, God can and will bring that dream into being as we respond in faith to him. Elizabeth's rejuvenation also involved the enlivening of her husband, in spite of his lack of faith. What joy—that it's never too late with God for the fulfillment of a dream, for the creation of life in the place of barrenness.

O God, I praise you that you are the God of the impossible.

MARCH 19   **YOUNG**

(Read Luke 1:26-35.)

"The angel Gabriel was sent by God to . . . a maiden . . . Mary. Gabriel . . . said, 'Greetings, lady of grace! The Lord is with you' " (Luke 1:26-28 Rieu).

Mary was a young girl, as far as we can tell, just at the beginning of adulthood. Betrothal in those times could be contracted when a girl was twelve to fourteen—an age we today consider far too young for marriage. Certainly we would consider a teenage girl quite the wrong person to be trusted with an important mission—mothering the Son of God.

The joyful news is, however, that we cannot be too young for God to use, just as no one is too old to be beyond God's power to touch and transform. Youth is also the time of dreams. When the angel called Mary "lady of grace," he started her on the journey to adulthood, to the fulfillment of her dreams with joy—and sorrow—in ways she could never have imagined.

Lord, I thank you that you use us even in our youth.

MARCH 20   **PREGNANT**

(Read Luke 1:39-45.)

"When Elizabeth heard Mary's greeting, the baby leapt in her womb" (Luke 1:41 Rieu).

In the first two chapters of his Gospel Luke gives us personal glimpses of the characters, taking us behind the scenes into their thoughts and conversations. Here we listen in on the intimate talk of two pregnant women sharing the joys, wonders, fears, and expectancies of this time that belongs so uniquely to women.

We women can be awed and joyful that in this Gospel our uniqueness becomes part of Scripture. And more than that, we can rejoice that God himself became part of us. "God sent forth his Son, made of a woman" (Galatians 4:4).

O God, thank you for using us in your worldwide plan.

MARCH 21   **OLD AND SINGLE**

(Read Luke 2:22-34, 36-38.)

"And there was Hannah, a prophetess . . . She was very old, having lived . . . by herself as a widow for as much as eighty-four years" (Luke 2:36-37 Rieu).

As a single person I sometimes wonder what will happen to me when I get old without a family. How will I manage, and what will I do? From Anna, as we know her in the King James Bible, or Hannah, her Hebrew name, I am given a clue. Hannah was either eighty-four (RSV) or else had been a widow for eighty-four years, which would put her in her late nineties or early hundreds. She had spent her life praying and worshiping in the temple. I'm sure she had friends and acquaintances in Jerusalem, but what gave meaning to her life was her connection to God, her "sacrifice of praise to God," as the writer of Hebrews puts it (Hebrews 13:15).

I see this same kind of connectedness in my father's life. Since my mother died, he has lived alone, but his life continues to have meaning through his constant prayer and his service in the church he has been a member of for over fifty years. Though he is in his nineties, he is still active and, like Hannah, is "never far from the Temple" (Luke 2:37 Rieu).

O Lord, I want my old age to be meaningful and connected to others. Help me now to create those connections by prayer and worship and by giving myself to your church.

MARCH 22   **JUDGING**

(Read Luke 6:32-38.)

"Do not judge and you shall not be judged" (Luke 6:37 Rieu).

In moving into my own house recently, I have had to clean heavy nicotine and grease stains from all over the kitchen and stove (I'm still not done)! When I first started the job I grumbled ferociously about the woman who never cleaned around her stove after she fried foods and never worked on the vent-a-hood grease trap.

Then it came time to move the last things out of the apartment I had lived in for two and a half years and to do the final cleaning there. As I ran the vacuum wand over the baseboards and up around the ceiling molding, I realized again how seldom I dusted. And then when I came to clean up the stove for the last time, I saw the evidence of another woman who neglected her stove and let the grease build up in the cracks. By my own judgment I was convicted and judged.

Lord, forgive me for my critical attitude that finds it so easy to see another person's faults and to ignore my own. Thank you that you do not condemn me. Help me not to condemn others but to love them.

MARCH 23   **LEAVING HOME**

(Read Luke 7:35–8:3.)

"He was accompanied by . . . some women who had been cured of evil spirits and infirmities—Mary surnamed Magdalene . . . ; Joanna . . . ; Susanna; and a number of others, who were in a position to minister to his wants out of their own resources" (Luke 8:2-3 Rieu).

I love to read this part of Luke's Gospel. It is so unexpected, so little known, so unconventional. Women traveling as part of a band of disciples. Women with money—their own, as Rieu's translation makes clear. Mary Magdalene we know from other accounts, but Joanna and Susanna are only mentioned here. Joanna came from Herod's court to be with Jesus on the road.

We don't know the circumstances of Jesus' calling these women to be his followers, yet I believe he did. Certainly they responded to his message and his person by leaving their homes to become part of an itinerant band. (Other disciples, like Mary and Martha of Bethany, stayed home.)

As these women traveled with Jesus, they served him with what they had—their money, their time, their presence—and so met his needs. What needs of his can we meet today in his service?

Lord, help me remember that as I help "the least" of people in need, I am helping you (Matthew 25:40).

MARCH 24   **DAUGHTERS**

" 'My little daughter . . . is at the point of death.' . . . 'Daughter, your faith has saved you.' " (Mark 5:23, 34 Rieu).

She was twelve—just on the verge of adulthood in the

Jewish world. She was the darling of her father's heart, his only daughter (Luke 8:42). Now the twelve years of childhood were about to be wiped out, canceled. The beloved daughter was dying.

She was no longer anyone's child, not a beloved daughter, not even a wife. For the past twelve years she had been a nobody, hidden away because she was unclean from her constant menstrual flow. Anyone—any man—she touched became unfit for temple worship.

The little girl was recalled from death and restored to her family, to grow as a loved daughter into womanhood.

The hidden woman was called out of her living death and restored to health. She was given back her identity as a beloved daughter of Abraham and of God and was restored to society as a whole woman.

Whether old or young, we women are God's loved daughters.

Lord Jesus, touch the parts of my life that are dead, restore me to life and health, and help me live as a loved and loving daughter of God.

MARCH 25   **HOMES**

(Read Luke 10:34-42.)

"He came to a certain village, where a woman named Martha made him welcome in her house. She had a sister called Mary" (Luke 10:38-39 Rieu).

When I finished graduate school and began to work, I used to imagine that I would marry. That, I thought, would be when I would have a house and set up housekeeping in earnest, because homes and houses were for married folk. But I didn't marry, and eventually, with much trepidation, I bought a house on my own. With the second house I even gained enough confidence to know how I wanted to decorate it, though I still felt a bit odd as a single woman owning a home.

It wasn't until I was well into my forties that I saw a significant fact in the accounts of Mary, Martha, and Lazarus. They were a family of singles—we don't read of any spouses—and the house belonged to Martha. Yet their home was one that Jesus loved to go to. He felt welcomed there, by Martha's hospitality and good food, by Mary's inquiring and responsive spirit, and by Lazarus' sympathetic understanding and friendship.

"Jesus loved Martha, and her sister, and Lazarus" (John 11:5). Perhaps because they didn't quite fit the stereotypical family of their day, Jesus felt he was with kindred spirits. The examples of their home keeps giving me courage and inspiration.

Lord, I offer my home to you as a place of refreshment and friendship for others.

MARCH 26   **MOTHERHOOD**

(Read Luke 11:27-28; 8:19-21.)

"A woman . . . called out to him from the crowd: 'Happy the womb that bore you and the breasts you sucked!' " (Luke 11:27 Rieu).

When I turned forty and realized I would probably never have children, I went through a period of deep mourning and grief. Briefly I even thought about adopting a child.

I don't remember reading these words at that time, but this brief exchange between an unknown woman and Jesus has a word I still need to hear. For this woman motherhood was the highest state. A mother was blessed, made significant, by her children, so how blessed must Jesus' mother be. From this point of view, I as a single woman could never attain such a high blessing.

Though Jesus honored his mother and in his dying moments arranged for her future care, he would not define either her life or his solely in terms of physical relationship. Motherhood, though high, is not the highest honor or achievement in the kingdom of God. The highest blessedness is doing the will of God. And those of us women who do that will, whether married or single, mother or childless, may have as close a relationship to Jesus as his mother, may become his mother. " 'Those that hear the Word of God and do it are mother and brothers to me' " (Luke 8:21 Rieu). There are times when it has been hard to believe that statement. But Jesus gives it to me as a fact on which to build my life.

MARCH 27   **FAMILY**

(Read Luke 8:19-20; 6:27-38.)

"Those that hear the Word of God and do it are mother and brothers to me" (Luke 8:20 Rieu).

When I was growing up, the importance of learning God's will for your life and then doing it was stressed continually—pounded into us. Jesus himself underscores how important it is. Our closest relationships are not as meaningful or as personal as doing God's will (Mark 3:35). Yet it seemed the hardest thing in the world to know what God's will for my life was.

Yet is it so hard? Luke sums it up in his abbreviated version of the Sermon on the Mount in chapter 6. The hard part is not finding God's will—it is doing it.

What is the word of God I am to obey?

"Love your enemies"—the unpleasant and angry neighbor, the "friend" who repeats everything I say with just enough twist to make it false, the person who challenges me and my judgments. That means praying for them and calling down blessings on them.

"Be compassionate."

"Do not judge."

"Do not condemn."

"Forgive."

"Give."

"Love one another" (John 15:12).

And the result? I will not be condemned or judged, but will receive far more than I have given. I will be helping to create the family of Jesus. And that is God's will.

MARCH 28 **CLEANING**

(Read Luke 11:37-44.)

"You have only to give in charity what is *in* your cups and dishes, and they will all be clean" (Luke 11:41 Rieu).

There was a time some years ago when I was extremely depressed. Though I never thought of actually committing suicide, I understood for the first time why people did. The world seemed so dark that the few periods of light (good times) only made the darkness blacker by contrast. I felt alone, unconnected to the human race; no one would really know or even care, I thought, if I should disappear or die.

Psychotherapy did no good (I wasn't really ready for it). The darkness began to lighten only when I admitted to myself and to God that I *hated* someone. (A Christian wasn't supposed to hate!)

In the years since then, as I have shared with others that first honest look at what was in me, which became my first step out from the bonds of depression, I have found that the cups and dishes of my life have indeed been coming clean. It's the dishonesty and pretense that keeps them dirty. Anger and hatred are part of the human condition—are part of *my* human condition. It's what I do with them that matters. I must *see* them in my cup. When I know why they have arisen, then I can deal with them in love. I have learned why I hated. I was really hating an unrecognized part of myself (the cute young charmer). Though I don't give it free rein, I no longer find that part of myself unclean, but rather a part to be loved.

Thank you, Lord, that you love me as I am, a very human person. Help me to keep on growing toward wholeness.

MARCH 29   **FREEDOM**

(Read Luke 13:10-17.)

"This woman, this daughter of Abraham, whom Satan bound . . . was it not right for her to have been loosed from those bonds of hers on the sabbath day?" (Luke 13:16 Rieu).

The reaction of the ordinary people to this healing was to think "with joy of all the glorious things" Jesus was doing (13:17 Rieu). But the synagogue rulers were frustrated that Jesus had broken the Sabbath again. Yet what better day than the Sabbath, the day of rest and re-creation, on which to free a daughter from her bondage?

Imagine for eighteen years being bent further and further over, head lower and lower, seeing only the ground, never the sky, the trees, or even other faces, except by severe contortions, living in increasing isolation.

How many of us have allowed ourselves to be isolated by our emotional burdens, problems we're afraid to share with others, faults we're afraid to admit. And so we hide our faces from one another and let our burdens depress us. We can no longer see the sun rise or set or receive love from the faces of others, because we are bent over with the weight of depression, anger, fear, and even hate.

Jesus comes to restore us not only to the human race but also to the family of God. This woman was a daughter of Abraham, and it was the work of Satan, the Enemy, that she was bent double. She needed to stand upright, to live erect and proud, grateful for herself, her family, and the One who set her free.

MARCH 30   **MOTHERS AND SONS**

(Read Matthew 20:20-28.)

"The mother of Zebedee's sons went up to him now with her sons . . . and made him a petition" (Matthew 20:20 Rieu).

Mothers are ambitious for their children. And too often they try to take their children's destinies in hand. I have wondered if James and John, who Jesus nicknamed "Sons of Thunder," weren't given to fits of sudden anger because their mother tried to control them or at least push them forward, and they had not yet declared their independence of her. When we cannot allow ourselves to be angry at our mothers' interference in our lives, we may find ourselves striking out unnecessarily at others.

Twice (in the King James Version) Jesus has to tell James and John that they don't know what they are doing or saying. The first time comes after a demonstration of the brothers' thunderous anger when a Samaritan village refused to let Jesus in (Luke 9:51-56). Jesus had to tell them they *did not know* what spirit they were made of. They were not in touch with the true cause of their anger, nor aware of how to use anger, and therefore did not understand Jesus' spirit.

The second time came when, following their mother's lead, they aimed for the top posts in the kingdom they were expecting. Again Jesus told them they *did not know* what they were asking for. Unrecognized anger and unexamined parental relationships blind us to reality and give us a distorted sense of our own importance.

James and John got their underlying request—to follow Jesus to his destiny. That was a martyr's death and victory beyond the grave, in a kingdom not of this world. But their mother—I wonder what she thought when instead of a minister's post, her son James was killed by Herod. For her, as for Mary, a sword pierced her heart. Did she understand the honor and accept it?

MARCH 31   **EATING**

(Read Luke 24:13-35.)
"He took his place at table with them and presently picked up the loaf and said a blessing" (Luke 24:30 Rieu).

Eating is the central act of Christian worship, the heart of the family of God. We come to a meal, at which Jesus is both the host and the food.

Eating—mealtime—is the heart of the family. And hospitality is the extending of family warmth to the outsider. Hospitality is love in action. We can begin to understand the importance both of eating and of hospitality to the first Christians when we realize that Luke has fifteen references to Jesus' eating or being invited to someone's home and gives an additional twenty-three references to food in Jesus' teaching.

When Cleopas and his companion—I like to think it was his wife*—opened their home to a stranger that first Easter evening, they discovered that they were entertaining Jesus himself, who not only graced their home but blessed the meal and became *their* host before he vanished.

Let us as Christian women continue to offer food and hospitality. And so may we discover that we have seen the Lord and been blessed by him.

---

*Even though both Rieu and the Revised Standard Version refer to "O foolish men" in verse 25, the Greek just has the adjective "foolish [ones]," though it is in the masculine plural.

Concerning Relationships

VERA CHAPMAN MACE

APRIL 1   **CHOOSING TO BE A FOOL**

The origins of April 1 as All Fools' Day are shrouded in obscurity. The timing may relate to the beginning of spring, when nature often fools us with sudden changes from shower to sunshine.

To me, All Fools' Day always brings vividly to mind the story of a woman who chose to be a "fool for Christ." She was Catherine Booth, who together with her husband founded the Salvation Army. At a time when women were supposed to be silent in church (I Corinthians 14:34), she had become deeply interested in a controversy about women being allowed to preach. Though virtually an invalid and the mother of a large family, she had made time to write a striking pamphlet on female ministry, but she had not applied her convictions to herself. After the birth of her fourth child, she felt a call from God to do so. To this she emphatically replied, "No! I would rather die than speak." As she told the story, "Then the Devil said, 'You will look like a fool, and have nothing to say.' " Those words triggered a response in her that has reverberated around the world ever since. "I said, 'I have never yet been willing to be a fool for Christ. Now I will be one!' " (A. Maude Royden, *The Church and Woman*).

Catherine Booth's decision took place in England more

than one hundred years ago. Does that mean it is no longer relevant today? Might it still be a valid example for us to follow?

APRIL 2   **ACCEPTING FOOLS**

It would be easy to dismiss fools as being of no account in today's world. Not so in early Christian times. Saint Paul commended the Corinthians for suffering fools gladly (II Corinthians 11:19) and declared, "God hath chosen the foolish things of the world to confound the wise" (I Corinthians 1:27 KJV).

Brother Juniper is, for me, the perfect example of that kind of fool. He was a follower of Francis of Assisi, who early in the thirteenth century received the Pope's permission to establish the Order of Friars, which is still in existence. So many amazing and absurd stories have been told about Juniper that today it is questioned if he really lived. While it is clear that some of the stories about him are sheer invention, surely there *must* have been a real person behind them.

Though his activities were inspired by his longing to be helpful, Brother Juniper was an exasperating person to his peers. For example, he was constantly giving away his clothes to beggars and having to be supplied with new ones. On one occasion, having heard the friar cook complain of too much work, he sneaked into the kitchen and, to be helpful, put the next meal into the oven to cook: unskinned rabbits, bread, and vegetables. "It wasn't I'd forgotten to skin the rabbits, but I thought their rinds came off in the cooking," he said.

Father Francis took Juniper's foolishness and, through complete acceptance, transformed it into humble, service-able love. Is there anything we can learn by acceptance of fools in today's world?

APRIL 3   **THOUGHTS ON MEDITATION**

In order to prepare these meditations, I have had to meditate myself on each one of the daily suggestions. Here are a few insights from so doing:

1. Meditation is not an alternative to regular prayer. Nevertheless it must be done regularly. Meditating occasionally may be enjoyable, but it doesn't lead one to the core of the art.

2. Meditation takes time, though not an excessive amount. One writer suggested fifteen minutes a day. My experience has been that when I meditated on a theme for the allotted time, I did not then forget it. It kept returning to my thoughts throughout the day (I'm a morning person, so I like to meditate in the morning), with new insights and further truths.

3. Because meditating must be experienced personally, the same exercise might turn out differently for different persons. Nevertheless, meditation does not mean isolation but rather leads to a universal relationship with God. An anonymous rhyme describes it thus:

> First find thyself, 'tis halfway house to God,
> Then lose thyself, and all the way is trod.

4. In meditation there is value in asking questions—childlike ones—not to increase one's knowledge but to widen one's understanding and experience.

5. Meditation is not for figuring out material advancement but rather a spiritual activity leading to an increase in the love of God.

APRIL 4   **THE BEGINNING OF HIS LAST WEEK**

The date of Easter varies from year to year. For this book it has been decided that we observe it during April. Thus we shall now consider the events of Holy Week from the point of view of relationships. It is hard to divest one's mind of a knowledge of what came later, but we must try.

It is Saturday evening, immediately before Palm Sunday. Jesus and his disciples are in Bethany, a village about two miles from Jerusalem. Simon the Leper is giving a dinner to honor Jesus. During the meal Mary, sister of Lazarus, anoints Jesus with very precious aromatic balsam, the scent of which fills the whole house.

It is easy to realize what prompted Mary to this generous act: adoring love of her Lord. Can we imagine the feelings of the other people there? Did Martha, her sister, who was serving at table, approve? Did Simon, the host, along with his gratitude for having been healed of his skin affliction, feel mild concern that Mary's anointing was stealing his show and lessening his honoring of Jesus? We know the disciples were highly indignant, complaining of the waste of the equivalent of a year's wages for a working man. Did they all feel genuine concern for the poor, or was this Judas' reaction only because he wanted some of the money?

Can I think how I might feel in a roughly parallel situation today? ———

APRIL 5   **ENTRY INTO JERUSALEM**

On Palm Sunday we celebrate the "Triumphal Entry." I would like to meditate on the responses of some who were there.

A great crowd had gathered on the Mount of Olives to meet Jesus as he approached Jerusalem. The atmosphere was one of high rejoicing; with abandon, some spread their coats on the road for him to ride on, while others spread leafy palm branches. With loud hosannas they proclaimed him the king who had come in the name of the Lord. Some of them were getting out of hand, and the Pharisees urged Jesus to control them. Some were just curious. They wanted to see the one who had brought Lazarus back from the dead. Most were amazed when they heard him teach.

His disciples were rejoicing too, but that is only part of the picture. Earlier on their journey they had become frightened by the awe-ful exaltation that filled their leader. Their fears were not dispelled when he told them about coming events. They were deeply concerned for his welfare but completely puzzled as to how this seemingly victorious entry into Jerusalem fit into the picture. Did they understand the sorrow in the heart of Jesus when he wept over Jerusalem? Do we? Could we substitute any modern city for Jerusalem?

APRIL 6 **SOME WELL-KNOWN CAREGIVERS**

"Caregiving" is so new a word that it is not in my dictionary, but it needs no definition. I like to think it carries with it some of the wider meaning implied when Jesus told Martha she was "careful about many things."

I have always been impressed that after deeply stressful days early in his last week, Jesus chose to leave Jerusalem and go to the home of two women—surprisingly unconventional behavior in the days when women were of no account. There he drew solace and strength from Martha and Mary. I am sure that, apart from supplying food and shelter, they were caregivers to him in the deepest sense.

Lazarus, very recently raised from the dead, was there too. He was a man whose experience was a confusing enigma to his friends and enemies alike. There must have been a special relationship between Lazarus and Jesus, a spiritual bond that for Lazarus found expression as caregiving at a deep emotional level.

Of all the disciples in Bethany then, I think of Thomas (Didymus) particularly as taking thoughtful care. He, perhaps more than the others, was facing the reality of what the future meant for them and making a tremendous outreach of trust out of his doubts and courage out of his fears.

Little Zacchaeus, who climbed a tree in order to see Jesus, became a great caregiver at this time, first of Jesus himself, then of those he had wronged as a tax collector.

Is the motivation behind our caregiving the same today?

APRIL 7   **SOME NAMELESS AND SOME MIGHT-HAVE-BEEN CAREGIVERS**

If you think today's meditation "all imagination," may I quote from George Bernard Shaw's play *Saint Joan?* Joan, similarly accused, replied to her judges, "Of course, that is how the messages of God come to us."

First on my list of nameless caregivers are some who made material provisions for Jesus' last week: the owners of the colt on which the Triumphal Entry was made, and the owner of the home in whose upper room the Last Supper was held. The strange way in which the disciples were directed to these persons suggests they had some relationship with Jesus, perhaps secret, that could be considered as caregiving.

Then there were those who had come to condole with Mary and Martha on the death of their brother, Lazarus. Were they influenced deeply enough to become caregivers? Were those who brought their children for Jesus to bless possessed of some understanding of what children meant to him, which was denied the disciples at that time? Could this be construed as caregiving?

The list is shorter for the might-have-beens. John's Gospel tells us of many among the ruling classes who believed in Jesus but kept it to themselves for fear of the wrath of the Pharisees. "They loved the praise of men more than the praise of God" (John 12:43). Finally, there was the rich young ruler who could not accept Jesus' challenge to be a caregiver in its fullest sense.

What messages do we have from God in modern caregiving?

APRIL 8   **THREE SILENCES IN HOLY WEEK**

Holy Week was a period of crowded activity. So much was happening so quickly that, meditating on those events, it is easy to overlook a number of significant silences. Three stand out clearly.

1. At the Last Supper in the upper room, Jesus had just told his disciples that one of them would betray him. There followed a stunned silence, in which the disciples were exceedingly sorrowful as "they looked one on another, doubting of whom he spake" (John 13:22).

2. In the courtyard of the High Priest's house, Peter had cursed and vehemently denied that he knew Jesus. Then the cock crowed and Jesus looked on Peter, who " . . . went out speechless from the face of all / And filled the silence, weeping bitterly" (Elizabeth Barrett Browning, "The Lord Turned and Looked Upon Peter").

3. Pilate was sitting in judgment on Jesus. He appeared to want to release Jesus. At heart Pilate was a cynic who despised the Jews, so he tried to hand Jesus over to the priests and elders who had condemned him in no uncertain terms. In the face of all this Jesus remained silent, to Pilate's great astonishment.

Each of these silences is different. The disciples' silence suggests they dared not face the knowledge of self that might reveal the possibility of betrayal. Peter's silence is from the brokenhearted depths of his grief. Christ's silence before Pilate is described thus by Ben Jonson, writing in the sixteenth century: "Calumnies are answered best with silence."

Can we identify with these kinds of silences today?

APRIL 9   **MAUNDY THURSDAY**

I have experienced two very interesting Maundy Thursday celebrations.

One of my most moving experiences took place on Maundy Thursday evening a few months ago. After receiving Holy Communion at our church, we shared in "the Stripping of the Church." Everything was removed from the altar and communion table—flowers, candles, communion vessels, linen, vestments, and even the Bible—as a dramatic way of portraying the desolation and abandonment of Gethsemane. This practice dates from the seventh century, when it was the custom to strip the church for cleaning in preparation for Easter. Now it has become a symbolic ceremony in its own right.

Fifty years ago in England I went to a Maundy ceremony at Westminster Abbey where alms were distributed to selected poor people by a member of the royal family. This ceremony is a relic of a former practice whereby sovereigns used to wash the feet of twelve poor men on Maundy Thursday.

How did this day get its name? It came from the first word of an anthem always sung on this day: *mandatum,* meaning "a commandment." "A new commandment I give unto you, That ye love one another" (John 13:34). This is the ultimate mandate for Christian relationships.

> Love as he loved! How can we soar so high?
> He can add wings, when he commands to fly.
>
> Love as he loved! A love so unconfined,
> With arms extended, would embrace mankind.
>   ("A New Commandment I Give Unto You")

APRIL 10   **GOOD FRIDAY**

The present name of the day of the Crucifixion probably derives from "God's Friday." That seems appropriate.

I have twice been privileged to see the famous Passion play in Oberammergau in the Bavarian Alps. In the early seventeenth century the people of Oberammergau made a vow that if their village was spared a visitation of the deadly plague, they would regularly give public thanks. They have done this every ten years (except for three interruptions caused by war) by enacting the Passion of Christ, from the triumphal entry to the Resurrection. This is not a commercial performance. The people of the village, usually over seven hundred of them, act all the parts.

The first time I saw the play was in 1934, a special performance to celebrate three hundred years of keeping the vow. It was in German, and as I did not have an English text, my whole focus was on what I was seeing. To live through the events, hour by hour, of the first "God's Friday" was an incredibly poignant, unforgettable experience. A line in Charles Wesley's hymn "O Come Ye Sinners to Your Lord" does it for me: "The speechless awe that dares not move."

Do these two profound experiences of the Passion play still influence me today? Yes, because they lead directly to the question posed by Sam Bradley, a modern Quaker poet, in "A New Gethsemane":

> Is our way
> At last
> To a cross
> Of choice:
> To obey
> Atom's blast,
> Or God's still
> Small voice?

APRIL 11   **THE DARKEST DAY**

The time between the Crucifixion and the Resurrection was a time of utter desolation. Humanly speaking, the hopes and dreams of the disciples lay shattered around them. Jesus had died under the vilest death sentence meted to criminals by Roman law and, in a way, cursed by God, according to

Jewish law. Can we even begin to imagine what the disciples were feeling and thinking then?

The Apostles' Creed, when it was established in the seventh century, included a phrase that seems to be omitted in some churches. Following the account of the Crucifixion, it said, "He descended into hell." That is how I learned it. To my teenage mind this seemed a vivid portrayal of the depths of degradation to which the cross had taken Jesus. The early church recognized this in its liturgy for Holy Saturday as *tenebrae*, Latin for "darkness" or "the infernal regions."

A light came into this desolation, symbolized today by the lighting of the paschal candle. Hope and faith were resurrected. Walter C. Smith, a nineteenth-century poet, expressed it thus:

> All through life I see a Cross
> Where the sons of God yield up their breath:
> There is no gain except by loss,
> There is no life except by death,
> And no full vision but by Faith.

APRIL 12　**THE GIRL WHO BAKED THE BREAD**

When all the wonder and radiance of Easter are filling my heart and mind, I like to meditate on a fictitious character in the drama who has become real to me.

I found her in Agnes Sligh Turnbull's book *Far Above Rubies,* in a story entitled "The Maid of Emmaus." She was an orphan, forced to work as a servant for uncaring relatives who had an inn about seven miles from Jerusalem. She was sent by them on an errand to the city, and there she heard Jesus speaking to a crowd. When the crowd moved away, he spoke just to her, changing her life completely. She longed to give him a gift but had nothing of her own but a little gold chain. Secretly, with this she bought the finest flour possible and made four perfect little loaves. She took her precious gift to Jerusalem only to learn that Jesus had been crucified. What should she do with her perfect loaves?

After her return home, she was beaten for running away and told to attend to any late travelers. There were three, two she knew and one a stranger. After an anguished struggle in her heart, she decided to give the travelers her precious bread, the gift to Jesus that could never now be given.

Besides the two disciples, there was a young servant girl whose eyes were opened that night. The face of Jesus, "shining, majestic and glorified, yet yearning in its compassion and love," was made known to her.

APRIL 13 SPIRITUAL RELATIONSHIPS—INWARD

There are two aspects of spiritual relationships, the inward and the outward. They have been described as two sides of a door, so closely related you cannot have one without the other.

We need to give up any misconceptions that the spiritual life is only a vague theological theory, very holy and remote. It is our relationship with God within, beyond, and above us. Paul refers to it often as "the Christ in you." Quakers have taken this relationship as their doctrine of the Inner Light, "that of God" in all of us. Evelyn Underhill, an English poet, described how God was making us for himself "not in some mysterious spiritual world that I know nothing about, but here and now where I find myself as a human creature."

Inward spiritual relationships are not achieved by our effort, though their consequences may be very costly in suffering and sacrifice. God is the Prime Mover in establishing spiritual relationships. What is required of us is *response*. As Frederick Hosmer puts it,

> Go not, my soul, in search of Him,
> ....
> But to thyself repair;
> Wait thou within the silence dim,
> And thou shalt find Him there.
> ("The Affirmation of the Divine Response")

April

For many years women were thought not to have souls; therefore, they could not have spiritual relationships. In theory all that has now passed, but does it still linger in practice, in your experience?

APRIL 14   **SPIRITUAL RELATIONSHIPS—OUTWARD**

It is sometimes difficult to recognize outward relationships as being spiritual. We may even think of them as an alternative to, instead of an expression of, inward spiritual realities. A good criterion for recognition is to examine our everyday style of living to see if it is a genuine expression of our inward relationship to God.

Most of us have had occasions of deep spiritual experience in our lives, which we could not explain in materialistic terms. How can we translate the inspiration we receive from these into a never-failing dynamic for living in our hectic world? We believe that we may become part of what has been called "the creative apparatus of God" or, more simply, the tools and channels of the will of God. Knowing and doing the will of God give all our lives direction and purpose, as we pray, "Thy kingdom come, Thy will be done," and live every part of our lives anchored in God. I believe that women have special gifts for interpreting and demonstrating this kind of living.

Though outward spiritual direction is primarily personal, there is no exclusion or isolation about it. It reaches greater depths when we recognize that it is for *all*. Dante said, "Directly a soul ceases to say Mine and says Ours it makes the transition . . . to the truly creative spiritual life."

What do spiritual relationships, inward and outward, mean to us?

APRIL 15   **HUMAN RELATIONSHIPS**

I chose the subject of human relationships for today's meditation, first, because of their universality. We are all

118

born as a result of a relationship (even in the anomaly of a test-tube conception!), and most of us live in settings where we have to make and maintain human relationships (as distinct from those we inherit by reason of race, blood, etc.). John Donne, the English poet of four hundred years ago, wrote, "No man is an island, entire of itself; every man is a piece of the continent, a part of the main. . . . I am involved in mankind."

Second, our need for relationships continues throughout life, following roughly three phases. The first is the dependency stage of early life, when relationships are mostly made *for* us, though even here the young start early in responding to relationships—or lack of them! I was stunned to learn from Dr. John Bowlby's studies that infants can and do die for lack of adequate relationships. They may be given sufficient feeding and their physical needs taken care of, but if they are not loved, held, fondled, and talked to, they can die of emotional starvation. In the second phase, as we become mature, relationships are made *by* us. Now responsibility takes the place of dependence. The third phase is often a mixture of the two prior ones, when some relationships are made *by* us, some are made *for* us. Often this is not an easy combination.

APRIL 16   **NEW EVERY MORNING**

In the small junior high school I attended in England, we began every day with an assembly that included the singing of a hymn. One of these puzzled me greatly: "New every morning is the love / Our waking and uprising prove" ("New Every Morning Is the Love"). How could God's love be new when I was being taught he existed "from everlasting to everlasting"? How could some essential part of him—his love—be new every morning? I wasn't very curious then about the nature of the love, except its strange fact of being new daily while it was really old too. In those days I knew neither the word "paradox" nor its meaning, so the old that could be new remained a mystery to me.

It was much later that I found answers to some of my questions. The hymn was based on Lamentations 3:22-23 (NEB): "The Lord's true love is surely not spent, nor his compassion failed; they are new every morning."

This passage was written in a time of utter desolation. Jerusalem and the temple were in ruins, and many people had been taken into exile. This was a time of unutterable grief, suffering, and despair. What remained? Nothing, humanly speaking. The only glimmer of hope was in the steadfast love of God, which could be re-NEW-ed every day—had to be, for the people to endure at all.

Our world today is living through comparable tragedies. How do we relate to them?

APRIL 17   **CRITICISM OR ENCOURAGEMENT?**

I was twelve years old. Because my father's work moved from the north of England to the south, I had to change schools in midyear. In my new school people talked differently, and my accent was wrong. As I was very sensitive, it is not surprising that I felt unaccepted, lonely, and unhappy.

One morning the vice-principal, who used to "prowl" around the classes, stood behind me as I tried to write up my first science experiment. Fixing her eyes on my page, in a loud voice she said to the teacher, "Miss T——, would you tell me what 'sluphic acid' is?" I'd never before seen or even heard of its being spelled "sulphuric" acid. (Today I'm amused that my American dictionary says, "This spelling is no longer admitted by scientific publications.")

Another teacher gave me my introduction to geometry. After a difficult lesson on a particularly intricate diagram, she said to me, "You ought to become an architect; you take such great care over every detail."

I have never forgotten those two experiences, and there is no doubt which of the two has had the greater influence upon my life. Through the years I have learned, too, that encouragement is not only a sound method of teaching children; it is also a way of cultivating relationships in all life.

APRIL 18   **RECOGNIZING CHANGE**

For us mortals, change is inescapable. It may be dramatic and sudden, but it is more likely to be slow and gradual and, for that reason, to go unrecognized for a long time. A pre-Christian Greek philosopher described change by saying no one could "step into the same river twice." He meant that the flowing river is constantly changing, and a human being is likewise changing.

The difficulty is that when life is very good for us, we resist the idea of change. Even though we know it is impossible, we wish that time, as we are experiencing it, could stop and our immediate life circumstances be guaranteed us forever. But to stop time would mean death.

Reluctantly accepting that kind of change, we ask if depth of a relationship can establish immunity to change. Robert Bridges, who was poet laureate in Britain early in this century, wrote: " . . . let truth be told / That love will change in growing old."

A church bulletin contained a quote from Anne Morrow Lindbergh, the beloved contemporary writer: "When you love someone, you do not love them all the time in exactly the same way from moment to moment."

What, then, must we do to relate to this possibility? First, we must recognize change is happening to *both* of us in the close relationship. Then we must concentrate together on making the relationship *now* the richest, deepest it can possibly be.

APRIL 19   HANDLING CHANGE

Although the philosopher Heraclitus recognized the inevitability of change, that was not the last word in his philosophy. There was "something" he called an "ever-living world order." A modern writer calls it "identity," that part of us which is ongoing, regardless of change. I would call it "spirit," defined by my dictionary as "that which constitutes one's unseen, intangible being."

In England in the mid-1930s I met a man nearing retirement from directing the manufacture of world-famous fine broadcloth. The climate was perfect for the weaving of the cloth, the local water perfect for the dyeing of its brilliant hues. So for over four hundred years his predecessors had supplied the cloth for uniforms for both gorgeous ceremonial occasions and everyday wear. Then came dramatic change; the army abandoned red coats, ceremonies became infrequent, and, most far-reaching of all, man-made fabrics were coming into widespread use.

Was this man bitter and resentful? No! Because he was a fine Christian, he was able to handle change in the spirit of caring for his employees, with pride in their craftsmanship and with determination that the traditional values underlying their work should continue. In all this he was motivated and sustained by a strong belief in the *unchangeableness* of God. "From everlasting thou art God, / To endless years the same" ("O God, Our Help in Ages Past").

Would a current counterpart of similar changes be found in what is happening today to those who have been tobacco growers for years? How are they handling change?

APRIL 20   RELIGION AND RELATIONSHIPS

My dictionary defines religion as "the expression of a man's belief in and reverence for a superhuman power recognized as the creator and governor of the universe."

"Belief in" and "reverence for" are both highly significant in relationships.

I once worked with questionnaires that asked the religion of the writer. One person wrote "gardening," explaining, "That's what I do on Sunday morning when other people go to church, so I figured that was my religion."

Religion is our way of life, based on the true values we hold, leading to right relationships and moral conduct. Religion is what we worship, that we have of "worth-ship" in our relationship with the "superhuman power" we call God. Religion gives meaning and dynamic to human relationships—in families and in institutions. Religion embraces the resources we bring to suffering and to that last, inescapable fact of life—death.

The history of Christianity's coming to northern Britain in the early eighth century tells of how the king called a council to decide if the realm should accept Christianity. One adviser likened life to a sparrow's brief flight into a lighted hall through one open door and out through another; he concluded "but of what follows or what went before we are utterly ignorant."

A thousand years later John Henry Newman answered: "He has not made us for naught; he has brought us thus far, in order to bring us further, in order to bring us on to the end." That's what religion is all about.

APRIL 21   **WORK**

Brother Lawrence, a Franciscan, served in the monastery kitchen where, he maintained, amid noise and confusion he "possessed God in great tranquility." Henry van Dyke wrote, "They who tread the path of labor, follow where my feet have trod." Are both these examples irrelevant to work in the twentieth century?

Is our motivation about work different today? The reasons why we work are many, but does God come into any of them? I feel he should. I started, first, my professional career; then, my married life; and have performed much public service since, in the very definite awareness that God was involved in what I was trying to do.

If that sounds facile, I assure you it was not always easy to keep it that way. The great musician Artur Rubinstein said, "If I omit practice one day, I notice it; if two days, my friends notice it; if three days, the public notices it." I have to practice the presence of God daily in my work.

Here are a few truths I've learned on the way:

— When we complain, it is often not our work that is wrong but our attitude to it.
— "God does not demand impossibilities"; so said Saint Augustine.
— "To be fatigued, body and soul, is not sin" (Elizabeth Prentiss, *Joy and Strength*).
— Beware of destructive haste—"haste of thought, haste of judgment, haste of manner, haste of speech" (William Bernard Ullathorne, *Joy and Strength*).

Most important of all, Thomas à Kempis said, it is not how much we do, but "how much we love" in the doing of it.

APRIL 22   **OVERWORK**

We think we know what overwork is, sometimes from personal experience, but we limit our understanding if we think of it only as having too much to do. An archaic form of the word was "over-wrought," meaning having too much work, resulting in excessive strain, agitation, inner turmoil, and restlessness. Today we talk about "burnout" and "workaholics."

I have recently been reading (in *Joy and Strength*, ed. Mary W. Tileston) the works of some eighteenth- and nineteenth-century devotional writers. Writing about people who had choice about working, unlike servants and slaves, one of them wrote: "Don't be unwise enough to think that we are serving God best by constant activity at the cost of headaches and broken rest. . . . We may be doing too much." Another man wrote: "Our object in life should not be so much to get through a great deal of work as to give perfect satisfaction to him for whom we are doing the work." A woman who lived earlier than either of these two men wrote, "It may be with some of us that it is more for what we leave undone than for what we do, that we shall be called to an account." A philosopher of that period wrote, "Lay your deadly doing down. Doing leads to death."

These thoughts raise a question: If in our work we could be more God-related, like Brother Lawrence in his kitchen, would we know how to avoid modern-day burnout?

APRIL 23   **HUSBANDS AND WIVES**

Some readers may be surprised that I have not written meditations directly on two most important relationships, those of husbands and wives, and parents and children. This is because these two subjects are too vast to permit of brief, daily consideration. Nevertheless, they would provide worthwhile themes for meditation. I have a concern about each that I will share today and tomorrow.

Society is rooted in relationships, and learning to relate begins in the family, which in turn begins in the relationship of two persons—a husband and a wife. This places marriage at the fundamental core of society. Does this mean, then, that the alienation, chaos, and war in today's world indicate unmistakably that inadequate marriages are producing inadequate families, with members who haven't learned to relate? Confucius, the Chinese philosopher, is reputed to have said, "When there is love in the marriage, there is harmony in the home; when there is harmony in the home, there is contentment in the community; when there is contentment in the community, there is prosperity in the nation; when there is prosperity in the nation, there is peace in the world."

It is an awesome thought that in order to contribute to world peace, we must offer help in building better marriages, particularly for those just starting, in whose hands the future of mankind may well lie.

The hour is late. Can we do more, before it is too late?

APRIL 24   **PARENTS AND CHILDREN**

My concern about children today is that so many of them are being deprived of their inheritance of the values and truths that make strong, joyful, caring citizens, capable of making right relationships.

The ancient Hebrews believed that God "visited the sins of the fathers upon the children." What happened to the values and virtues of the fathers and the mothers? It was the parents' responsibility to pass these on from generation to generation. Throughout biblical history, and since in the Christian church, bearing children was considered to be the first and main purpose of marriage. In our day we have switched the focus in marriage to the relationship of the couple, but society's dependence on parents as the transmitters of the culture still remains as central and imperative as ever, especially in a time when so many of the great values and truths are being ignored or denied.

I have before me a copy of *Time* for August 8, 1988, part of which is devoted to the article "Growing Up in America Today" as seen "Through the Eyes of Children." In it, Lance Morrow writes of "a child's struggle to understand right and wrong in a society that has lost its bearings," leaving today's children exposed to "alcoholism, child abuse, young runaways, social breakdown, violence, hypocrisy, racism." What a legacy!

What *must* we do for today's children, remembering that

what we do is a payment to the future for a debt we owe to the past?

APRIL 25   **USING ANGER CREATIVELY**

Some of us were taught that anger in interpersonal relationships is bad. (There are other kinds of anger.) Some of us learned that anger is sin. If so, how should we explain the fact that in the Bible God is often portrayed as being angry?

Of itself, anger is neither evil nor good. The trouble is in the way we use it. It is a normal, healthy emotion that, if understood and used rightly, can help our relationships.

We need to understand that anger is a secondary emotion, triggered by some deeper cause. What *do* we do when we are angry? Generally we usually react in one of two ways. Either we clam up, thinking that we are controlling anger, which is rarely true since buried anger accumulates and leads in time to catastrophic explosions. Or we attack the person with whom we are angry. That leads to counterattack and destructive fighting, which do not deal with underlying causes and only leave scars and bitterness for the fighters.

What *could* we do?

1. Recognize that it is normal for us to get angry, and give ourselves and others permission to do so.

2. Commit ourselves, in angry situations, to together find the underlying causes of our anger, *without attacking each other*.

3. Through resources available today, learn how to negotiate and deal with the underlying causes of our anger in relationships.

Easy? No! Very hard, but worth every effort.

APRIL 26   **NOT LISTENING**

My husband and I watch a television news program during breakfast (not an arrangement to be recommended).

Recently I said (during a commercial), "What was he saying about the man from ———?" My husband replied, "I don't know; I wasn't really listening."

Just as "not listening" can be a part of interpersonal relationships, so it is often a part of relationships with God in prayer. Imagine someone lifting the phone, pouring a torrent of words into it, and then hanging up. We would think that ridiculous, but it aptly describes some praying. As a preacher expressed it a hundred years ago, "When we fail to hear his voice, it is not because he is not speaking so much as that we are not listening" (Charles H. Brent, *Joy and Strength*).

Another way of not listening might be better described as not hearing. An example of that is taking one's problems, one's difficulties, to the Lord, asking for guidance and help with their resolution, and then, not hearing an immediate answer, taking them all back again! I've done that.

We often excuse our not listening and our not hearing because we do not have enough time. I learned the truth about that years ago from a quotation by Ghazzali in a church service paper: "If you are never alone with God, it is not because you are too busy; it is because you don't care about him, don't like him. And you had better face the facts."

APRIL 27   **JOY**

To the early Christians the advent of Jesus was God's great redemptive act, the occasion for an outpouring of human and heavenly joy.

At their last meal with Jesus, the disciples were bewildered and fearful. After Judas had gone from the meal, Jesus talked intimately with those who were left, and with us also, when he said, "I have spoken thus to you, so that my joy may be in you, and your joy complete" (John 15:11 NEB).

Some equate joy with pleasure. Lecturing in Australia in 1964, the Quaker Kenneth Boulding said, "Man will shortly be able to run an electrode into the pleasure center of his brain, and enable anyone who wishes to enjoy a lifetime of utterly meaningless ecstasies." It may have happened, but that is *not joy*. Joy is more than happiness, because it includes happiness but extends beyond it. Joy also includes true, honest, and wholesome laughter and fun. Francis of Assisi often rebuked his followers for solemnity.

Saint Paul stresses the paradoxical idea that joy can be experienced in affliction. George Matheson, the young Scottish preacher, was moving toward the height of his powers when he was struck with blindness. The girl he expected to marry forsook him. Then he wrote in his great hymn: "O joy that seekest me through pain / I cannot close my heart to thee" ("O Love That Will Not Let Me Go").

What kind of joy do we have in our relationships today?

APRIL 28   **AFFIRMATION**

Affirmation is the positive expression of affection, approval, tenderness, and love. As most people have these feelings, why do so many find it hard to express them? Why is it easier to express negative feelings of blame? It may be that we have been brought up in families where affirmation was reserved for public occasions only and was considered sissy in the home and quite unnecessary in close relationships. Yet it has been found that the supreme quality in strong families is that they constantly affirm each other. Or it may be that we try to justify ourselves when expressing negative feelings, by calling them "constructive criticism."

Who needs affirmation? All of us. When? At least daily. Timing must depend on sincerity. Affirmation must be the warm expression of sincere approval and not merely the repetition of a cold formula. There are other forms of affirmation, but still with the same motivation. There is conditional affirmation, given to get something in return— not the best kind, but not to be ignored if one is *learning* to express affirmation. Then there is the special affirming of someone who is going through deep grief experiences. This affirmation is the giving of comfort, meaning "giving strength." This is often hard, not because we don't feel deeply, but because we find it difficult to express our feelings.

Why affirmation? An anonymous writer answered thus: "We are all lonely personalities; seas roll between us and our nearest; but remember He can walk on the waters."

APRIL 29   **RELATING THROUGH SILENCE**

Today we live in a hectic world, bombarded by sounds. Most young people have not known any other. I remember that when, fifty years ago, we got our first radio (known in England then as a "wireless"), our two-year-old daughter was fascinated. When a visitor arrived, she asked, "Shall I put the wireless on so that Mrs. B—— can hear the noise?" How the volume of "the noise" to which we are exposed has increased since then!

This means if we want creative silence in our lives, it must be intentional, and we must use it positively. Some kinds of silence, as, for example, that of a deep hatred, can be used very destructively. As Robert Louis Stevenson expressed it, "The cruellest lies are often told in silence."

Silence is not just an absence of sound, when nothing is happening. It is an activity of the mind and heart used creatively; the sentry on duty, straining every nerve to hear the slightest sound; the Quaker at worship, relaxed but concentrating on hearing "the still, small voice."

The positive, creative potential of silence is great. Think of the silences of great love—true friends do not need to talk all the time; or the silence of great sorrow when words fail us; or the silence of a spiritual crisis when the message comes to us, "Be still and know that I *am* God."

Do you need that kind of silence in your life? I know I depend on it.

INTO THE FUTURE

The distinguished British historian Arnold Toynbee, at the end of his monumental *Study of History,* tells of a dream he had. He dreamed he was precariously clinging to the cross above the high altar of the Benedictine abbey in Ampleforth, Yorkshire, when he heard a voice say, "Cling and wait." At the end of his book, he took this as his message to Western civilization: "Hang on, wait, and pray."

When I was six years old, we went to live at Ampleforth for a year. My father was a builder and an authority on stone, and he went to Ampleforth to do some special work. Even though I was so young, I still remember my feelings of awe when I was taken to see the church there, so I readily identify with the setting of Professor Toynbee's dream.

In a world of so much chaos, cruelty, and conflict as we have today, and when the human race is even threatened with annihilation, I cling, not in despair but in tremulous hope, to the message, "Hang on, wait, and pray." And I am reminded of a woman almost of our generation, Minnie Louise Haskins, who wrote: "I said to the man who stood at the gate . . . 'Give me a light that I may tread safely into the unknown.' He replied, 'Go out into the darkness and put your hand into the hand of God' " *(The Desert)*.

Blossoming

MARI GONZÁLEZ

MAY 1   **ONE OF THOSE DAYS**

May Day, I woke up with all the excitement I had had as a child, expecting a sun-drenched day, lots of wildflowers, and that intense feeling of being 100 percent alive.

But when I sat up in bed, I faced a windowful of gray. Then I heard it—the wind howling across the fields. The calendar said May, but winter wasn't through with us yet.

The day grew grayer as I went to work. And that grayness seeped inside me until I felt ugly inside and out. Fortunately, I have an office all to myself!

By the time I got home, I felt as listless as the sky. I didn't want to cook, I didn't want to clean house, and I most assuredly was in no mood to put up with a husband and two kids.

That's when God intervened.

"Mommy!" Maridee shouted. (My kids only talk in one volume.) "Look at the rainbow."

A rainbow? Tonight?

Wanting an excuse to leave the dishes, I looked out the front door toward the Tetons. The sky to the southeast was almost black, but to the west it had cleared enough to give the sun the final say on the day. Where the two met, just beyond the canal and towering willows, arched a double rainbow.

"Thank you, God," I prayed silently, as I thought of all his promises to me. I knew, no matter how ugly I felt, inside or out, I would always be special to God.

MAY 2   **APPLES AND ORANGES**

I was reading Galatians 5:22-23 the other day. You know, that long list of the fruits of the Spirit.

Those attributes—love, joy, peace, long-suffering, gentleness, goodness, faith, meekness, and temperance—have been my goal most of my Christian life. But I have to admit, it's not a goal I've been able to reach. I don't think too many people have.

The only person I've ever met who comes anywhere close is Grandma Farley. I've never heard her complain, gossip, or say a bad thing about another person. Her faith and trust in God are almost childlike. And, unlike me, Grandma doesn't seem to have a problem with spiritual pride, thinking she's "arrived."

Even if Grandma weren't a Christian, she would be a good person. That's just the kind of woman she is. But then, those attributes wouldn't spring from her relationship with God, so they couldn't be called the "fruit of the Spirit."

If Grandma weren't a Christian, she'd be like a withered branch, incapable of bearing any fruit that has its seed planted in a God-centered life.

It's kind of like apples and oranges. An orange tree will never grow apples. It takes an apple tree to do that. And it takes a true Christian to produce the fruit of the Spirit.

Of course, not all apple trees produce delicious apples.

MAY 3   **SHORT ON PATIENCE**

I love my husband. But there are days when I take him for granted, kind of love him, or wish he'd go to the timber for another twelve hours.

Lately, it's been more the latter. After two months of waiting for the spring thaw to dry up, Joe is logging again. The first month is always the hardest.

Every spring, our finances reach all-time lows after months of surviving on my paycheck. So when Joe starts up, he pushes to the edge of endurance—mine—to make up for those months of poverty.

He gets paid by the piece. That means he puts in twelve-hour days, six days a week, to recoup our losses. When he gets home, all he wants is supper, a shower, and bed. The few words he mumbles are complaints.

I endure it for a few days. But it doesn't take long of playing career woman, housewife, mother, and father for my patience to evaporate.

By then I'm so deep in self-pity that even God has trouble getting through. There's a passage he uses to challenge and shame me. In Ephesians 4:1-2 Paul urges us to walk worthy of our calling "with long-suffering, forbearing one another in love." (I think "long-suffering" says it better than "patience.")

That "forbearing one another in love" means "putting up with each other because you love each other."

So for the spring endurance test, I need to pray for more patience to put up with the man I love.

MAY 4   **LEARNING TO LOVE**

When I was growing up, I never doubted my love for my parents. I have great parents, so it wasn't difficult to love them.

All that changed the night my daughter was born. As I held that little, red, wrinkled bundle, I was consumed with a love I had never felt before. I knew that Maridee, with her bald head and round chunky cheeks, would not win any beautiful baby contest, but to me she was magnificent.

The love I had for my daughter overwhelmed the feelings I

had toward my parents, so that I felt guilty when I thought of all Mom and Dad had done for me. With tears in her eyes, Mom told me she understood exactly.

Kids don't love their parents as much as their parents love them. And until they become parents, they can't comprehend all the pride, sense of responsibility, and total giving that is expressed in parental love.

When I held that helpless baby in my arms and realized I would give my own life for her, I also began to understand a little more clearly God's love for us. More so than any earthly parent, God takes pride in his children. He hurts when we hurt, and he wants to protect us from all the danger that awaits us. But just like our earthly parents, God knows we have to make our own decisions, even though we may end up learning the hard way.

MAY 5   **GIVING IT ALL**

I thought I had seen poverty. Hadn't I driven through the slums of Philadelphia and been in Chicago's Cabrini Green?

I still wasn't prepared for Mexico. We drove through village after village of squalor. The best houses would have been condemned in this country.

I shuddered at the thought of living in one of the adobe houses with thatched roof, holes for windows, dirt floors, and no electricity or water.

Then we came to a neighborhood of houses made of sticks tied together. To block the mountain breezes, the owners had filled the cracks with mud.

It got worse. Sloping up toward a city was a hillside littered with cardboard nailed loosely to poles to form small paper houses.

As we reached Joe's hometown, I was indignant. When he showed me the cathedral, my indignation grew.

Freshly whitewashed, the cathedral looked like a diamond glittering in a coal mine. Inside, the blue mosaic floor led to an altar alight with gold. The only sign of poverty was in the weathered face of an elderly worshiper. Wrapped in a shawl, the woman silently prayed, her gnarled hands clasped in reverence.

I didn't see the reverence. My eyes focused on her tattered clothes. "How can the church take their money when they have so little?" I whispered to Joe.

"They want to give their best to God."

That silenced me as I thought of my tithe, calculated to the penny and recorded for tax purposes. I didn't know the meaning of giving to God.

MAY 6   **ON FIRE FOR GOD**

The sky over Yellowstone National Park hung so heavy with smoke it was impossible to pinpoint any one of the wildfires burning through the park until we reached the peak of a high mountain road.

From our vantage point at the north end of the park, we looked out over a panorama of smaller peaks and wooded canyons. Gushing from one of the canyons and consuming half a mountain was the billowing smoke of a forest fire.

The smoke mushroomed toward the gray-cloaked sky, part of the haze settling over the park. Every few seconds, a tongue of orange flame licked into the smoke, consuming another lodgepole pine. One at a time, the flames spread from one tree to the next as the fire claimed an even bigger portion of the park.

Spiritual revival is much like the forest fires that ravaged Yellowstone. The spark of revival starts with one person who is totally on fire for the Lord. Fanned into flames by a zeal to share God's Word, the revival spreads to relatives, acquaintances, and friends.

Though still a part of the world, those who burn with the desire to follow the Lord will be distinct from the world as they let their flames shine.

When Yellowstone caught on fire, almost ten thousand firefighters tried to control the blaze. But they were powerless against the forces of nature.

When Christians catch on fire for the Lord, not even a million troops will be able to beat back the forces of God.

MAY 7 **PULLING GOD DOWN**

Every man-made religion that's ever been imagined has one thing in common. It strips God down to the level of humankind or promotes humankind to God's level.

That's to be expected. The human species has this innate curiosity of wanting to know how things work. There's power in understanding the intricate workings of the universe.

In the self-centered realm of human knowledge, there's a prevailing philosophy (though seldom acknowledged) that if we can't explain something, it can't be possible. This philosophy makes humans the source of all knowledge.

As Christians, we self-righteously sniff at these humanistic ideas, smug in our knowledge of God. But we who personally know God often demean him the most.

The Bible is full of concepts foreign to humans. Take the Trinity, for example. When was the last time you met an individual who was three distinct people simultaneously?

When faced with such concepts, we have three choices: Deny them, try to explain them, or accept them.

In our zealousness to make the Bible more palatable to a lost world, we strip God down to our mortal level. We forget who is Creator and who is creation. It's like expecting a computer to understand its programmer. The computer can understand the program, but the machine cannot understand the human who programmed it.

We can comprehend God's message to us, but we will never fully comprehend God until we meet him face to face.

He tells us that in Deuteronomy 29:29: "The secret things belong unto the Lord."

MAY 8   **FEMINIST OR FEMININE**

From the day I started shaving my legs, I was labeled a feminist. I guess that's because I say what I think.

When a man in our church heard I was planning a career, he suggested I read Proverbs 31 and learn my place.

I read it. That virtuous woman was quite a gal! Not only was she a good wife and mother, she was an astute businesswoman in her own right.

When I pointed this out to Dean, he stammered, "Well, the Bible says women are to submit to men."

"Scripture and verse?"

He spouted Ephesians 5:22.

"Wait a minute," I interrupted. "That says I'm supposed to submit to my own husband, not to every man I know. And what about Ephesians 5:21? It says we're to submit to each other. It would be easy to submit to a husband who's willing to submit to me."

Dean shook his head and walked off. But I thought of another instance he had ignored. In Matthew 25 Jesus talks about the servants who were given talents according to their ability. The servant who buried his talent was condemned. The servants who used their talents for their master's glory were rewarded.

I would not be a good steward if I used my gender as an excuse not to develop and use my God-given talents. And when I get to heaven, I doubt God will say, "I wanted you to bury them. You're just a woman."

MAY 9   **LITTLE MIRACLES**

Whenever it was testimony time at camp, I felt cheated. I didn't have a spectacular testimony. I didn't come from a broken home, my parents weren't alcoholics, and I had never strayed from the straight and narrow. My testimony was humorous. When I was little, Mom led me to the Lord as she bathed me.

Sometimes I told about the miracles in my life. They weren't miracles on the scope of parting the Red Sea, but they were miracles.

The first one happened after Dad was laid off. We moved to Milwaukee where he could find work. That move took most of our savings. Though Dad was working again, payday was several days off. The only food in the house was some sugar. For supper that night, we had a tablespoonful of sugar.

Dad was too proud for welfare or to ask for money, so no one knew of our plight. We went to bed with stomachs rumbling.

In the middle of the night, we were awakened by a noise. We got up to find two bags of groceries by our front door.

We learned that a woman from the church we had joined had awakened with an undeniable urge to buy food for the Farleys. She had tried to ignore it, but God wouldn't let her.

There were other such miracles in my life. But I know now that the greatest miracles were God's keeping me on the straight and narrow and giving me a Christian family.

MAY 10   **TIME ALONE**

In Mexico they don't mess with the calendar like we do in the United States. There, Mother's Day comes every May 10. It's easier for my husband to remember that date than to chase down the second Sunday of May.

The best Mother's Day present Joe ever gave me was when he took the kids fishing so I could have a day to myself. At first I didn't know what to do. I had never felt the house so quiet.

Since this was my day, I decided to enjoy it. But as I settled down with a book, my sensible side suggested, "You ought to clean the house while no one's tracking in."

I ignored the suggestion. But the minute Joe's pickup pulled into our lane, I guiltily shut the book and started cleaning up.

Sometimes this supermom mentality goes too far. We get so caught up in our jobs, our families, our homes, and even our churches that we forget us. We are so busy nurturing everything else that we are too tired to nurture ourselves.

When Jesus came to the house of Mary and Martha, Mary couldn't drag herself from the Master. She sat at his feet, nurturing herself on his words. Meanwhile, Martha fumed in the kitchen as she singlehandedly prepared the meal. Jesus told Martha there were more important things than worrying about a clean house.

We shouldn't wait for Mother's Day on any calendar to find time to nurture ourselves.

MAY 11   **MALIGNED**

The Bible is full of women who glorified God despite hardships. Then there's the one who didn't.

Throughout history, Job's wife has had a bad press. She's been placed in league with all the bad mother-in-law jokes as the epitome of a nagging wife. As women we turn away from her, refusing to see our reflection in her grief, her weakness, and her doubt.

Job's wife had everything wealth and love could bring. Her husband's prominent position made her the envy of many a woman. Her day revolved around her husband, her children, and her home. She drew her strength from Job; he was her spiritual leader.

In one day, her world crumbled. Her children killed, her wealth destroyed, and her position of pride turned to that of ridicule, Job's wife clung to him for support. That last crutch fell when Job was plagued with boils from head to foot.

It had been easy to serve God when everything was great. But why should she serve God when he treated her so shabbily?

Seeing her once-great husband sitting in the ashes, scraping at his open sores with a broken bit of pottery, was more than this woman could endure. She turned on her husband, voicing her own human frustration: "Just curse God and die."

Maybe that's why Job's wife has been maligned for all these centuries. Maybe we see our own human shortcomings portrayed—all too clearly—in her.

MAY 12   **WAITING FOR MOTHERHOOD**

We had been married two years and yet there was no sign of a much-wanted child. There had been false alarms—so many we didn't get excited about them anymore.

Day-to-day life left few voids, as both Joe and I had our jobs. But the holidays and family gatherings were torture. My younger sister had two daughters and my brother had one. Then another sister announced she was pregnant.

I did my big-sisterly duty and planned baby showers and wandered through the baby department for gifts. The whole time, my arms ached to hold a baby of my own. Somehow, cuddling a niece wasn't the same.

Then one wondrous morning, the false alarm became real. At long last, I anticipated being a mother.

Our two years of longing pale beside the lifetime of yearning of Sarah and Abraham. For Sarah there had been lots of promises but no delivery. It's no wonder she sought a surrogate mother. But the surrogate brought only problems to Sarah's marriage.

Then two men visited their encampment and told Abraham that within a year Sarah would have a son. Sarah, ninety years old, couldn't help but laugh; she'd heard such promises before.

But this time was different. This time, there was a time frame. And sure enough, within the year Sarah's arms lovingly embraced her baby son. At long last Sarah knew the miracle of life and learned to wait upon the Lord.

MAY 13 **ONE WOMAN**

In Romans 5 Paul discusses how by one man sin entered the world and how through another man came eternal life.

Behind those men were women. One was a wife, the other a mother. Both women made their own choices.

When Eve was tempted in the garden, she thought only of herself. The forbidden fruit looked so delicious. Surely God wouldn't punish her—not for one little bite. Dismissing the consequences, Eve bit into the lush fruit.

Eve's sin wasn't complete until she shared the fruit with Adam. From the moment Adam bit into the fruit, their relationship with God, each other, and their inner selves was strained.

Eve remembered her selfishness with each child she bore. As she watched her children quarrel, get angry, and turn their backs on God, she felt responsible.

Centuries later, an angel appeared to a virgin, asking her to put her reputation, her future, on the line for God. Mary knew she could be shamed, put away, or even stoned if she bore a child out of wedlock. But Mary wasn't thinking of herself. Dismissing the consequences, Mary paved the way for God to bridge the gap Eve had helped build.

Neither Eve nor Mary had an easy life. Eve grieved when one son murdered another. Mary sorrowed as her firstborn hung on the cross. In thinking only of herself, Eve helped condemn the world and lived a life of defeat. But in forgetting herself, Mary discovered victory and brought new promise to generations to come.

MAY 14 **ALL THE RIGHT STUFF**

When I was in grade school, my best friend was Diane Passmore. Diane was everything a proper little lady should be—blue-eyed, blond, dainty, and very feminine. Of course, Mrs. Passmore got a lot of credit. Every morning she got up early to curl Diane's hair into perfect ringlets (this was before electric curling irons). My mother had a hassle getting my thick brown mane into a ponytail.

At Halloween Diane was the envy of the class. Every year Mrs. Passmore spent hours making Diane's lavish costumes.

My mother, an ace scholar, flunked Home Ec. She had a tough time sewing on buttons. But what Mom lacked in sewing skills, she made up for in creativity. In just a few hours Mom could pull together this and that to transform me into a prize-winning Martha Washington or Little Bo Peep.

Once, Mom, tired of me raving about all the beautiful dresses Mrs. Passmore had made, went through the torture of making me a sleeveless shift. From the remnant she made a drawstring purse.

The dress had no lace, no intricate stitching, but to me it was the most beautiful dress I ever owned.

I always admired Mrs. Passmore; she was an inspiration. But I never wished she was my mother. God gave me the best mother I could have. In Mom he gave me a godly teacher, a writing partner, and, most importantly, a best friend for lives.

MAY 15   **JUDGE NOT**

Appearances are everything in this world—even in church. Many Christians choose a church by its clientele. Do we want a church with a name? Or one that caters to the country-club set?

Is our involvement in church another part of our respectable facade, a facade used to capture that success that's always just out of reach?

How many of us would feel comfortable sitting next to a prostitute, drug addict, or town drunk? Would we look down our self-righteous noses, expecting them to clean up their act before entering church? If they did get their lives turned around, would we want it known that a person of that reputation was worshiping with us?

In reading the Bible, it's easy to gloss over the many ardent followers of Jesus who were the scum of their land. Mary Magdalene, the Samaritan woman, and the woman caught in adultery had hit rock bottom. They let Jesus give their lives meaning. And because they followed Jesus, they were accepted by the likes of Jesus' mother, Paul, and other stalwarts of the early church.

While the prostitutes, tax collectors, and other undesirables had their lives changed by Jesus, the self-righteous, influential people of the day condemned the Savior because of his followers.

Today's Pharisees sit in the pews of Christian churches, happy in the knowledge that their church, at least, is safe from all those undesirable elements of a lost world.

MAY 16   **PUT IN PLACE**

When I attended Bible college, I would get a big head about all the biblical knowledge I had amassed. Whenever I discovered something new in the Bible, I couldn't wait to share it with a nonstudent.

Grandma Crawford was the most accessible. Since she lived three hours from college and my parents lived three days from the school, I spent most of my holidays with Grandma.

Grandma had lived alone since Grandpa's death sixteen years earlier, so she looked forward to my visits. We spent the entire vacation talking. Grandma would sit in her recliner, Bible opened on her lap and reference books strewn on the lamp table beside her.

I'd curl up on the floor near her chair. Then we'd talk about the classes I was taking. I'd share something from a book I had read for a class. Grandma, a seventh-grade dropout, would quote from it.

Once, when Grandma went for the mail, I browsed through the books piled on the shelves lining her living room wall. There—dog-eared, underlined, and thoroughly studied—were the same books I had been assigned as texts and required reading in some pretty tough courses.

All my pride melted to shame. I never would have read those books had they not been required. And yet Grandma, thirsting for knowledge about her Savior, had sought out the books on her own and studied them.

My college studies were mere book learning. But Grandma, delighting in God's Word, meditated on it day and night.

MAY 17   **FINDING GOD'S WILL**

It was easier starting out in life when there were few choices for women. When Mom graduated from high school, her biggest choice was whom to marry. She made that decision before she got her diploma.

Mom went from her parents' home to her husband's home with no stops in between. She had a scholarship, but that wasn't a consideration then. She had the skills needed to be a secretary so she could put hubby through college.

When I was in high school twenty years later, diamonds had little importance. My friends discussed ACT and SAT scores, college catalogs, and which major to take. The diamond became more important in college, but it still fell behind career choices and job offers.

Those college years were tough. Filled with youthful idealism, I felt like the rope in a tug-of-war, with causes and lost souls tugging at either end. I waited for a momentous tug on one end to decide the outcome.

With so many life-determining decisions to make, I kept God and my older friends busy with questions about determining God's will. The best advice was from an instructor who had ended her engagement to serve as a missionary to India. She said to take every opportunity God allowed us to have and use it for his glory.

I never did get a road map pointing out the routes my life would take. But God has given me plenty of exciting opportunities.

MAY 18   **LIGHT AT THE END OF THE TUNNEL**

The tunnel seemed to go on forever—long, dark, and dank. At the very end, as tiny as a freckle, a speck of light promised an end to the darkness, held out hope for warmth.

Stumbling against the clammy sides of the tunnel, I hurried toward that speck, longing for that promise to wrap me in its brightness.

I shuddered against the tunnel's chill, my eyes fixed on the ever-growing light. No longer a speck, it entered the tunnel as a diffused ray, dispelling some of my gloom and hinting at greater warmth to come.

Exhausted and bruised from my long trek through the tunnel, my body begged to stop. But my eyes clung to that light growing brighter with every step I took.

Gasping for fresh air and rest, I finally reached the opening. I fell outward, stretching toward the light and its warmth. As I lay there on the fresh earth, bathed by the gentle heat of the sun, I knew it had been worth all the effort.

Before we meet God's Son, we struggle through an endless tunnel of sin. When we glimpse the truth, we're drawn toward it. If we continue to control our own lives and do things our way, we feel only God's diffused blessings. But when we yield our lives to him, we will bask in the full radiance of his Son.

MAY 19   **THE LONELINESS FACTOR**

I spent my high school years alone, but not by choice. I enjoyed being alone when there was no one around. But being alone in a crowd was murder. I envied the popular kids and those who shared classes with friends. They were participants in a life I seemed destined only to observe. Inwardly, I fought that destiny.

I wanted a quick fix to my loneliness. I expected someone else to rescue me from isolation—a boyfriend, a relative, anyone but me.

Deep inside, I knew the problem was me, but I didn't know what part of me. I blamed all my problems on my looks, something I couldn't change.

From there, it was a quick little hop to blaming God. After all, he was the one who made me. But God doesn't make mistakes.

In my loneliest hours I turned to God and did some soul-searching. The first thing I had to learn was to love myself, inside and out. In both the Old and New Testaments God tells us to love our neighbors as we love ourselves. I couldn't love anyone else until I loved myself.

The next step, the step that formed the bridge from inside me out to the rest of the world, was even harder to take. Secure in the knowledge of my love for myself and my position as a beloved child of God, I had to forget myself and reach out beyond the loneliness of others.

MAY 20   **WEDDED BLISS**

Statisticians say most marriages ending in divorce do so within ten years. That means my marriage probably will survive.

Now that we've been married more than a decade, Joe and I don't think in terms of honeymooning. I mean, we're hardly newlyweds anymore. We can answer most of the questions on "The Newlywed Game" and get them right.

The flames of romance still glow; they just don't flicker as much. But with two kids in tow, there isn't as much oxygen to stir the flame.

Familiarity hasn't bred contempt. It's created a web of love spun with threads of companionship, security, and friendship. No longer do we have to fill the gaping silences with pratter of newfound love. Those once-awkward silences have become treasured moments of communion.

Our romance has taken us from the banks of Mesa Falls, where he first proposed, to a kitchen filled with dirty dishes and forgotten toys, from the heights of the Juniper Mountains to the bedside of a sick child, from a float trip down the Moose River at the base of the Tetons to an enjoyable jaunt through life.

There have been rocks. Sometimes they seemed insurmountable. But our marriage is based on a shared faith in God, our home established on God's Word. With both of us believing God has united us, divorce is not an easy option. And that forces us up and over the rocks instead of around them.

When two people are joined by God, their marriage is stronger than statistics.

MAY 21   **TOO HASSLED TO WORSHIP**

It was potluck Sunday. I'd gotten up an hour early to get everything ready. Now I was five minutes late.

Juggling potholders, casserole, and condiments, I stumbled out to the car. We live within an acre of the church, but that's too far to walk with arms full of food and kids.

I rushed back to the house for my Bible, the kids, and the car keys. Finding the Bible and kids was easy, but the keys? Then I remembered, Joe had driven last. The keys were probably in his pocket, and he was at work.

I handed Maridee the Bible and unloaded the car for the trek across the field to church. Two-year-old Tommy demanded to be carried. I left him standing in the field while I hurried to church with the food.

Service hadn't started yet. Everyone was outside, talking.

Tommy's yells drowned them all out, but no one offered to get him or relieve me of the food. By the time I had the food downstairs and reclaimed my son, church had started.

While everyone sang, I smoldered—about Joe, Tommy, and the thoughtlessness of the congregation. After an hour of fuming and wrestling with two toddlers, I came out of church exhausted. Church had been an obligation instead of a special time of worshiping the Lord.

Too often, we're so busy preparing for church that we forget what church is all about. Instead of giving God the first fruits of our energy, we give him the leftovers.

MAY 22   **MANSION HUNTING**

We were driving along Grandview Drive in Peoria. It's one of those roads littered with the homes of the ultra-rich, interspersed with thick groves of shade trees and overlooking the Illinois River.

Maridee, who's a princess in her fantasies, fell in love with a castle complete with turrets, wind-blown banners, and a moat. While she fantasized, I enviously compared the mansions to our mobile home situated on an acre of rural Idaho desert.

Knowing we would never live in such a house, Joe and I took the sour grapes approach. "How could you keep it clean?" I asked. (I have trouble with only seven rooms.)

"They have servants, dear," Joe replied.

"I don't think I'd like that. You'd never have any privacy."

Maridee took our banter seriously. "Well, which one are we going to buy?" she asked.

"We couldn't even pay the taxes on one of those," Joe answered.

No, our home is no mansion. But after two weeks of living out of suitcases, we were happy to be home, no matter how modest it was.

Our house is more than a mansion; it's a home. Every inch

of it is stamped with our personality—right down to Maridee's fingerprints on the windows and Tommy's scribbles on the wall.

Though I'll never live in an earthly mansion, I'll be content with what God has given us. After all, I've got a mansion waiting in heaven with my name on it.

MAY 23   **LOOKING TOWARD TOMORROW**

One of the luxuries we take for granted is planning a future. From the day I started talking, adults asked me what I wanted to be when I grew up. That simple question opened a world of possibilities.

Not everyone gets asked that question. My husband grew up in a poor family in Mexico. No one asked him that question. For him, there were no choices. He would do whatever was available.

Joe was twenty-one before he was asked that question. He had come to the United States and learned several skills. The world opened to him as he realized he had job choices.

Now he's asking our kids that question. Maridee had us worried when her only ambition was to become "a teenager like Aunt Becky."

Late at night, Joe and I lie in bed, sharing the day's events. Sometimes he asks me what I want the kids to be. The possibilities flit through my mind, but I come up blank.

When I was young, Mom wanted me to be a writer; that's what she had wanted to be. But I am what I wanted to be; I have no unfulfilled desires to pass on to my children.

As Maridee's and Tommy's personalities emerge, I see specific job possibilities. But that choice will be theirs.

I don't care what they do for a living; that's not important. What is important is that they grow up loving and serving the Lord. Then the future will take care of itself.

MAY 24   **TOO SECURE**

The caterpillar twisted in her cocoon. She was tired of this confining shell; she wanted a change.

Before she had entered the cocoon, she had crawled tediously through life, longing to soar to the treetops like other insects. Now, stuck motionless in the tight cocoon, she wished she were back crawling through the dirt.

She stretched. Oops! She had punched a hole in the cocoon. She could get out! She wriggled toward the opening to peep at the outside world. She blinked at the blinding sunlight and sighed. She couldn't go out there. What if she were still a little green worm destined to crawl while others flew? Clinging to anonymity, she snuggled back into her secure cocoon.

Security. It's more important to us than our own happiness. It was the security of his wealth that kept the rich young ruler from following Jesus. It was the security of home and comfort that made Lot's wife look back toward Sodom.

Today, the security of being accepted by our peers keeps us from witnessing and inviting people to church. Job security gets in the way of God's leading. Wanting security for our family makes us ignore God's call to full-time Christian service.

In clinging to the security of her cocoon, the caterpillar denied herself the life of a butterfly. In clinging to the false security of the world, we deny ourselves the blessings that come with fully following God.

MAY 25   **A LIFE OF DESTRUCTION**

The Bible defines sin as anything, action or thought, that displeases God. Throughout its pages the Bible lists many specific sins. And throughout history Christians have added to those lists.

While compiling sins that aren't mentioned specifically,

we ignore one that is mentioned repeatedly, along with being drunk and lazy. That's the sin of gluttony.

A glutton is much like a drunkard. A drunkard drinks too much. A glutton eats too much. Both sins will damage, if not destroy, the body God has given us.

I don't always eat right or get enough exercise. But I didn't know I had a problem with gluttony until years of abuse caught up with me. It wasn't until my blood pressure soared, my waistline doubled, and the scale groaned that I admitted I had a problem.

Then the doctor checked my cholesterol and had a serious talk with me. I could either do something about my weight and eating habits or I could die at a young age.

Despite the doctor's ominous incentive, I haven't found victory over this sin. In I Corinthians 10:31 we're told: "Whether you eat or drink, or whatever you do, do all to the glory of God" (RSV). My eating habits and the damage they are doing to my body do not glorify God.

I need to etch that verse in my mind and think about it with every bite I take. With God's help, I will win the battle of the bulge.

MAY 26   **ANOTHER PERSON'S GARBAGE**

Getting into a trashy car is an ordeal. I don't care what the car looks like on the outside. I just don't want to sit on a pile of garbage.

It doesn't bother me when the garbage is in my car. I know whose lips have drained the dented pop cans, whose noses have blown into the wadded tissue, and whose fingers dropped the sticky candy wrappers. True, I'd rather all that garbage be in the back where I can't see it.

Riding in someone else's car is another matter. As I climb in, I surreptitiously check the seat for gooey masses that could transfer to my seat. My feet wade through the soiled napkins and crumbs, trying to take up as little space as size ten clodhoppers can. The whole time I wonder how anyone can live with such a mess.

It's easier to overlook our own garbage than put up with someone else's. That's true about garbage, and that's true about sin.

As Christians we spend a lot of time worrying about someone else's sins. We don't "gossip" about it. We phrase it as a prayer request. "Would you pray for so-and-so? The poor soul. You wouldn't believe what happened . . . " All the while, we're keeping our sins out of sight in the back seat.

In his Sermon on the Mount Jesus talked about this human trait. In essence he said, "Why worry about the splinter in your brother's eye, when you don't see the beam in your own eye?"

MAY 27   **CONNECTED**

My family sank its roots into Bloomington Hill three generations before I was born. Great-grandpa bought his farm and then subdivided it among his children. Some of them sold their heritage.

Uncle Herman built a subdivision on his, saving a lot for each of his kids. Grandpa farmed his, saving an acre for each of his children.

My parents built their house on Mom's acre, next to the house where Mom was born. Great-grandpa's house had been sold years before, but it still stood about a half mile from us.

I grew up surrounded by my grandparents, aunts, uncles, and cousins. It was a sheltered life. I went to the same high school my parents and all my aunts and uncles had graduated from. It had grown since their day, but many of the teachers were the same. My classmates were the children of their classmates. And in all the trophy cases were the marks left by my family.

They've all moved from Bloomington Hill. The houses they built are still there, but the heritage won't pass on to another generation of Crawfords. My children and my cousins' children will go to schools unhaunted by earlier generations of family. They'll grow up without that sense of belonging, of stability.

As society becomes more mobile, the only way our children will keep that stability is in a firm family unit built on a foundation of Christ. Then they will have that sense of belonging—to the family of God.

MAY 28   **DEALING WITH TIME**

The time was when a birthday was something to look forward to. Now it's an event I hope everybody forgets.

When we're young, a lifetime seems like forever. But with every birthday, the shorter forever becomes.

Birthdays are ego-bashers. On the inside we're the same as when we first set out on our own—maybe wiser, less naïve. Since the internal doesn't change, we pretend the external isn't aging until a birthday jolts us to reality.

I usually spend May 28 looking for gray hairs and wrinkles and bemoaning the loss of my girlish figure. After agonizing over appearances, I play through my memories, assessing where I am after thirty something.

There are accomplishments I'm proud of and quite a few I'm not so proud of. But I wouldn't relive a day of my life. I've got too much to look forward to to waste time worrying about the past.

According to statistics, I've got half a lifetime ahead. But statistics aren't guarantees. I may have half a lifetime; I may have a few days.

Whenever I face Jesus, the length of my life will be unimportant. The wrinkles and gray hairs will dissolve along with all my worldly success. It won't matter if I leave my mark on the earth. As I face eternity, my earthly achievements will be an unheard whisper. But the moments I've lived for God will echo through the ages.

MAY 29   **PRAYING FOR PEACE**

My brother was a Marine on an aircraft carrier passing through the Suez Canal when the United States retaliated against Libya.

When I heard what we were doing, my thoughts flew across the continents to the USS *Enterprise* and Jeff. I could hardly sleep that night, I was so worried about him.

Throughout Jeff's hitch with the Marines, he hit several hot spots of terrorism. All I could do was pray for his safety. And I prayed for Mom and Dad's peace of mind. If it was this hard being a sister, how much tougher would it be to be a parent with a son the likely target of a crazed fanatic?

Then I thought about my son, my precious little Tommy. I cherish his childish antics, his innocence, and those strong boyish hands that someday may have to hold a gun. I don't want him to become target practice for terrorists. And I don't want him to have to kill another mother's son.

Some day Tommy may have to carry a weapon to defend his homeland. While I can't prepare him for actual warfare, I can see that he marches off in the armor of God.

In the meantime I pray—for peace, for understanding, for tolerance. But man-made peace will always be tenuous. Only in God is there true peace. Only in God is there real understanding. And only in God is there no male or female, Jew or Gentile.

MAY 30   **GIFT OF A SON**

For nineteen years Uncle Roger was Grandma's pride. In one day the battle of Iwo Jima reduced him to a cherished memory, two purple hearts, and a photograph of a fresh-faced boy playing dress up in a Marine uniform.

Grandma prayed three sons off to World War II. The other two returned, but they were never the same. One contracted tuberculosis and lost a lung. The other, the oldest, had watched helplessly as Roger was buried alive in a foxhole.

The men and women who have fought for freedom, including the ones who have returned, have paid a dear price. But they aren't alone in the sacrifice.

For every soldier who's answered the call of his country, there's a mother who knows her child's dreams may never be realized. Ignoring her breaking heart, she waves her child off to battle. When the peace treaties are signed, she knows her sacrifice and that of her child weren't totally in vain.

God, his heart breaking, sacrificed his only Son to free mankind from a spiritual death. Though the treaties have been signed in Christ's blood, so many of us stand hopelessly by, observing that death as a historical casualty.

When we refuse to look beyond the death to the significance of Christ's resurrection, God's sacrifice has been in vain. In so doing, we make Christ's death a mere memorial rather than the victory it is.

MAY 31

ONLY THE BEST

All a would-be entrepreneur has to do to make her fortune is come up with a new self-improvement gadget. We humans are obsessed with improving our bodies, our status, our homes, our kids, our love lives. You name it and we want it, new and improved.

We women especially spend hundreds of dollars to look the best we can. We pour money into perms, cosmetics, and clothes. We agonize through endless hours of aerobics and dieting.

On lists of best-selling books and videos, the how-to's

have replaced literature. Every day a new one comes out, telling us how to dress for success, improve our money management, shape the perfect figure, raise the brightest kids.

From the adolescent to the college student to the housewife or career woman and even up to the grandmother, we are besotted with making ourselves the envy of others.

But in all this striving for self-betterment, we forget our souls. To be sure, there are books on how to live a more spiritual life. We may buy the books; we may even read them. Then they go on the bookshelf, and we go back to improving a decaying shell while our eternal being stands stunted.

If we would spend even half the time on the spiritual that we spend on the physical, we'd win the world to the Lord just by our example. But God doesn't want half-hearted effort. We as earthly parents expect 100 percent from our children. God expects the same from us.

Reflections

CAROL GOLL BURRIS

THE CHEERLEADER

At the end of the school year our twin daughter, Susan, was just completing the eighth grade, and she decided to try out for freshman cheerleader. Because she was so young, I didn't think her chances were very good, so the morning she was to try out, I made sure to prepare her for a gracious loss.

When she came home, I said to her, "How did you do?"

She answered me with excitement in her voice, "Mom, you didn't tell me what to do if I won!"

She *had* won, and she was right. I hadn't prepared her for winning. As we sat down at the kitchen table together to talk over her winning, we both decided that winning shouldn't be looked on as a chance to be overly proud. Her peers had given her something precious, their trust, by selecting her to represent them, and she owed them her best in return, as thanks.

As I reflect on our talk about winning, I can't help but think of the times I've been ungrateful when I've enjoyed good fortune. I have received so many blessings from God throughout my life but have not always accepted them. A lot of times I did not take the responsibility that was entrusted me.

Blessings are gifts from God, freely given, and I try to be worthy of them.

I hope, for all the blessings God gives me, that I will not fail to give my whole heart in return.

JUNE 2   **HOPE, A MYSTERIOUS AND WONDERFUL POWER**

Hope is the most mysterious and wonderful power we are granted. If we fail to use it, we become handicapped and weakened. People who possess hope can endure incredible burdens and overcome tremendous odds. That is a medical fact that has been proven over and over.

I've been around many people who have been faced with terrible illnesses. Some of them died, some got better, and some knew they would never be cured. A lot of those people exemplified positive attitudes. They showed love, continued to laugh, smiled a lot, and possessed a far-above-average ability to hope, by never giving up. It was hope that kept them going, and much of the time it was hope that kept them alive.

Hope, as the Bible says, is the twin sister of faith. It is wishing for a dream to come true and believing that dream will come true. It is fear that has said its prayers. The impossible happens when people wish strongly enough and believe firmly enough. Jesus is our hope and salvation. We must always be thankful for that.

"Not only so, but we also rejoice in our sufferings, because we know that suffering produces perseverance, perseverance, character; and character, hope" (Romans 5:3-4 NIV).

JUNE 3   **THE GOOD SAMARITAN**

One day while I was extremely busy attending to our six children, the telephone rang just as I was ready to go out the door to take the girls to Brownies. It was a friend from church who was upset because her husband had left her.

My life was in constant turmoil, and I did not want to set one more moment aside for another unsolicited interruption, so I said, "I don't have time to talk, because I'm just ready to leave to run an errand."

I hadn't driven more than a mile before I was forced to come to a standstill due to a road construction project. I waited for over thirty minutes, and my having to sit at an idle for so long caused the car to overheat, and, sure enough, it stalled. I got out of the car, started waving my arms in the air to every passing motorist along the highway, and no one would stop. Finally, forty minutes later, an elderly man pulled over, assessed the situation, and drove to the nearest filling station for some water. He came back and worked with my radiator until he got the car started again. After the man finished and was ready to leave, I said, "Thank you. I hope I haven't made you late for an important engagement."

He answered, "No problem, I was just on my way to the hospital to visit my wife, who had major surgery on her back yesterday. Besides, I couldn't just drive by without helping." He bid me a good day and left.

He was certainly a Good Samaritan. I told the children what a kind man he was for helping us and started down the highway again. Of course, we didn't make it to the Brownie meeting, so I got off at the next exit and headed home.

After supper I decided to visit my troubled friend. We spent over three hours together, and I didn't feel rushed at all. I learned from that experience that the more love I give to others, the more room I make for God's love.

JUNE 4   **LET'S GO CAMPING**

I never thought I would get hooked on camping, but we certainly did a lot of it when the children were small. Always when the first beautiful warm weekend would break through, all six of them would beg us to go camping. That meant loading the station wagon with two tents, eight sleeping bags, and all the other paraphernalia that goes along with camping. We usually packed some food and stopped for a picnic on our drive to our favorite camping site.

"What have you gotten me into, God?" I would say under my breath. "I'm not a camping-type mother. I don't like bugs, mud, toads, hard lumpy ground for sleeping, cooking out, or dirty hands."

It was pleasant to view the surroundings each time we arrived at our chosen spot. I so loved nature and peaceful lakes. We picked wooded areas so the tall trees could protect us from the sun. We loved to wade in the creeks and walk through the woods, and in a short time, somehow, I managed to overlook the children's dirty hands when we would eat.

I was always hesitant about going camping, but each time we went, the trips turned out to be a total delight. Those fun times together as a family provided us more time for communication.

The children always thanked us when we returned from our primitive outings and would tell us they didn't know we could be such good sports, so that made the sacrifice worthwhile.

Those camping experiences reminded me that there would be many unique experiences God would give us as a family, if I would just check with him every day. God's ideas are always better than mine, so I try to keep open to them.

JUNE 5   **MY FRIEND WAS TRULY A FIGHTER**

For over a year a friend of mine fought a battle with cancer. During the eleven months of her illness, she never complained or stopped doing for others. One day I asked her, "How do you keep going? You are so ill, yet you never give up. Why?"

She replied, "I never want to be totally helpless or dependent on others, because when I stop being able to do things for myself, then I won't be able to do things for others, and my greatest need is to be around people and to do things for them. Besides, when I'm doing for others, I don't think so much about my disease or myself."

She spent much of her time laughing, joking, and cheering

up people, and, in turn, she was being cheered. Because of her, lives changed. She taught people the value of life. Her attitude of courage helped others to be healthier and happier. She made me more aware of how, inescapably, we influence everyone we come into contact with. Her illness brought those people who surrounded her closer to God. Bitter feelings did not occupy her mind, even though she knew there was no cure for her disease. God had given my friend patience, the main ingredient needed to keep going. Throughout her illness she refused to give up; she took her suffering and used it as a source of hope for others.

The people who supported her, sharing her pain with gentle touches and comforting words, were her reason for not giving up. She knew she really mattered. Hindrances became a way for her, obstacles became open doors, and daily setbacks became merely disturbing interruptions in her life.

My friend's death reminded me of my one-way ticket through life. I must never defer any kindness I can show or good I can do for any living person. I must never neglect being attentive, for I will not pass this way again.

JUNE 6   **PLEASE, GOD, I WANT A BICYCLE**

When our eleven-year-old son, Mark, asked the mealtime blessing one night, he added at the end, "And please, God, thank you that you are going to help me get a two-wheel bicycle." His Dad explained to him that we did not have enough money for a bicycle. That same night while he was saying his bedtime prayer, he prayed, "Thank you God, that you will keep working on my Mom and Dad so they will change their minds about my bicycle."

Mark soon got a paper route, making only three dollars a week. He went out faithfully in all kinds of weather to earn that three dollars. By the time fall approached, most of his friends had signed up to play football for the local community center team. We discouraged Mark because he was so small. All of the boys his age outweighed him by at least twenty pounds, so we offered him the amount of money we would have spent for him to play ball. He was thrilled with our decision; "Good," he said, "I can add that to my bicycle savings." I told his Dad, "Well, if I have to make a choice between a bicycle or a football, I'd much rather Mark have a bicycle."

In less than eighteen months Mark saved enough money to pay for all but twenty dollars of the cost of the bicycle. He was so excited on the way home after the purchase that he hung his head out of the window, never taking his eyes off of the shiny red bicycle tied to the top of the car.

We all learned a lesson from our child's determination and faith. When we want something we feel is impossible to obtain, we are reminded of how an eleven-year-old boy thanked God for a bicycle, even before he had a nickel, a job, or our blessings.

JUNE 7   **MUSIC TO MY EARS**

About twelve years ago a friend of mine gave me a transistor radio, complete with earplugs and a tape player. I have enjoyed the service it has given me through the years. But last winter while I was on vacation, basking in the Florida sun on the beautiful St. Petersburg beach, I noticed that because of its age the radio had lost most of its energy, that the music no longer came through very clearly. From time to time the music sounded clear, but most of the time it sounded fuzzy and faded. Every time I held my hand on the radio, the sound would become clearer.

Well, just like my radio, I'm getting older too, and often I tend to lose much of my energy. I forget easily, tire more rapidly, and my bones and muscles complain a lot, especially when I'm climbing stairs.

My radio and I have found the same cure—the touch of a

hand. I certainly need the touch of God's gentle hand daily, and I get that touch through the love of his people. Their special caring words, touches, and hugs keep me going and reassure me. I thank God for his people who help me to live my life better and am more fulfilled and happier because of them. Without the touch of a hand, my life would be meaningless. With the touch of a hand, I am continually revitalized and brought closer to God.

> Two are better than one,
>   because they have a good return for their work:
> If one falls down,
>   his friend can help him up.
> But pity the man who falls
>   and has no one to help him up!
>   (Ecclesiastes 4:9-10 NIV)

JUNE 8   **CHANGES ARE DIFFICULT,
                            BUT NOT IMPOSSIBLE**

Several years ago when I was diagnosed with an incurable disease, I was forced to change my life-style from one of extreme activity to that of being sedentary. At first I was rebellious and bitter, but reality forced me to accept my situation, and when I chose to do that, I became productive again. My first inclination was to pray for myself, but I found it too difficult to do. It made me feel like a hypocrite. But my friends from all over the United States prayed for me, and I'm sure it was their prayers that brought me out of a deep spiritual depression. Knowing they cared kept me going, and it meant a lot to me when they would say, "Don't give up; we love you and need you." I always answered them with "I won't, I promise." After all, they cared, because they were praying for me. My friends also did a lot of listening during my time of confusion and shared their own stories of how praying for themselves had helped them through their own personal traumas. Soon I was able to pray for myself, without feeling selfish or guilty. I prayed silently when in public and aloud when alone.

My disease has since gone into total remission. I have experienced the healing power of Jesus, and through that have learned what Paul meant in I Corinthians, chapter 13, about love never giving up, and I have discovered how powerful and sustaining prayer can be.

Perhaps there are people on your prayer list who are at a standstill in their lives, or even you yourself need to be spiritually renewed because of some personal crisis. Don't hesitate to ask other Christians to pray for your real needs, and don't feel guilty about praying for yourself, either. Remember, prayer heals not only the one who is prayed for but also the one who prays.

"Meanwhile these three remain: faith, hope, and love, and the greatest of these is love" (I Corinthians 13:13 GNB).

JUNE 9 **THE QUESTIONS PEOPLE ASK ABOUT LIFE**

One day while I was outside taking my daily walk, I stopped to talk with Norbert, an old gentleman of ninety, who was also out walking, taking advantage of the beautiful day. He said, "Hi, pretty one. You know, I don't know whether I'm coming or going. I'm too old to remember where I came from, and I really don't know for sure where I'm going, so it frightens me a little."

I said to him, "Norbert, you are on your way home, because you are practically in front of your house."

He answered, "I sure hope I'm on my way home," and pointed to the sky above.

After leaving Norbert, I thought about what he had said and realized that older people probably do get a little fearful of how they will die, not knowing whether it will be quick or if they will suffer.

We all go through adversities in our lives, but if we believe in God and eternal life, he will provide us with the courage we need to handle those adversities when they occur. We cannot allow ourselves to rely on our own inner strength, or we will most certainly be afraid. Our fears will leave us, if we make the choice to rely on God and trust that we are in good hands, because God never gives us more than we can handle.

By believing and not doubting, we are assured that God will be with us when we need him the most. After the storms have passed, we need to live each day to its fullest, making sure we are enhancing our personal well-being and not fearing what new adversity may befall us tomorrow. It is only through faith that we can trust and believe that God will give us strength and courage sufficient for the time.

JUNE 10   **SUCH GRACE AND BEAUTY!**

I first came to love dancing when I went to my cousin's recital. I noticed that most of the dancers were having a marvelous time performing their various routines. I was especially thrilled by the grace and beauty of the ballet dancers, as they leaped and pirouetted around the stage, and was amazed at how the acrobatic dancers kept from flipping right off of the stage onto the floor below. I wondered how those dancers kept from losing their balance while performing these special acts.

The following fall I enrolled in a dancing class, and the first question I asked my teacher was "How do the ballet dancers keep their balance?"

He answered, "Oh, that's easy. The dancers first fix their eyes on one particular spot and return to it with each whirl and flip. As long as they do that, they can keep going without losing their balance."

My dance teacher's words left me for several years, until one day when I was doing some shopping in Chicago. I wasn't used to such big cities or rushing crowds, so the going was rough. I was unable to keep my balance, because I was pushed and shoved by several impatient shoppers as I walked from store to store. Just as I was about to lose my temper and say some very unkind words, my eyes caught sight of a beautiful cross silhouetted against the sky at the top of a large church, and my bitter thoughts suddenly turned into feelings of peace. I stopped in the midst of all of that confusion, took a deep breath, and said a little prayer. "God, fix my eyes on Jesus, so I can keep my balance in this whirling, twirling, dizzying world. Help me not to lose sight of you, especially when I'm running around in circles."

After I finished my prayer, I continued my shopping. In fact, I actually enjoyed it, and the unkind words never came.

JUNE 11   **EXERCISE AND EAT RIGHT**

We are living in an age when we read a lot about physical fitness and continually hear about the importance of good health habits. We cannot pick up a newspaper or magazine or tune into the television without hearing or reading about how important it is for us to stay healthy. These programs and editorials give us hope, because we are assured that good habits will lengthen our life-spans. These sources also remind us of how we are shortening our life-spans through obesity, smoking, alcohol abuse, lack of exercise, and too much stress.

Most of us are aware of how much older we are by our cholesterol levels and blood pressure counts, and all of that is fine, but how do we measure our spiritual age? Just as bad habits age our bodies, bad spiritual habits age our souls, and we become lifeless. We can go to the doctor or the bathroom scales to check on our bodily age, but we need to attend church regularly, fellowship with our Christian friends, attend Bible studies, read the Bible regularly, pray consistently, or talk with our minister, in order to check on our spiritual age. Somehow that does make a difference.

When we do these things, we are not merely reading or

mumbling a few words, but we are disciplining ourselves, and self-discipline requires pain and the agony of thinking. When we think prayerfully, we can use God's gifts wisely. We can bring joy to those who do not have a good life. We can share God's peace through the love of others. We can easily continue to love and to forgive. We can better understand God's love and respond to his call. These sources are privileges that anyone can enjoy. They disclose what the divine mystery is all about. It is only when we grow in spirit that we will be able to hold the goods of God's universe in trust. If we stay in close touch with God, we will remain young forever.

JUNE 12   **WHY A CAT?**

When our children were small, a friend of ours gave them a beautiful long-haired cat. We already had a dog, a snake, a guinea pig, a hamster, and a rabbit, and I wasn't open to the idea of housing another pet. At first my husband and I treated the cat, whom we named Necasion, like an outsider, because we did not welcome the new intruder into our home and certainly didn't take into account how happy the children were with the new pet.

I did take on the responsibility of feeding Necasion in his own special dish on top of the washer, but he always seemed oblivious to my protective care and presence. He managed to eat in fearful haste, nervously glancing at me from time to time, yet I had really never given him anything to fear.

It didn't take me long to realize why Necasion reacted the way he did. It was because my husband and I were avoiding him. We were not neglecting his physical needs, but he sensed he didn't belong in his new environment.

We decided to start working at enjoying having the cat around, and soon he began to come to us, lie on our laps, and purr his happy tune.

People are a lot like Necasion. When they feel rejected,

they start to carry a chip on their shoulders. We all need love, but it is much easier to accept it than to give it. With God's help we are more able to allow our love to spill out onto others, and God is the only one who can teach us the difference that love can make.

JUNE 13   **MY FLOWER GARDEN**

One very warm summer day when I was outside working in my flower garden, it suddenly occurred to me how much I had learned from my grandmother. She was such a patient woman with me and later with my six small children. She was always so willing to give of her time and love, never expecting anything in return. How my life had changed because of her. She taught me to appreciate the little things of life. I would have missed so much if I had not experienced her enthusiasm. I remember watching her hunt down her favorite things in secondhand stores. I remember the intense smell of her homemade apple dumplings and going to her house for many family Thanksgiving and Christmas dinners. I loved to sit with her on the front porch swing and discuss things that were exciting to me. We would swing and talk for hours at a time. Her attitudes and philosophy helped to shape mine, and through her I developed so much confidence.

As I pulled the weeds in my flower bed, I began counting up those contributions and suddenly wondered what effects I had had on my children and grandchildren. How much help had I provided? How many of my self-imposed opinions possibly colored their views? How far would their lives widen because of me? What kind of influence did I have on the friends they were choosing? Were any of them healthier, happier, or wiser because of me?

Pausing to take such an inventory was very refreshing. It gave me a new appreciation of my importance and made me realize how influential I am to others and what an incredible responsibility I have.

JUNE 14 THE LEGAL SECRETARY

On my first job, fresh out of business college, I worked for two attorneys as a legal secretary. During the first week I went to court to take notes for the senior partner on a case assignment and was unprepared for the fierce, aggressive confrontations that took place. During the hearing the opposing lawyers became the angriest men I had ever seen. The trial went on for over an hour before the judge pronounced his sentence. My boss won his case. After the trial my boss told me he was going to lunch with the other lawyer. The two of them left just ahead of me and to my total surprise walked side by side down the stairs, talking like friends. I couldn't believe my eyes. Just before that time, they had shouted, clawed, and verbally abused each other. What hypocrites they were!

As I sat at my desk later that afternoon, I said to myself, "They're not enemies; it was just their job to try and influence the jury in order to win in court. They had to have a difference of opinion, but that didn't mean they couldn't be friends."

We would probably all be better off if we copied the characteristics of those lawyers. People should not be considered enemies just because they do not agree with us or have opposing opinions, religions, or political views.

Since that time I have been aware of the friends I could have lost, simply because I hadn't liked their opinions. We are taught to live peaceably with all people. We need to love people for the goodness that is in their hearts. By practicing that, I can love my friends without loving every word they say.

JUNE 15 MOVING CAN BE REWARDING

Because of my husband's profession, we've moved many times, praying fervently each time that everything would turn out right. But when it was time to pack and say

171

good-bye to the known, loved, and familiar, in exchange for the strange and uncertain, it always seemed wrong. When we moved a few years ago, I swore it would be our last move. As I stood in the front yard, gazing at the beautiful farmlands, I was thinking, "I really don't want to hang another picture," and I meant it. Tinker, our little poodle, saw me and came running, carrying a well-nibbled rubber ball in his mouth. I looked at that awful ball and went inside to get a new one to take its place. "Wait until he sees this," I thought.

I took the ball outside and called Tinker over to me. I held the ball out to him, but he wouldn't take it. Instead, he just held on tightly to that bleached-out, chewed-up rubber ball and wasn't the least bit concerned as to what I was offering him, nor was he about to trust me enough to give up or trade the well-worn familiar ball.

But I realized I wasn't trusting God either—not enough. I was rejecting all of the good things God had in store for my husband and me in our new home, by resisting the move.

I left the new ball on the ground for Tinker to play with when he was ready and went back inside to continue packing, and I began to trust God again for that day and, of course, for tomorrow also.

JUNE 16   **A COMMON CAUSE**

Recently I went to Senior High Institute along with my husband, who was the keynoter for the week. Those 240 campers had so much vitality and spirit. They were working together for one common cause, and that was to witness openly for their beliefs.

During the week I took the time to notice the beauty I had been too busy to notice before. Every day I viewed the violently colored sun as it rose and set in a brilliant, burning copper sky, and throughout the days I particularly enjoyed watching the birds flit about from limb to limb, cawing, chirping, and screeching. The week was incredible.

I was enthralled by the competitive spirit displayed among the campers and counselors that week. The young people were fun to be around. They made me feel like one of them when I sang songs with them in the assembly hall and entered into their response groups. They were quite assertive and had so much energy. They were bold, honest, and earnest. They seized every minute of the days and part of the nights, engaging in activities with enthusiasm. They were continually galvanized into action, and their energy caught on. The whole experience of being with those young people left me with a sense of completeness and rightness.

How wonderful it would be if all God's believers used the same assertiveness and showed as much spirit and energy as those young people did. Binding together and making each moment of life count should be everyone's priority. When we join others by working together for the common cause of witnessing openly for our beliefs and honestly speak out with boldness, we will most certainly gain strength in God's sight.

"For 'In him we live and move and have our being'; As even some of your poets have said, 'For we are indeed his offspring' " (Acts 17:28 RSV).

JUNE 17   **THE BIRTHDAY PARTY**

When our youngest son, John, was approaching his fifth birthday, his Dad and I decided to give him a party. A couple of weeks before the day of the party, I shopped, cleaned, planned, invited, decorated, and baked. I kept so busy that I hardly had any time for myself, my husband, or my other five children. In fact, I felt like backing out of the seemingly never-ending situation.

The time came much too quickly, and almost all of the twenty children I invited showed up. The party lasted two hours and the young guests were very active and messy.

After the last party guest left, I instantly began cleaning up the mess, hurrying around like a madwoman. As I pounced on the half-eaten cupcakes, broken balloons, and torn party favors, I noticed little John sitting in the middle of the floor, surrounded by a bed of ribbons and wrapping paper. I was just about to shout at John to help me clean up the mess he and his friends had made when I looked over and saw my husband smiling lovingly at him. I quickly held back my anger, then took a look at little John, myself, and at what my husband and I both saw was sheer happiness and contentment. John looked at us with such innocence and said, "I'm feeling really good. I had a wonderful party!"

So often I tend to rush into a panic when it's not really necessary. Then I later wonder why life has to always be so hectic. Why couldn't it be as simple for us as it was for John? We could just sit down and feel good about God's generous love, if we did not allow panic to set in. We should never drive through life so fast that we are unable to see the beauty along the way.

JUNE 18   **A GREAT VACATION**

When the children were small, my husband and I spent a week each summer attending a church camp. The log cabins we were furnished were small but quaint, and all noises were accented. I never had to do any cooking because we ate in the mess hall with the campers, so that allowed us to spend the week resting and recreating.

One year we had a dreadful storm in the middle of the night, which frightened the children, and there was no way their father or I could calm them down. Reading always worked when they were upset, but that wasn't the answer because the power had gone out. The bolts of lightning were so severe and loud that it made the children shiver with fright! They ran into our bedroom, screaming and crying, and leaped one by one into our arms. In a matter of seconds, our bed was overloaded with children.

"What if the lightning kills me, Mommy?" Susan cried out in fear. I held her tightly and told her, "Don't worry, it won't."

"How do you know?" spoke Debbie in haste.

I answered the children. "Do you remember learning in

Sunday school about how Jesus calmed the storm by commanding the wind? He said to the wind, 'Be quiet,' and then he said to the waves, 'Be still,' and then the wind died down and there was a great calm. The men were terribly afraid and said to one another, 'Who is this man that even the wind and waves obey?' Those men needed more faith so that they could believe that Jesus would keep them safe."

After a little pleading on my part, the children finally calmed down, and I tucked them into their beds. Soon they drifted off to sleep.

The next day was absolutely beautiful. We all went to the lake. The children and their father swam, and I lay in the sun. They asked for me to join them, but ever since a near drowning accident when I was small, I had managed to stay away from water over my head.

"No thanks, I'll just lie here and get some sun," I said.

A short time later, Paul, our six-year-old twin son, came over to me and said, "You're afraid, aren't you, Mommy? Why don't you have enough faith to believe that Jesus will keep you safe, like you told us last night?"

I had no answer, so I followed Paul into the water.

That leap was a leap of faith, and it proved to me that the power of Jesus to calm all fears is a comfort as well as a challenge. It's a leap we can all make when we are assured he is watching over us. We cannot be afraid when we have faith.

"Jesus got up and commanded the wind, 'Be quiet!' and said to the waves, 'Be still!' The wind died down, and there was a great calm. Then Jesus said to his disciples, 'Why are you frightened? Are you still without faith?' " (Mark 4:39-40 GNB).

JUNE 19   **OH, HOW I HATE BUDGETS**

I am a thrifty person by nature, so each payday I have developed the depressing habit of making out a budget. Somehow I always manage to overshoot my projected expenditures, which fills me with concern as to how I'll make the money stretch until the next payday without going into the red. There just never seems to be enough money to go around. Well, this time I got so discouraged that I just shut the book and gave up.

That same afternoon I went to lunch with my dear friend Blanche, and during our conversation she told me about her sixteen-year-old neighbor boy who had been in a motorcycle accident and as a result had lost both of his legs.

"How terrible," I said; "that poor boy, how will he ever be able to continue on with all of his normal peers and his life?"

She answered, "Oh, he's having no problems at all. He has mastered walking on his artificial legs so well that people hardly notice his handicap, and he has a terrific attitude. He is quite a survivor. He has transferred most of his activities over to his hands. He has taken up sculpting, is very creative, and does a beautiful job. His sculptures really come to life."

I thought of how well off I was, and it brought to reality Paul's words from I Corinthians 7:7: "Actually I would prefer all were as I am; but each one has the special gift that God has given him, one man this gift, another man that" (GNB).

That evening after supper I was able to readapt myself to finish my budget, and the problems that had been overwhelming earlier in the day seemed so small. As I closed the ledger, I said to myself, "I am bigger than all of the difficulties that stand in my way."

JUNE 20   **THE SOUR PICKLE**

The other day I busily set out to can pickles. I was my usual enthusiastic self at first, but before the project was completed, my disposition changed to a rather bad one. When I can pickles, I try to can both sweet and sour ones all in one day, which always turns out to be a big mistake because I manage to turn into a sour pickle myself. If people

would happen to be around me when I'm in such a bad mood, they would put me in a jar and seal me up, because when I'm like that, I'm no good to anyone.

As my mood continued to worsen, I thought of the many people I have come into contact with daily whom I would have liked to shut off, but it's never that simple. It takes a lot of patience to get along with so many different types of personalities, and we need to work daily at developing the kind of patience God expects of us.

Finally, after the canning was successfully completed, I went out onto our sunny patio with a good inspirational book in hand and read for about an hour. Before I had finished, I found renewed peace and joy and became the whole person God intended me to be.

When I returned to the kitchen to prepare our supper and viewed my hard work, I merely said, "Thank you, Lord, for the strength and knowledge you have given me, because those pickles sure look tasty and beautiful, and I couldn't have done it without you."

JUNE 21 **THE GARDEN MUST GROW**

Several years ago my husband was transferred to Detroit, Michigan, and we bought a home out in the suburbs northwest of the big city. The yards in the neighborhood we moved into were very small. The neighbors called them "postage stamp lots." Before that time we had always lived in the country, with at least half an acre of ground, so we decided to plant a garden in our small yard, hoping that we could bring some country atmosphere to the city. We didn't have very positive attitudes about our garden and worried about rabbits, and sure enough, they destroyed it. We also had a large Bing cherry tree just outside of the patio door but believed that we would not get any cherries off of it, and sure enough, the birds managed to eat them. We really weren't very happy about moving to a big city, after having lived in

small towns for so many years, and I'm sure that our unhappiness caused us to develop a lot of negative thoughts. We couldn't help but notice, though, that the people who had lived in our home previously must have had green thumbs and good, positive attitudes, because their perennials blossomed beautifully without any special effort on our part.

I believe that it was our discontentment that unnecessarily caused us a lot of misfortune that summer. We allowed our excessive worry and negative thoughts to obscure God's loving desire to take care of us or to give us what we wanted, so the opposite really happened. We failed to consider what Peter told us in I Peter 5:7: "Cast all your anxieties upon him, for he cares for you" (RSV).

We need to do just that, and the way we can is to relax and not give ourselves permission to worry about tomorrow. When we can enjoy the many gifts God bestows on us each day, no matter what environment surrounds us, then we can most assuredly let go and let God take over. God only wants the best for us, and from now on I'm going to live each day as if I believe it.

JUNE 22 **RESPONSIBILITY HELPS US TO GROW**

When I was ten years old, my Dad bought my sister and me each a rabbit. We devoted ourselves to those rabbits. We faithfully fed them and cleaned out their cages every day. We were so responsible with our rabbits that he decided to get us some chickens. We were fascinated with the chickens, and when they laid their first eggs, we gently turned them every few hours to check the temperature and just counted the days until they would hatch. It was so exciting to hear the pecking inside the shells. We wanted to rush the time for them to hatch, but our Dad told us if we did, the chicks would not be strong enough to live, so we patiently waited. My sister and I had so much fun caring for those rabbits and chickens, and

while doing our chores learned patience along with responsibility.

I was taken back so many years today when I thought about those pleasurable moments my sister and I spent caring for those chickens and rabbits, as I was trying to help a friend break through her resistance to Jesus. I was indeed confident in my capability to surround my friend with the warmth of Christian love, and I knew if I provided the warmth, that God would certainly provide the inner strength for her rebirth. God has taught me that love is patient and kind.

JUNE 23   **PASSING LOVE ON**

When our twins were born prematurely, we were quite anxious about their survival. How small and frail they looked in those incubators! As we stood outside of the room watching them, we scarcely noticed an interested woman who had come to stand beside us. "Would you mind if I said a prayer for your babies?" she asked. Of course we didn't mind. A nurse later told us that the woman we were talking to had been visiting her own baby, who had been in the hospital with a severe heart condition for over three months. During the month our twins were hospitalized, that very same woman took time out of her busy schedule to check on them each time she came to visit her baby, pouring out her special feelings for their well-being.

After the twins left the hospital, we never saw the woman again. We had gotten to know her name and had made conversation with her, but we lived in another part of the state and never kept in touch. Now when I look at our healthy adult twins, I think often of that woman, a perfect stranger, who showed such care and concern, and I can't help but feel thankful. But I cannot be any more thankful for her prayers and concern than I can be thankful for and think kindly of all of those other people who took care of our older son and who brought meals to us while our babies were in the hospital. There were so many who lent helping hands. We cannot really repay those kindnesses, but we can pass them on.

Now each time I take soup to a sick friend or say a special prayer for someone who is suffering, I know I am passing on the love that was shown to us when we needed it. There have been times when I have wanted to do kind things for others and have been unable to for one reason or another, but it seems like there is always someone who reaches out and lends a helping hand to me when I am in need, and when they do I find that I am able to accept their help graciously. I no longer catch myself saying to them, "You shouldn't have" or "How can I ever repay you?" I've learned that it is as important to be a good receiver as it is to be a gracious giver.

Perhaps when the kind woman prayed for our frail, sickly twins, she was passing along the concern that was shown by Jesus long ago. I want to always be a link in the chain of kindness that connects us all to God, when I am needed. I hope also that as I become more dependent on others I will not develop feelings of unworthiness that would cause me to block out my ability to be a gracious and thankful receiver.

JUNE 24 ## THE PEACEFUL LAKES

I love it when I have an opportunity to go to the lakes. The world always looks so great, wide, and beautiful when I sit in the sun looking at the shining light reflecting on the water, giving it the appearance of bobbing diamonds. I sit at the water's edge for hours, taking it all in, wanting to embrace it somehow. I derive so much joy from feeling the cool blue water on my feet and hearing the grass rippling in whispers behind me. I am overwhelmed by the formations of the clouds floating above, in silence. It makes the whole world seem like a huge, bright, invitation from God.

But there are people who do not really see or feel the world. They huddle in their towels, with umbrellas overhead shielding the sun, slapping the bugs, not really involved with life. They are just living on the surface. Of course, I myself have fallen into those subtle ways from time to time by giving in to inertia. There have been those rare times when I've allowed the wonder to dim, and my awareness to slip away, too.

When Jesus spoke of abundant life, he said, "I am come that they might have life and have it more abundantly." He was trying to wake us up to the joys of existence, where we would view all the world as a miracle and enter in. He was trying to coax us into an involvement with life. But it's up to us whether we choose to float on the surface of life or take the plunge to dive deep.

JUNE 25   **FIXING THE CAR**

When our son Mark was a teenager, he spent a lot of his spare time fixing up his car. Less than a month before his seventeenth birthday, he wrecked his car. Luckily, Mark was not hurt. The insurance company determined that the car was totaled, but Mark didn't agree with their decision, so he got a friend of his to help him put the car back into running order. After they finished the job, the car really didn't look too bad, and the engine sounded pretty good. Mark even had enough money left over from the insurance settlement, along with some money he had saved from detasseling corn, to buy some fancy seatcovers. I had my doubts in the beginning, but Mark convinced me his plan would work, and it did.

After that experience I have learned that whenever I have a falling out with someone or start to feel a little impatient about their actions, I know it's fixing time, forgiving time, putting the relationship back together time, and I know my forgiveness and acceptance will create a strong deep love and openness to those around me that nothing can wear away. I also know that when I work hard at fixing up relationships, I will become stronger in my broken places.

JUNE 26   FLYING IN A PLANE

Whenever I fly in an airplane, I look out the window, down at the earth below, and am overwhelmed by the beauty spread out before me. All of those tiny houses and buildings standing in neat little rows remind me of a patchwork quilt. When God looks down on his world, it must look something like that. I sit there and imagine, while I am looking at those homes, that in some of them people perhaps are offering prayers up to God, and can see in my mind those prayers surrounded by a double black line. When recollecting how small everything looks from an airplane window, I remember a minister saying in a sermon one time, "God always takes time to listen to your prayers, even if they are little ones."

Now when I become frustrated with unsolved problems, or I am driving to the store and in a big hurry, or my husband and I simply can't find enough time to be together, or I can't keep up with life's daily demands, I remember the view from the airplane window when I am flying. I see water, houses, buildings, and streets, and then I see my prayers rising up. "Lord, help me not to be in such a big hurry that I miss the simple things of life." And suddenly I find peace, because I just know God hears me. And during those times when I am feeling small, like those objects from the airplane window, I know that I am always large in God's eyes.

JUNE 27   LET'S GET OUT AND SELL

When I was twelve years old, our church youth group took on the project of selling lint chaser brushers. Our goal was to raise money for church camping scholarships. We had a number of youth signed up to go to church camp, so we needed to sell a lot of brushes. I didn't do too well the first day because I was so frightened. Our youth leader told me not to give up and to try again the following day. I said, "Not me, it makes me too nervous."

She explained to me that it would get easier and that my giving up would display weakness of character.

I thought about what the youth leader said and was determined not to give up, so I did go out the next day, although it was very hard for me. I had to literally force myself to keep selling those brushes. As the youth leader had said, it would have been much easier for me to give up, but by continuing on I gained more courage each time I knocked on a new door and ended up selling a lot of brushes.

Since that experience, I have learned that God doesn't want us to be fearful. He wants us to be courageous instead. He wants us to believe in ourselves, and it is our duty as Christian followers to stay near him and to not stray away.

JUNE 28   **SUPPER TIME AGAIN**

The other evening while I was dishing out the food onto our plates for supper, I was complaining about a string of minor misfortunes that had seemed to zero in on my little corner of the world. The medical bills were piling up to the place where we had considered borrowing from the bank to pay them. Our grass was dying from some unknown infestation. Our car was in much need of repair. My list went on and on. I silently asked the Lord, "Why me?"

My husband interrupted my deep thoughts and said in his usual joking way, "Why are you giving me burned lasagna? Don't I deserve better? After all, I work hard for the money around here." I had burned part of the lasagna and was dishing out the bad portion to him.

"Sure, you deserve better—it's just been a bad day all the

way around, and I'm not paying any attention. Here's mine, I'll trade you."

"No, don't trade," he said. "Just relax, give me a big hug, and let me know you love me. It's okay."

"You know I love you," I said, as I hugged him.

Strangely, his words kept repeating themselves in my mind, and suddenly the question came to me, didn't God love me? Of course. Then the medical bills, the sick lawn, the loud muffler, the burned lasagna, and all the other petty annoyances were okay. I wasn't being singled out by God, or by anyone or anything else, for that matter. Those petty little things just happen to pop up from time to time, and when they do, I need to use my confidence in God's love to help overcome them. I know God loves me, even when I'm in a bad mood, so everything's okay. I reached out and gave my husband another big hug.

JUNE 29   **A WASTED DAY?**

What a wasted day this has been. I am exhausted and haven't accomplished one single thing. I've answered the phone many times. Six of the calls were from a relative with anxieties of her own, and my friend stopped to share her worries about her wayward teenage son. My husband popped in for lunch, filled with enthusiasm about his accomplishments on the job, and the sixteen-year-old neighbor boy came over to show me the car he had just purchased. My daughter called me long distance to share with me all of the new things our beautiful granddaughter had mastered. Another friend called to tell me about a trip to the Bahamas she and her husband were planning. Tonight our women's church society is holding its monthly meeting, and I am responsible for the refreshments, and I even feel too tired for that.

Finally I managed to make the bed and straighten up the clutter, and while I was putting things into order, my Bible fell onto the floor. When I picked it up, a scripture passage from the book of Job jumped right out at me: "Hear diligently my speech, and let this be your consolations" (Job 21:2).

A wasted day? Perhaps not. I certainly didn't accomplish everything I wanted to, but I have listened all day. If I have consoled just one person and made him or her feel loved or happier by listening, then this has been a day of accomplishments, and one of my better days.

Sometimes when I'm busy listening, I forget that I'm doing something, but listening is by far the greatest gift of love we can give.

JUNE 30   **PETS HAVE THE ANSWER**

Our little poodle, Tinker, has become a big part of our lives. He hardly ever goes outdoors, sleeps in whatever bed he chooses, lies on his favorite living room chair, and spends a lot of time on the back of the couch looking out of the big picture window. There is always food and water in his special dishes, and he is loaded with toys. He certainly does not want for love. He has made his way into our hearts and very well knows it. In other words, he is in charge of the house and allows us to live in it.

The day my mother-in-law moved in with us, she brought her cat, Penelope. When Tinker first saw Penelope, he barked loudly, growled a little, and then ran under the bed. He would not come out from under the bed, even to eat. He lost weight and was not his usual happy self anymore. Once in a while he would venture out into the living room, and instantly Penelope would spring forth, ready to get acquainted. Tinker would growl and bark at her and run under the bed.

Penelope never gave up on becoming friends with Tinker. Whenever she got a chance, she'd go toward Tinker in a hopeful way, and Tinker would just growl, bark, and run.

Finally Tinker relented and stayed out from under the bed, but he still growled and barked a lot. Nevertheless, Penelope was excited and watched Tinker's every move, careful not to venture too close. Tinker would look back at Penelope with narrowed eyes and growl with his leave-me-alone warning.

But very slowly Penelope got Tinker to come closer, by pretending to be asleep. One day I caught them eating together. Another day they were both sleeping in Tinker's favorite chair. Tinker finally stopped growling and barking.

Too often, I'm like Tinker. I pout when I think someone else is getting the love and affection I deserve. How much better it would be if I were like Penelope, who never worries about how much love she deserves but instead concerns herself with how much love she can give.

Journeys

BARBARA OWEN

JULY 1   **ON THE GO**

We think of ourselves as a mobile society, and indeed we are—moving often, traveling away from home for weekends and vacations, carpooling, constantly on the go. But this is nothing new. The people of Bible times were also on the move. The Old Testament folks are called seminomadic people. Throughout their history God's people were on the move, much as we are today.

And for them, as for us, times of travel could be times of blessing, confrontation, fresh insight—times of awareness of God in their lives. For us and for them the travel may be for a move (Abraham and Sarah) or for business (Paul) or part of the daily routine (the woman at the well). It may be for spiritual restoration (Hagar) or to attend an exciting event (the boy who took his fish and bread lunch and went to hear Jesus).

Something special can happen during travel times. During July we can see in our own lives, as in the lives of biblical people, that there are moments during travel when God brings about something new for us. We can be awake to what God may have for us on our next trip down the street, across town, out of state, around the world.

JULY 2   **SIGN ON THE BUS**

Years ago I rode the bus to my first job. The advertising signs always caught my eye. Ads for suntan oil, cigarettes, milk. Public service signs saying "Don't Litter" and "Give Blood." And then there was the Bible verse sign. If I sat on the long front seat that ran sideways, my attention was forced to this sign above the heads of passengers on the other side of the bus. It said, "What shall it profit a man, if he shall gain the whole world, and lose his own soul?" (Mark 8:36).

I was a searcher at the time, not raised in a churched home, wondering about God. These words caught me up in more wonder. Surely I wouldn't want to lose my soul, but what did the words mean? I didn't suppose I could save my soul either. God would have to inform me about this.

It would be ten years before I was baptized and understood something of Christ. But I reflect happily on that sign on the bus, something ordinary in my daily commute to work, that opened my mind to think more about life with God. A few words caught "on the go" can make a difference.

JULY 3 **THE WOMAN AT THE WELL**

The woman in chapter 4 of the Gospel of John must have made the trip to the well often. Yet this trip, on the day she met Jesus there, may have been an extra one, since no other women seem to have been there drawing water. Like going to the store for an extra jug of milk, perhaps she had need of extra water that day. And she met Jesus there at the well. He spoke, and his words proved a turning point in her life.

Has not something similar happened to you too? It may not have been such a life-changing event as happened to the woman at the well. But has not Jesus, living in the heart of a believing stranger, offered a word of blessing, a drink of living water to bring new life on a dry day?

You head for home, knowing your extra trip "to the well" that day was not by accident. The Lord of whom you ask "daily bread," of whom you beseech "thy kingdom come," had sent both to you that day. Your meeting did not seem as dramatic as that of the woman at the well, but it was just as real, prompted by the same love.

It could happen even today. Or the reverse might happen, too, and you might bring Christ to another during one of your routine trips.

JULY 4 **BABEL, PENTECOST, HEAVEN**

I was at worship in a large chapel on a seminary campus. The bulletin noted that one of the presiding ministers was visiting from Germany. I knew that this happened occasionally; a visiting instructor would come, often bringing some of his own students.

We sang the hymns and chanted the psalm. Soon we were going to the altar for Holy Communion. We stood in a circle around the altar. "The body of Christ, given for you," said the officiant to me.

"Amen." I accepted the bread.

"Das ist der Leib Jesus Christus," said the officiant to the young man next to me.

I blinked in surprise, but the young man smiled and accepted the bread offered in German. He had sat in our pew, seemingly alone in his thoughts till now. Suddenly, by use of his native tongue, he was brought into the fold. Wondrous thoughts of our great God washed over me—of the immensity of the kingdom of God, including people of many languages.

The people in Jerusalem on the first Pentecost felt some of this as they heard the gospel in their own language. The Tower of Babel experience had divided them, but the Pentecost experience made them one again, this time in Christ.

And I was one with this young man from Germany, as we shared the body and blood of Christ in different languages. I thought about heaven, our destination, where we will all have one language again.

JOURNEY THROUGH A
DIFFICULT TIME

Here was a different sort of journey—one through a difficult time of life. The separation came after twenty-six years of marriage. It had been her decision after much counseling. The deep problems in the marriage were affecting her mental and emotional health.

There was some release and ease there in her own apartment. She knew a sense of moving forward, and yet there were times of painful emotional swings. Books she read reassured her it would be like this—hurtful for both parties in a separation or divorce, the one who left as well as the one who was left.

After some months she began keeping a special journal suggested by a friend who taught journal writing. This journal was a page of questions to answer each day: *(1) Words that were important today:* Each day she wrote different words. *(2) An observation, an idea I heard, something I read, that opened up new doors in learning:* She watched for newness in her days. *(3) A problem that came up today:* One day she thought especially hard to answer that. Finally she laughed aloud, writing, "My omelet turned to scrambled eggs."

Life *was* getting better, she knew, if that was the biggest problem of her day. The God who makes all things new was active in her life, renewing, restoring, healing.

TO A NURSING HOME

I went with the pastor to visit an elderly parishioner who was spending her last months in a nursing home. There were several halls to walk down on the way to her room.

My pastor strode along, then stopped a moment to greet a woman wearing a brightly colored duster and seated in a wheelchair. "Good morning," he said. "You look lovely."

The woman stared at us for a moment, then smiled. "Thank you," she said.

We walked on, the pastor greeting patient after patient—a frail man, bent over and struggling with a walker; a vacant-faced woman seated in a chair in the doorway of her room; two patients sitting on a sofa in a hallway, waiting for the lunch signal.

Most responded with words, a nod, a smile of pleasant surprise, or a flicker of light in the eyes. I'd been in nursing homes before and always hurried to see the person I would be visiting, passing by the others I didn't know. In my own uneasiness, it never crossed my mind to say hello or smile at someone along the way. I had been like the priest or Levite in Jesus' parable of the Good Samaritan. But the pastor did not avert his eyes or walk by on the other side. He spoke a friendly word; he smiled and recognized the humanity of each patient we passed.

"Good morning," I said at last, smiling at a tiny, balding old lady. She blinked, straightened a little, and smiled back. And I was blessed. After that, it was easy.

JULY 7   **TAKING OUT THE GARBAGE**

The day was full of problems. There'd been the disagreement with her husband that morning. Why did he have to be so stubborn, not wanting to accept the dinner invitation for Saturday? The girls had squabbled over who was wearing what for school, and then they said, "Tuna fish *again?*" after looking into the sack lunches she'd packed.

Now here she was carrying out the garbage, doing her son's job because he forgot. She grumbled all the way to the outdoor cans.

A cardinal sat on a branch of the evergreen, looking like an ornament on a Christmas tree. She stopped to enjoy the sight. A breeze blew the scent of honeysuckle to her. She dumped the garbage and quickly replaced the lid to give priority to the honeysuckle smell. The spring sun warmed the tense muscles of her shoulders.

"The sun doesn't shine for itself," she thought, remembering Martin Luther's words. "Water does not flow for itself" (Barbara Owen Webb, *100 Devotional Thoughts from Luther*). She looked around at the morning. "The sun is shining for me. The cardinal is cheery for me. God's love comes through God's creatures." Peace settled over her, and she laughed. God's peace was always coming to her if she had the heart to see it. It was not dependent on circumstances. God was loving her despite circumstances.

JULY 8   **SOUVENIR**

He had been on a trip to the Holy Land, and among the souvenirs was a small wine jar from Cana, 0.75 liter by today's standards, I supposed.

"The women carry them on their heads at weddings," he explained. He held up the terracotta jug, pointing to four little holes that would hold flowers and to a place at the top for a candle.

"But where does the wine go?" I asked.

He turned the jug upside down and asked for a cup of water to demonstrate. In the bottom of the jug was a deep hole. He poured in the water, then turned the jug right side up.

I gasped, expecting the water to rush right back out the hole. But no, it didn't.

Now he poured from a spout on the side of the little jug, then from a twin spout on the other side. How amazing! He was the hit of the party, showing off the little jug.

As I thought about the little earthenware vessel later, I thought about God's love coming to us. As he pours in his love, it doesn't rush right back to him. Like the water, it goes out in different ways to others. They, in turn, will praise God.

"But we have this treasure in earthen vessels, to show that the transcendent power belongs to God and not to us" (II Corinthians 4:7 RSV).

JULY 9   AWAY FOR A MENTAL HEALTH DAY

Aren't there times when most of us need to get away? When everything is going wrong on the job, and we can't handle it another minute? One way or another, we manage to take a few hours off. Some call it a "mental health day." It might be called a spiritual health day.

Hagar, in the Genesis story of Sarah and Abraham, had such a time. She had been performing her duties as slave to her mistress, even sleeping with Abraham to provide an heir. But her success in becoming pregnant led to disrespect of her superior, Sarah. And with Sarah's harsh treatment, Hagar left work, deciding to "get away from it all."

Her solitary journey led her out to a lonely spot. An angel of the Lord, whom we are to understand as a manifestation of the Lord himself, spoke to her there, giving comfort, reassurance, and instruction. Hagar, lifted in spirit after seeing the "One who sees me" (i.e., provides for me), returned to carry out her responsibilities at work.

Like Hagar, we may meet God in our time alone. It may be through prayer, reading the Word, meditation. Peace comes unexpectedly but is most welcome. A new understanding of our role at work may come. Like Hagar, we can return rejoicing in our God, who sees us and provides, time and again.

JULY 10   **TO A WEDDING**

"This, the first of his miraculous signs, Jesus performed in Cana of Galilee. He thus revealed his glory, and his disciples put their faith in him" (John 2:11 NIV).

It's not difficult to imagine the joy of the guests at the wedding in Cana. Such wonderful times of celebration must have been welcome indeed. But when something goes wrong at a wedding, how nervous both the host and guests become.

So Jesus performed his first miracle for this joyous family occasion, giving what to some might seem a frivolous gift in using his power. But he gave more than wine. He gave joy and faith. What a wonder for his disciples who were starting on an unknown journey with him.

Weddings are times of many emotions. Sometimes we attend out of duty, other times with a great desire to rejoice with friends or family. Have you not heard the Word afresh at such a time? Christ is there, not just for this couple getting married but for people in all sorts of conditions. A divorced couple meeting for the first time in months at the wedding of their child find a reconciliation—not one that will bring a new marriage, but one that brings friendly relationships in dealing with family matters. Another couple decide to have a ceremony to renew vows. A husband and wife each vow silently to be more forgiving in their marriage.

Miracles still happen at weddings because Jesus is there with his love and power.

JULY 11   **MOVING**

Some people move to a new place of residence every few years; others stay put for a long time. Those who move frequently develop a method to take some of the hassle out of moving. But from talking with Christians, I've heard the greatest help in moving is going to worship.

Abraham and Sarah did this. When they reached Canaan, the land to which the Lord had called them, Abraham built an altar for worship. For us, worship in our new place gives a sense of God having gone before and meeting us there.

I moved once to a new state. Towns were called boroughs, the state was called a commonwealth, taxes were different, the driver's test was different, insurance regulations were more complicated. The local radio and television stations were suited to the farming community, not the metropolitan area I had left. It seemed almost like a different country. But at worship I grasped the familiar hymnal, sang the liturgy, and found that the experience of shared faith crossed many barriers.

It is good to worship the Lord very soon after moving. It is good to be with God's people.

JULY 12   **A SHORT WALK**

There is something in the rhythm of walking that helps people to ponder or meditate. Writers will take walks to think through story problems. A teen may go for a walk, trying to sort out the contradictions in his or her life. A patient out of bed soon after an operation takes a short walk down the hall and back, slowly getting body and mind working together again.

Today we hear so much about walking for exercise. We see people busily concentrating on walking style; others wear earphones, doing other "work" while their bodies are walking.

But the short walk for mind and body is still appropriate, particularly after some overwhelming event. After Jesus' Ascension the disciples had a short walk from the Mount of Olives down the hill and up into Jerusalem, to the upper room where they would pray. Who can know their thoughts on that walk? And yet it must have prepared them for the concentration of prayer in the upper room.

I sometimes walk for exercise, but more often I stroll on a daydreaming or pondering walk. There is something quite satisfying in walking and letting the mind play with thoughts. Perhaps it is a form of prayer.

JULY 13   **BRINGING CHILDREN TO JESUS**

"They were bringing children to (Jesus), that he might touch them. . . . And he took them in his arms and blessed them, laying his hands upon them" (Mark 10:13, 16 RSV).

In the summer we often take children to vacation Bible school or special church camps. We see posters showing a welcoming Jesus. Youngsters go and read stories, do crafts, play, and worship.

Do we realize how wonderful this is, bringing children to Jesus? In biblical times Jesus healed and preached, showing the love, concern, and power of God in the lives of ordinary people. People wanted their children to be near him; perhaps he would touch them! He did more; he welcomed the children and took them in his arms. Surely the parents and children had much to talk about later.

Do we too? Or do we miss the wonder of Jesus in our midst? Jesus is welcoming children at vacation Bible school. If our children had been to see the president for a morning, we'd be eager to hear everything. Can we not see the great value in bringing children to Jesus?

JULY 14 _____ **GOING TO CHURCH**

Most of the time I agree with the psalmist who said in Psalm 122:1, "I was glad when they said to me, 'Let us go to the house of the Lord!' " (RSV).

But the exclamation point sometimes gives me trouble. *That* glad? This psalmist is exclaiming with great joy. Yes, I'm usually glad to go to church, looking forward to the worship and eager to participate in the Lord's Supper. But *that* glad?

Two thoughts have helped to make the psalmist's joy mine. The first is a passage from Martin Luther's writings. He wrote of God's presence for us in worship: "It is true that you hear a human being when you are baptized and when you partake of the Holy Supper. But the Word which you hear is not that of a human being; it is the Word of the living God. It is He who baptizes you. It is He who absolves you from sins. It is He who commands you to hope in His mercy" (*In Christ, My Lord—100 Devotional Thoughts from Luther*).

Seeing God in the service this way can produce joy like that of the psalmist, or like that of a two-year-old girl waiting on her front steps for her grandfather's arrival. He saw her there as he drove up. To his amazement, she squealed with delight and started jumping up and down when she saw him. "That's for me" the grandfather thought incredulously. And because he is a pastor, he also thought, "Oh, that we could greet God on Sunday mornings with such joy."

JULY 15   **TO THE DOCTOR**

The woman with the flow of blood (Luke 8:43-48) had been going to the doctors for years before she was healed by faith during her encounter with Jesus.

The sick man in John 5:2 had been lying by the pool of Bethesda for thirty-eight years, hoping to be healed by the waters. Jesus told the man to take up his pallet and walk.

Naaman, commander of the Syrian army, asked the prophet Elisha to heal his leprosy (II Kings 5:1-14). Elisha sent word that Naaman should dip himself seven times in the Jordan River, and he'd be clean. Disgusted with such a simple procedure, Naaman wasn't going to bother. But his servants prevailed on him to try it. He did and was made clean.

What may happen on our own visit to a doctor for healing? Perhaps we'll be told to wait, things will be better. Or we'll receive a prescription—"Be sure to take it all," we're cautioned.

Very often we have in our minds what the doctor will or should do. But faith in medical science and in God's using it for our good may call for us to abandon our ideas of what will make us well or better.

A woman with back pain expected the sports medicine doctor to take strong measures. She was sent to a physical therapist. "I'll be on a rigid program, seeing the therapist often," she assumed.

But he gave her three simple exercises to repeat three times a day. "That's all?" she thought. But her faith made her open to God's working in this simple way. In two weeks she was feeling better.

Faith is openness to God's many ways of working.

GO HOME AND TELL

The Bethlehem shepherds were at work at a rather grubby task on a forlorn hillside. We must see them not as depicted in so many nativity sets and paintings, with fluffy white sheep. Shepherds were hard-working poor people, laboring at a dirty job, caring for grey-brown, scraggly sheep.

The angel of God said, "Go and see the Savior." And they left work to see. What joy and amazement! The scene at the stable was just as the angel had said. How they laughed with hearty joy at the wonder of it all. They had been the first to know. They had been visited by God's angels. They had seen the Savior!

As they returned to work, they told everyone. What good news!

It can happen today. A hospital worker saw a traveling exhibit of a model of the Sistine Chapel ceiling. Back at the hospital, he spread the word, and others took time off work to see the exhibit.

"Go and see," the friend had said. They went and came away with fresh joy, telling others what they had seen.

There are times when we will see faith-building art such as this. Or we may hear a faith-building concert or see such a play. Like the shepherds who were the first evangelists to share the news of Jesus' birth, we can tell others what we have seen and heard, not keeping our joy to ourselves. Friends of faith will be glad to hear. Friends who don't know God may have something new to ponder. Our joy may make them want to see and hear, too.

JULY 17   ATTENDING A LARGE-CROWD EVENT

The small boy was there at the front of the crowd with his sack lunch. Perhaps he'd come out with his family or friends, but as children are wont to do, he squirmed his way up front to see.

The day must have been long, but the boy had been so fascinated with this Jesus that he hadn't bothered with his lunch. And then Jesus and his friends were talking about food for everyone. The boy overhead; he wanted to hear everything this Jesus had to say. He'd give his bread and fish if Jesus wanted some food. "Here! I've got something!"

Then what a blessing Jesus provided. What awe the boy must have known when he saw the power of God. This was a trip he'd never forget.

We sometimes make such trips out in a large crowd, to attend an exciting event. And while there God nudges us to share something we have with another. It could be simply a coughdrop or our program guide, or an umbrella at an outdoor event. Perhaps we share a word of joy and encouragement, or merely directions to the interstate highway. We recognize that we are not alone in the crowd but part of a family, interacting, blessing, and being blessed. God is there.

This might be a time to reflect on large-crowd events you've attended. Have miracles happened that you haven't thought about before? O God, when we go out to hear or see, let us be as ready to share as the boy with the bread and fish.

JULY 18   GONE FISHING

Jesus seems to have enjoyed the sea. We don't read of him actually fishing himself, but he chose fisherfolk for his companions. We read of him out in boats and giving suggestions on where to lower the nets.

My son Steve used to fish commercially from a workboat

managed by two people. Steve would come home at evening, telling wonderful stories of following schools of fish. One night he pushed aside his dessert plate and started telling of a school of fish they'd chased early in the week. He sounded like a young man seeking after his beloved.

"There they were, everywhere, runnin' into each other," he said, waiving his hand in a circle. "But all we had on board was six-inch net. If we'd had three- or four-inch, we'd have cleaned up. And the next day when we had it, there wasn't a fish anywhere. We chased after 'em all day. They was just gone, and we didn't see no more like that the rest of the week."

Steve was still on my mind Sunday when the pastor read from Luke 5:1-11 (RSV), "[Jesus] said to Simon, 'Put out into the deep and let down your nets for a catch.' And Simon answered, 'Master, we toiled all night and took nothing!' " "He sounds like Steve," I thought. "They enclosed a great shoal of fish; . . . their nets were breaking . . . filled both the boats . . . when Simon Peter saw it, he fell down at Jesus' knees." Yes, yes, what an awesome gift that no one else could give—the very fish themselves! "And when they had brought their boats to land, they left everything and followed him." Of course! So would Steve. It wasn't simply the miracle that won Peter, it was the gift! Jesus gives what is most sought after, what a fisherman speaks of most affectionately—the fish themselves. If Jesus could give the fish, could he not take care of everything in life, no matter what? Of course Peter left everything and followed!

I look at the gifts of Jesus in my own life—forgiveness of sins, peace, fellowship with God and with other people— gifts no one else can give. I too can follow.

JULY 19   **A FAVORITE RETREAT**

Although we need to be in community and our lives are shaped by our relationships with other people, there are times when we need to be alone. We need to retreat from the world and responsibility. Our fragmented selves are pieced back together so that we are ready to give of ourselves once again.

Jesus' favorite retreat spot seems to have been the Mount of Olives. There, among the sturdy olive trees on a hill overlooking Jerusalem, he would pray, speaking with his Father. But often when he would retreat, he soon would be surrounded by disciples or others in need. It seems a few quiet minutes would have to do.

And so with us. We may have a special place we go to after much preparation—a cabin, a condo, a camper. But I'm thinking of little daily retreats. Where can we go during the day to find a few minutes alone to pray, ponder, find new strength? For some the place is in the home, made private by their getting up earlier than others of the household. For those living alone, who may need to escape their aloneness yet still have a private time, it may be breakfast at McDonald's, alone yet together. For some busy parents, the bathroom with a locked door provides the oasis.

Our need is as great as our Lord's. We will find our place, perhaps without thinking of it as a retreat, but we will go there and be renewed. Perhaps you are at your place right now. Thank God for helping you to find it.

JULY 20   **TO A FUNERAL**

"Lenora's husband died last night," my friend told me. I knew the middle-aged man had been sick with cancer for many months.

"Poor Lenora," I said. "It's been tough." I had met Lenora through a writer's group but didn't know her well. Some of the poems she read for the group spoke of the agony of cancer, and we had talked after meetings occasionally. "I'll send a card," I said.

But my friend said, "Let's go to the funeral; it's tomorrow at one. I'll pick you up at 12:30, okay?"

Surprised, I agreed. "We didn't know Lenora that well," I thought. She would have lots of friends and family there. We would almost be like outsiders. But I went with my insistent friend.

I'll never forget the grateful look on Lenora's face when she saw us there. We hugged like old friends. "We were needed too," I thought, looking around. We were support from a special area of her life. That one day brought us closer; I didn't feel outside Lenora's life after that.

"It was *important* for us to be there," I thought later. And I remembered fifteen years earlier at my mother's funeral. "Who are all these people?" I had wondered. People from the rural county came up to me. "My son would never have learned to read 'cept for your mother," one said, and others repeated this over and over. Mother had been a home teacher and reading tutor. How important for me and my family that they took the time to come to the funeral of someone they didn't really know.

I remember these episodes when deciding whether or not to attend a funeral. Now, when possible, I go.

JULY 21   **POSTCARDS**

I love to send postcards when traveling. And here I was in Europe for the first time, debating over a rack of wonderful postcards. Carefully, I chose ten out of the fifty varieties, making a mental note of to whom each card would go.

But later, in my hotel room, with the cards spread on the bed, I debated. Perhaps Russell would enjoy the picture of the old fort better than the river picture. My roommate Shirley bought all one kind of postcard so she wouldn't have this problem. But I needed variety. I'd asked friends and relatives at home to save the cards for me. These pictures would then supplement my snapshots.

At last I decided, addressing each card before writing a message. There were so many things to tell. The first cards got filled with thoughts of the trip. But by cards eight, nine, and ten, a few lines, written large, seemed to do.

I think of another correspondent—Saint Paul. He was a great letter writer. If he sent anything as short as a postcard, we don't have it recorded that way. But the rather personal closings of his letters show the same warmth of feeling that we feel for our friends and relatives. Often he sends greetings to several people, and then he may mention several people with him who want to be remembered to his readers.

"I send greetings to Priscilla and Aquila, and to the family of Onesiphorus. . . . God's grace be with you all" (II Timothy 4:19-22 GNB).

I fan through my cards again. O God, go with these postcards to bring a blessing to Russell, Marilyn, Wanda, . . . Guard and keep us till we meet again, for Jesus' sake. Amen.

JULY 22 **TO AN ANCIENT CIVILIZATION**

The morning we went to Knossos on the island of Crete, I had read Psalm 77. Verse 5 came back to me later: "I consider the days of old, I remember the years long ago" (RSV).

I had never really *considered* the days of old—thinking about them and pondering ancient civilizations. Not when reading history books. The words didn't seem to involve *me*. But now I have walked broken streets planned by civil engineers of old, visited buildings planned by architects without a B.S. degree, wondered at the arts and crafts of people of thousands of years ago. The people of antiquity built with forever in mind.

I put myself back into their time. The years seem to melt away. If only someone from their ancient civilization were here, we could talk and see how similar our times are in their hopes, their dreams, their longings.

And God was busy then, too, pouring blessings on the just and unjust, calling people to himself. It is in him that time fades, and I stand with people of every age. The old times become my times. I buy a booklet with pictures and history notes, to consider the days of old.

At evening I pray: O God, you have seen all civilizations that have come and gone on earth. They have made you glad or angry, but always you have cared and called people to yourself. I rest in the peace of knowing you have always been Lord of all. Amen.

JULY 23   **OLD CATHEDRALS**

"Watch over this Temple day and night. . . . In your home in heaven hear us and forgive us" (I Kings 8:29-30 GNB).

What majesty we have seen in old cathedrals today! Art, sculpture, architecture of incredible grandeur and yet great sensitivity. Some of us took pictures where allowed. Others bought postcards, all to remember what we've experienced here. But what I'll most remember is the feeling of being in those huge homes for God—the awe and wonder that envelops one, standing in the nave of a cathedral.

The feeling comes from more than the beauty or an appreciation of the craft of the builders. It also comes from the link with other Christians. They worshiped here, in some cathedrals for hundreds of years, in others for a thousand. It is that kinship that envelops one and gives an inkling of what the body of Christ really is—people gathering for centuries, praising and thanking God, asking him to "hear us and forgive us."

The forgiveness is experienced once again in the cathedral. Everywhere a cross mediates God's Word. These are buildings of love and hope, built by and for God's own people, who rejoice in what God has done for them in Jesus Christ.

How can I take it home with me, this sense of awe and kinship? I will walk into my small, modern church building, bringing a link with the past to today's members of the body of Christ.

JULY 24   **TRAVEL BY SEA**

The great swells of the sea caused even our cruise ship to roll and sway. One member of our group stayed in her room for a day, nursing a queasy stomach.

Yet to stand here looking out over the rail, seeing the blue-green depths, swaying with the roll of the ship, it seems we are in the very palm of God's hand. "The sea is his, for he made it," I remember from the liturgy and psalm. The sea is animated when experienced like this, not merely a lovely picture but a great wonder that moves and seems to have a personality. Is it the magnificence and power of its Creator that it reflects?

This sea is his, this very sea, for God made it. God knows every drop of water here and the hiding place of every creature in the sea. He has spread forth this beauty for us.

And yet, to paraphrase the old hymn, Jesus is fairer, Jesus is brighter. Even the sea points us to him.

O Jesus, you stilled the waters of the sea; you traveled the sea in boats, seeing the beauty and bounty of your creation. And now I see and thank and praise you. Amen.

JULY 25   **STAINED-GLASS WINDOWS**

"I will call to mind the deeds of the Lord; yea, I will remember thy wonders of old" (Psalm 77:11 RSV).

When we went into the church on the tour this morning, the guide pointed out the stained-glass windows, briefly giving the story each told. She also noted the craftspeople and composition of the windows. But it was the story that caught me. Perhaps I had put myself back in time so much on this trip, into the shoes of others, that the stories in the windows were vivid to me.

Saint Francis was there with his little animals, and Peter with his fishing boat, and the women at the foot of the cross. Why have I not taken more time to see the windows, the

Christian art and symbols in my home church? Do we grow so used to seeing visual art everywhere that now we blank it out as we do Muzak on an elevator?

I buy postcards of the windows to remember them by, to ponder the stories they tell. Windows to call to mind the deeds of the Lord—his wonders of old. It is good to have time to stare, to search out every symbol. In a church service I'd be staring at the hymnal, not wanting to seem to be gawking around at the windows. But now I drink in the art and the story.

I resolve that when I get home, I'll take a tour of my own church during a quiet time, finding all the symbols and works of art—those in plain view and those in corners and crannies. They are symbols that help me to see the light of the world—Jesus Christ.

JULY 26 VISITING A CHILD AWAY AT SCHOOL

We are getting her ready to go off to college next month. And I'm reminded of Hannah in I Samuel 1 and 2—how long she prayed for a child, how she rejoiced in her pregnancy, how glad she was to bear the child Samuel. And he was given over to the service of the Lord. Hannah cared and prayed for her son. She went to visit him each year, bringing a little coat she had made.

My heart is close to Hannah's. I pray for this child going off to college, away from home. I am already planning the goodies, the surprise gifts I'll bring when we visit in October.

We did so for her older sister too. Each child is such a separate person, each with different needs. The prayers will be different for each, and the gifts will be different. But the visit will be full of the same strong emotions of joy and love.

Perhaps we learn from our heavenly Father's care for us, so individual, meeting our needs, yet for each of us the supreme model of giving love is the love of Christ who gave himself for us.

JULY 27   **FAMILY REUNION**

She told me of the family reunion they had every five years. Relatives from all over the country made the journey to the East Coast beach. Member families grew and changed, but her father's people were always there.

However, large families are never like the Waltons, the television family that a generation came to love. My friend's family was like other real families. The love and joy were tempered by grudges and occasional disharmony.

This summer two brothers weren't speaking. One said perhaps he wouldn't go, but he was prevailed upon to attend. The tension in the air almost crackled every time the two brothers had to be near each other during the week. But they were there; they nodded, barely cordial. Others surrounded them, loving each, enticing each to try volleyball or Scrabble or softball.

The reunion ended without the miracle some had prayed for. It came later when the older brother decided to send a Christmas card to the younger. A tiny miracle, a first step in communication between the two, which may never be easy. But it was a recognition of being brothers, part of a family. The family reunion had done its part in helping this to happen. Had either brother stayed home, how would love have worked?

JULY 28   **A CHANGE OF MIND AND HEART
                    ON BUSINESS TRAVEL**

She told me of her decision when she came home from a three-day business trip. Sitting in LaGuardia Airport, waiting for the limo, she had thought about her life. The briefcase of business papers was at her side. The papers had been studied on the plane. Now was simply a time of waiting for the next part of her business trip.

Maybe she was ready for the next part of her life too. She had been in turmoil ever since the separation. She had wept and prayed and sometimes shouted in anger, alone in her apartment.

But now, in the airport waiting room, with life going on around her, she knew it was time to get on with her life. She prayed silently for strength; peace came. In her mind she had taken the first step toward a fresh start. She would see the attorney when she returned home.

When I heard this, I thought of how conducive to making decisions travel can be. In new surroundings, a new perspective can come. Answers to prayer can break through our everyday mind-set.

We may not have as dramatic a change as Paul, also a business traveler, had on the Damascus road when he met the Lord; his whole life got turned around. But God meets us too, with surprises, new insights, answered prayer, and fresh blessings for the ability to make hard decisions for our lives. Business travel can be for more than business.

JULY 29   **TO A FRIEND'S HOUSE**

Mary could not contain her excitement after the visit from the angel Gabriel. She traveled miles to see her cousin Elizabeth. They had so much to share, with both being pregnant in such wondrous ways.

We make trips to share news, joys, and sorrows with friends and family. Sometimes the trip is nearby, stopping in for a cup of tea on the way to the store. Sometimes the trip involves longer travel. The important thing is that we do it. I have seen friendships slip away because one friend doesn't take the time and effort to visit, leaving the initiative to get together to the other friend.

A little trip to stop by to see a cousin, a brother or a sister, a grown child, a parent—each little trip is part of the cement that holds a relationship together. Sometimes these trips have to be made by letter or phone call, it's true. But for folks close enough for a real, face-to-face visit, such a trip is worth

the effort. Out of such trips come visits that make memories, or, as Elizabeth Yates once wrote in her book *Nearby,* "moments of joy that [will] lengthen into memories."

Such memories give strength for living. Our God is one who wants us to remember his acts of love for us, to keep us close to him. Memories of times with family and friends keep us near to them too, enriching our lives and thus the lives of others.

JULY 30   **TO THE LIBRARY**

When visiting a little town where I'd be moving soon, I checked out the library. Other places of interest could wait; the library was first on my list. It was small but served by pleasant people who assured me they'd be glad to order books from other branches, making much more available than the volumes on the shelves. Satisfied and comforted, I sought out a real estate agent to talk about housing.

Two elderly friends retired to a small town with a tiny library. They visited it twice a week, bringing home several books each time. After a few months, they were asked to serve on the library board, to make suggestions on the running of the library. "After all," they were told, "you use the library more than anyone else in town. You know what the library needs."

Even in this television age, many people of all ages still rejoice in the written word. And many have discovered something my father told me when I was a child. "If you ever want to know something," he said, "go to the library. Surely someone has written a book on the subject." From gardening to finance to raising children to coping with tragedy, on and on, the books are there, fiction and nonfiction, waiting to fill needs.

If it is true about the ordinary things of life, it is certainly true about the most encompassing things of life—those that pertain to faith. John must have understood when he wrote

in his Gospel, "Now Jesus did many other signs in the presence of the disciples, which are not written in this book; but these are written that you may believe that Jesus is the Christ, the Son of God, and that believing you may have life in his name" (John 20:30-31 RSV).

JULY 31   **TRAVELING OUT OF ONESELF
                                      IN PRAYER**

In the sixth chapter of his letter to the Ephesians, Paul speaks about the spiritual conflict Christians face. "Put on the whole armor of God," he says: righteousness as a breastplate, the gospel of peace as your shoes, salvation as a helmet, faith as a shield.

But in this armor we are not to cower, staying closed into ourselves. We take the words God's spirit gives as a sword against evil, and we go out of ourselves to others in prayer. Our look is outward, not inward. We travel out of ourselves each day, as we "pray at all times with every kind of spiritual prayer, keeping alert and persistent, [praying] for all Christ's men and women" (Ephesians 6:18 Phillips). We use our armor that we may be free to come out of ourselves for others. Prayer is the journey almost every Christian can make, even those who are housebound.

A woman at home in a wheelchair kept the church sick-and-shut-in list on her refrigerator door. Every time she came to the kitchen, she traveled around the city, state, and country, as she prayed for people on the list.

God gives us the joy to leave ourselves and care about others in prayers of intercession and supplication. Even this is part of our armor against evil.

Today I pray for you, that these journeys of July may have provided times of reflection on our loving God at work in your life. Blessings!

But Not Alone

KÄAREN WITTE

AUGUST 1   **THEY JUST DIDN'T KNOW**

I burned. My cheeks flushed, my throat clutched.

After all these years, I still remember the incident.

At fourteen I felt shy and vulnerable—painfully so.

My strong, masculine dad wasn't in the classroom to defend or protect me. For if he had been, he would have stood up and told them I was bright, witty, and talented and that they were just too dense and undiscerning to see it!

"Käaren!" The science teacher screamed at me. "Tune in to this lecture! Witte's mind is always out on another planet! Look at her, dazed and glassy-eyed," he elaborated, mocking me dramatically.

The class howled at his clever comedic word coloring and delivery.

No, I wasn't the adorable, petite, kitten-type adolescent who knew about eye contact and sex appeal and the effective use of such techniques for the melting of male teachers' hearts.

I was simply the kid who did the work, made good grades, and made no waves.

But on that painful day when the class with the jocks and the cheerleaders laughed at me, I assured myself that they did not know something important about me: My grandmother, who had lived with us, had left our family. My laughing peers didn't know that the week before she had slipped into a coma and died.

So my dazed little mind, at that moment in the class, only saw the empty Boston rocker where she rocked, as I gleaned and pondered stories about her life and loves and immigration decades ago. Sometimes, alone in the after-noon, we would eat butter pecan ice cream. We'd savor and smile at each other. She'd rock. We'd talk.

But on that long remembered day in Worthington Junior High, room 135, the people just didn't know.

"If you forgive other people their failures, your Heavenly Father will also forgive you. But if you will not forgive other people, neither will your Father forgive you your failures" (Matthew 6:14-15, Phillips).

AUGUST 2   **JESUS PLAYS ON MY VOLLEYBALL TEAM (OR SOMEBODY WHO JUST ACTS LIKE HIM)**

In the brutal gym heat people in my church, Christ United Methodist, play volleyball; they sweat, stretch, strain, fall, scramble, slam into one another, hit the wall, and mash their fingers for three hours twice a week.

The rules are (1) three people must hit the ball, and (2) one player can't be a hero and clobber the ball *alone*.

When people fall, they get pulled up by at least one other person, but usually the whole team. Even the strongest, most rugged men get a hand. If somebody is even possibly hurt, the whole team stops and diagnoses the injury. The game resumes only after the victim reassures the team that he or she is okay.

Do you know how much better a shoe can be tied when *two hands* tie and another person holds the lace down? A superior tying! Sometimes, too, players wear tops that require buttoning from behind by another team member.

"I can't play very well!" a new player will say.

"Don't worry! We'll help you!" another announces.

"There is no way you can look bad because the others will rescue your bad shots and bunglings. They will make you look good!" another assures.

Players huff and pant and push their bodies to the limits while calling to one another, "Nice shot!" "Yeah, Mary!" "Yeah, Sandi!" "Yeah, Val!" "Yeah, Team!"

Incidentally, our team progresses to winning only as fast as the weakest player can learn. So that's why we encourage and cheer every *good play*. Then the new player feels he or she has done something marvelous for the whole team. (And it's true.)

I think my volleyball team's team work is what Jesus had in mind for his entire church.

AUGUST 3   **IT PAYS OFF**

Bruce. Blond. Big. Strong and warm. He sang and played the guitar at college functions. For five dates, including a Christmas banquet when he played and sang—often directly to me, and everyone saw it—Bruce was my boyfriend.

"Käaren is too Christian! Look, I'm young and just not ready for that. I mean, don't get me wrong, Käaren is a pretty girl and fun to be with, but I'm not ready . . . if you know what I mean," Bruce told another. The words were verbatim, my friend told me.

"Hey! Here comes Käaren Witte! Let's make it look like we're having Sunday school!" one of the guys joked, as I entered the college snack lounge. Bruce was sitting among them.

"She's sweet, but not 'with it!' I mean, this is 1970!" Bruce said, as if giving some explanation for his apparent dissolving of our relationship.

He winked at me while he said it. I smiled and gave a little laugh too. But in my head I determined, "It will pay off to follow Christ's teachings. Maybe not fully this year or the next, but it *will* pay off."

Nearly twenty years later, I ran into, "by chance," one of those popular, outgoing "sharp guys," as we called them.

Unsuspectingly, in that "orchestrated moment," he gave me glimpses into the lives of the people we had known: "The ol' 'lounge pack'—ah, let's just say they all have had mixed up lives so far. One's tallied four marriages, another five," he said. He continued to disclose details about their children—and his—who now live with divided loyalties and resentments in the wake of broken homes and broken lives.

The man was Bruce.

This time I confidently said *out loud*, "Bruce, I lived *on faith* twenty years ago. Now I can prove that it pays handsomely to believe and follow Christ's teaching."

"You have escaped our devastation," he whispered as if to say he knew the truth now, as he held my hand in his.

"You will keep on guiding me all my life with your wisdom and counsel" (Psalm 73:24 TLB).

AUGUST 4   **LOVE**

Tiffany bore an elegant name. The very sound bespoke savvy and continental flair.

Tiffany knew somehow that her name was too grand for her appearance.

But she had lofty ideals: depth in loyalty, love, and sacrifice. In fact, she loved so purely that her elegant name and unrefined, chunky appearance seemed a perfect fit.

Tiffany—part collie and parts unknown—arrived in our family as a puppy in total fur and two pitiful eyes. She was always hopping into our laps and beds, making certain none of us was ever lonely or alone.

Since her puppyhood she sensed that she wouldn't be show dog material or a dog destined for television commercials. So she loved.

She hated to do tricks. Her legs were stubby and her torso too heavy. Nonetheless, she would do them while seemingly saying, "I'm happy—I'm just not exactly grinning right now."

We'd laugh, cheer, and applaud. She'd comply, receive a treat, and, nonverbally begging for permission, lie down after the evening's live entertainment.

Entering the house one afternoon, I found my dad kneeling over Tiffany.

"She's throwing up and very sick," Dad choked out.

Dad loved the big, furry pet. "Call the vet, Honey," he said. "Father, heal her. She hasn't sinned against you. Touch this friend of ours," my dad prayed.

"Jesus is healing you. He loves you." Dad spoke quietly to her, while he stroked down the fur on her head.

Tiffany whimpered and tried to lick his hand. In response? We believed so.

Tiffany recovered within a few days and continued doing task and wagging her magnificent tail so hard we thought it would lift her off the ground. She continued wearing ribbons and bows around her neck, sunglasses and hats, and posing propped up, for pictures.

Love bears all things, doesn't it?

"Love never gives up: its faith, hope, and patience never fail" (I Corinthians 13:7 GNB).

AUGUST 5   **THOSE WHO CAN . . . TEACH**

Every teacher remembers the students who taught her. I remember Ronald.

"These kids will make emotional mincemeat out of a junior high kid with a trembling, deformed body and a tongue that falls involuntarily out of his mouth when he tries to talk. Why, God?" I gasped and prayed.

On the inopportune day that he rolled into the class via his wheelchair, my students were selecting participants for a play contest group in the drama class. When the groups were chosen and Ronald wasn't, he asked to speak to them:

"I know I'm different from the rest of you guys. I can't talk very well. And I know you might think that it would be a drag to have a guy in a wheelchair in your play. But I could help direct. And, well, the friends I have say I know how to be a good friend. And they're guys like you; I mean, they don't have wheelchairs or crutches and stuff. So I know I could be a good friend to any of you, too. And look, if you think my shoes are funny, well, pretty soon I'm going to get shoes just like you boys wear."

After a twenty-second silence, one student director slammed his fist on his desk and shouted, "I've got a great idea for a play! We want Ronald!"

On the performance day, Ronald's group was to appear last. I agonized inside when the director got up to announce the play.

"This play is an original mystery detective story! And it stars Ronald Laffle as—*Ironsides!*"

I cried and laughed—no, make that howled—as I threw my head back and applauded. All at the same time.

After the play I sat alone in the empty theater, reviewing the incredible experience. "God," I prayed aloud quietly, "thank you for helping little deformed boys to be so brave. They teach us so much. Ronald will never earn a letter in sports or date the adorable cheerleaders. So just keep him encouraged and proud. You can do it in other ways. We need him. He helps us see your faithfulness."

AUGUST 6   **FAR-REACHING FORGIVENESS**

I grew up shy, plump, withdrawn, and bookish. How I wanted to be one of the extroverted, doe-eyed little cheerleaders about whom the teachers raved.

However, for some unknown reason, one teacher, Mr. Dean, thought I was a sparkling whiz kid.

I didn't question his perception. I just cherished the attention when he would share his M&M's with me and laugh as he asked me to describe the cafeteria food (Gravy Train du jour).

"If Mr. Dean, a strong, popular teacher, showers Käaren Witte with approval and attention, then she must be great!" I imagined the other teachers and kids saying.

Mr. Dean discovered my awesomeness in my sophomore year, and he carried me to new heights in the self-esteem department for three years.

Why the attention? I never knew.

Anyway, how long would my wave of unmerited good fortune last? Living in the world of fickle adolescents, I was conditioned to losing the painfully elusive commodities of attention and acceptance.

"Mr. Dean thought I was the smartest and cutest kid in Worthington, Minnesota!" I recalled one day to my dad, far into adulthood. "Dad, I never knew why! But I appreciated it more than anyone could believe, at that age!"

"I know why," my dad, moved by the love I had received, began. "We were having trouble with your brother. Nate Dean, who was also a deacon at church, just walked by our business place one day. I ran out the door and yelled, 'That's right, Nate, you just keep walking by just like the rest of them!' " my dad softly yet painfully shared. "The next day I drove to his house and asked for his forgiveness."

"Stay true to what is right and God will bless you and use you to help others" (I Timothy 4:16 TLB).

AUGUST 7   **GOD IS NEVER SILENT—
LISTEN TO THIS**

I thought it would be my dream job. Within a few months it became clear it wasn't.

I watched others in the company get the promotions and

the recognition and the laudings. I felt as if I were outside, looking into a room through a window.

On weekends I'd be asked to speak around the country. The host cities' media interviewed me and asked my opinion. I autographed books for long lines of affirming people.

But on any given Monday morning, no one knew.

I even skipped vacations. I worked on days off. I worked late hours.

"Inside," the staff sat secure, tight. Belonging.

"So who would reach out and 'risk' to a person like me who is apparently not politically advantageous?" I thought.

"You need a mentor," Joan, an older lady on the staff, advised.

"God isn't silent. He's arranging. You're going to change the world," a friend named Doug counseled.

"The world?" I questioned him, disbelieving, feeling he grossly exaggerated.

"The world," he repeated, unmoving.

I resigned within a year and began writing news stories. Assignments took me around the *world*.

At one point, when I was an international correspondent, my own parents wondered about my exact location.

"Oh! There she is!" my dad exclaimed, seeing me reporting for NBC news from London!

"I saw your daughter from Jerusalem on CNN," a friend informed my family. "I understand she even entered Lebanon!"

God isn't silent. Not to the believer. He sends mentors too—even to fledglings.

And a word about trust.

"Trust the Lord in the darkness of your soul. Use your emotional energy, which doubt steals, for creative pursuits that you and God cooperatively are creating," my friend Judy once told me.

"What is faith? It is the confident assurance that something we want is going to happen. It is the certainty that what we hope for is waiting for us, even though we cannot see it up ahead" (Hebrews 11:1 TLB).

WHY GOD? (HERE'S WHY)

"Why, God? Why am I not enjoying a lovely Sunday brunch with some fine man and a little family?" I lamented, lectured, and petitioned in a distress prayer, as I analyzed my appearance in my full-length mirror after church. "What is wrong with me? I am over thirty-five and still single," I questioned further. I headed for a Chinese carry-out—alone.

"Good food, already prepared, plus I don't have to sit and eat it there and be reminded of my fate." I continued selling myself on my purchase, as I dragged my defeated body to the car.

I stopped with my hand on the ignition.

I studied the man in front of me as he lumbered up the stairs of a vast apartment complex. Saliva ran off his chin. He huffed. His unyielding legs trembled as he clutched the railing. He'd conquer two steps and then pause. His total concentration on scaling the steps prevented him from noticing me, as I watched only a few feet away. After several minutes he reached the door, and his shaky hand cajoled his key.

"Alone on Sunday? Single? Yet he probably knows more pain than that. Look at his daily, moment-by-moment struggle," I thought.

As he went inside the door, I continued watching, lost in flying thoughts and searchings.

My thoughts were jarred when he came to the window—no, not to watch me but to open it. After the same caliber struggle, he succeeded.

"What? Is he singing?" I asked myself.

Yes. On that quiet, uncommonly still Sunday, I heard the garbled but recognizable words, "Great is thy faithfulness, O God, my Father."

AUGUST 9 ONLY A GOD-FOCUSED LIFE
MAKES SENSE

Show me strong people. People who walk in an aura of undeniable, inexplicable strength.

As a speaker I occasionally sit at a head table in a banquet hall. I watch the people file in.

"Who is that woman? Tell me about her. I sense something rare, an unshakable confidence. What has she experienced?" I will question the chairwoman or leader.

"Just as I thought," I remark to myself, when I hear her story of overcoming.

JoAnn, a friend of mine growing up, lost her first husband. Her second husband, another excellent Christ-following man, was also killed in a car accident.

Today, as a speaker and singer, walking in "that aura," she sings, "Because he lives, I can face tomorrow." She knows. She is the voice of credibility. People around the world believe her. She is God's living example.

"Don't ask why. Just ask what," my mother would say. "For every obstacle, every difficulty, every adversity becomes a tool in the hands of God." For the God-focused person, it does.

When my friend Evelyn bore a handicapped child, she prayed over his crib, "Lord Jesus, use this circumstance. If you can use it to transform me, then do it. You can bring a dream out of this." The dream? Other handicapped children found their way into her home and heart through the years. "Somebody has to love him," she said over one sleeping child.

The words of those great believers are forever etched in my memory. What an awesome privilege to be one of God's living testimonies, to prove God to the doubting world.

AUGUST 10 WHO ME? SCARED OF OLD AGE?
(NOT NOW)

"Surprise! Happy birthday!" My friends applauded as I blinked at the surprise party.

I was thirty-five. The fear of middle age and old age haunted me. I didn't want a party.

"I didn't trust the Lord when I was eighteen. I was panicky about life, about finding the right job, getting married, raising children. But now I am eighty," Marie, my friend, testified. "I see how God has kept every promise in my life. He promised never to leave me. And he hasn't. He promised to meet every need. He has. Rejoice and celebrate every year you walk with the Lord. You will grow richer and more beautiful," she said, hugging me and laughing.

"You're the voice of credibility," I said. "Your life proves what you say."

My own mother wrote a letter to me before she died. She said, "As I come to the end of my life's journey, I look back in wonder. God carried us through every sorrow and problem just as he promised he would. My only regret is that I didn't trust him at the *beginning* of every conflict, crisis, and hurt!"

At my birthday party everyone shared fears and concerns in life. They then personally illustrated how God had arranged and delivered his promises. They talked about provisions for jobs. For husbands. For the right wife. For sick children. For courage to overcome an addiction. For the ability to forgive another. For the gift of singing. "It had to be God. There is no other explanation," one said. "God proves himself through miracles," another confirmed.

One birthday card had this verse written by an ancient voice of credibility: "For no matter how many promises God has made, they are 'Yes' in Christ. And so through him the 'Amen' is spoken by us to the glory of God" (II Corinthians 1:20 NIV).

AUGUST 11   **GOD KNOWS WHAT HE'S DOING**

I grew up in a small town in Minnesota in the late sixties. Most young women there married after high school.

I approached twenty-five as the perennial bridesmaid who

always caught the bouquet. (One time I was so depressed I threw it back—slam dunk—to the bride. Yes, I was that discouraged.) Nothing extraordinary had happened in my life—not so far. But God was planning, dreaming, and arranging in his style "far more than we would ever dare to ask or even dream of" (Ephesians 3:20 TLB).

"But there are *no indications* that God is connecting and making a dream for me," I continued to cry to my parents.

"Darling, God knows what we do not know. His answer of no is a part of the dream for your life. Whatever he does, he does in love. Even when we don't understand him," my mother comforted.

A decade passed. Yes, God knew what he was doing.

"How perfect your plan was for me—tailor-made. You never made a mistake, God," I now pray.

"You have lived around the world, worked as a correspondent for some of the largest newspapers in the world, written books, and hosted television productions. How perfect was the plan for your background, personality, and temperament!" a friend observed. "If you had been living in suburbia with a stationwagon, contemplating waxy build-up and fabric softeners, you would have said, 'God, why me? Why couldn't I be a journalist and television host and live in Seoul or Rome?' my friend continued.

"I'm so glad God doesn't listen to my puny whining," I answered her.

"I know, O Lord, that thy judgments are right" (Psalm 119:75 KJV).

AUGUST 12　　A REAL MAN IN TODAY'S WORLD

I don't remember not loving Robby Creager.

"Pray for a thirty-two-year-old single businessman who was just sent to prison for drug violations," my pastor's wife pleaded. "His parents were members here."

A year later Robby spoke to the congregation. "I

discovered the devastation of drugs and alcohol and immoral sex, the destructive false 'highs.' The *real* life that God dreams for me—to be a *real* man—that's what I want. No more false rainbow ending or hollow relationships. I am a new person," the handsome, tall, impeccably groomed man articulated.

Jarred, I realized I had often swallowed the world's pathetically false definition of what a *real man* is.

"But wait! Is this the prisoner for whom I prayed? Is this the life for whom I petitioned at the altar? I was staggered by Robby's appearance. Having been involved in prison ministries, I had been expecting a ravaged man, wasted and derelict.

"I am a new man. I'm not ashamed to say I follow Jesus Christ," Robby softly, with traces of emotion, testified to God's grace and power.

Tears surfaced on faces around me.

"God, what does the future hold for this man? A real man, man enough to identify in this world with the most controversial figure in all of history: Jesus Christ," I prayed. "Robby, you're going to change the world!" I telegraphed mentally from the congregation.

And you know what? He has. He started with me.

"When someone becomes a Christian he becomes a brand new person inside. He is not the same any more. A new life has begun!" (II Corinthians 5:17 TLB).

AUGUST 13   **THE REAL PROOF OF LOVE**

"How do you prove love? What are the real secrets of success?" I asked a wise older woman from my church.

"Accept each other. See the other person as wonderful and say so. Provide security by ensuring that even in the face of failures, you will never notice because you are so impressed with his or her wonderful virtues!" she said.

"Honor one another. I studied a wife once who literally gave her husband 'status' in the family. She advised mothers to tell their children *who* the father is," she continued. "Reverence, revere, and respect are the three *R*'s."

"Serve each other," she added. "I love this bumper sticker: 'If you love Jesus, help me move my furniture. Anyone can honk!' "

I remembered a man who helped me move once. He was merely a friend of a friend. For hours in the brutally hot Oklahoma sun, he lifted my boxes and belongings, carried them two flights up, and loaded and unloaded his truck. Love spoke that day!

Once a young woman was thirty pounds overweight. Every day her father, in acceptance, only told her how pretty she was. When she lost the weight, she explained to her father, "After all, you made me see how pretty I really was, and should a pretty girl be overweight? Impossible!"

I was that young woman.

When we accept, honor, and serve each other, we give of our time. And time is our life. Only when our sacrifice cuts into our personal comfort does love get proven. When someone claims to love us, we really only believe it when they have sacrificed for us.

"Love each other with . . . affection and take delight in honoring each other" (Romans 12:10 TLB).

AUGUST 14   **OUR WORTH**

Reading the evening newspaper—an inalienable right for a dad, and usually a highly protected one. But if I needed to talk to my dad during that sacred time, he'd put the paper down. He was emotionally available. He listened, and his intensive listening gave me the message that I was worthy and important.

A seventeen-year-old boy beeped his horn outside our house. He was collecting me for a movie date.

"Isn't he polite enough to come to the door?" my mother asked, shocked.

"We're late!" I covered, as I paced the floor for a few seconds.

My dad went to the window while the guy's horn blasted long, loud honks.

"You forgot your purse, Honey," my mother called, as I whisked out the door in a sprint.

"Excuse me, Skip, but I won't be going. You see, I am worth more than this kind of treatment. My parents have been watching. Look, I must be important because my dad spent his life listening to me and praying for me. I must be worth it. I must deserve treatment like you would give a cherished, beautiful lady, because in my parents' eyes I am," I softly raced, pleading for understanding as I looked into his eyes. "They cannot bear to see me treated this way. I hope you understand."

"I'm sorry," he began. "I just didn't know this about you."

"I guess I never realized it or had to put it to practical use before," I answered.

"If they love you a lot, then you should," he said with surprising wisdom and understanding, his eyes downcast.

"When people sacrifice for you, I mean sacrifice their rights and life's blood, you must be worth a lot even if you don't see it for yourself," I concluded.

"Thank you," he said, biting his lip.

"No, thank you, Skip." I touched his arm and returned to the house.

"You stoop down to make me great" (Psalm 18:35 NIV).

AUGUST 15   **YOU NEVER KNOW**

The casket now rested in the grave. Silent. Final. Unspeaking. I walked away in grief and disbelief. This was not somebody else's loved one. Not today.

My friend Ruth Peterman pressed a Bible verse in my hand and said, "My deepest sympathy. You know your mother is in God's presence." The verse read, "God is our refuge and strength, a tested help in times of trouble" (Psalm 46:1 TLB). Had Ruth known personally that God was a refuge and strength? Yes. She had told me about it.

When Gus, a dear old man alone in the world except for the Peterman family, lay close to death, Ruth whispered in his ear, "Are you going to be with Jesus, Gus?" The former skid row bum, who accepted Christ in his old age and began a new life, smiled and said yes with his eyes. "Give Jesus my love," Ruth said, realizing Gus was a personal emissary.

Hours before my mother's entrance into Christ's presence, she promised to carry a message too. "Mother, you're going to be with Jesus. Tell him we love him," I whispered. "I will, Darling," she said, barely able to speak.

Ruth Peterman's words provided a life script for me at my great moment of sorrow . . . sorrow that changed into hope.

Gus never knew how his life, his belief in Jesus, his witness to the message, would provide such encouragement and the script—the lighted path—for thousands of grieving people like me.

But maybe he does.

You never know.

AUGUST 16　**THE STUFF DREAMS ARE MADE OF**

"How will you keep your dreams alive now?" a friend questioned after I confided about my difficult situation.

"I don't know," I cried. "I've persuaded readers and audiences to hang onto dreams, to put work clothes on dreams and give them all the love they need. But now I can't seem to keep my own advice."

Within that year, the Reverend Doug Burr "found" me and went into action.

At church he would gather groups of people around us. "Hey, Lois, Bob, you folks . . . come over here! I want to tell you about Käaren! Have you met her?"

The first time, I giggled with embarrassment. (Only the first time.)

"This young woman is outstanding! She is a writer of best-selling books! She's lived all over the world! Have you read her books? I hope she writes more!"

The "audiences" seemed not only amused but blessed. They saw the "picture."

"We were impressed with your credentials, Käaren, but we were also blessed and encouraged just by watching the remarkable Doug Burr affirm you in his inimitable style," one of the women told me later.

"I know how you feel—healed. Because that's what I feel. You know, the great yearning of us humans is to have people accept us just as we are—not only accept us but believe in us for great dreams for us. My dreams were dusty with discouragement. Today they live," she continued, her voice cracking with emotion. "I completed nurses' training when I was forty-eight years old. When someone like Doug Burr tells you you're great, brilliant, and that you can do it, then you do it! You believe him!"

People like Doug Burr make us say, "Oh, I see. That's how God is!"

A lifted spirit and a resuscitated dream makes us better at seeing even more opportunities and pursuing them. I know.

"Praise her for the many fine things she does. These good deeds of hers shall bring her honor and recognition from even the leaders of the nations" (Proverbs 31:31 TLB).

AUGUST 17   **CALLED AND "CAN DO"**

"I'm called! I can't explain it, but it will become apparent," I announced to my questioning missions director.

A few months later I was living in Israel and believing moment by moment for income and opportunities as well as for my "higher calling"—sharing my faith.

"This book can make a difference! It is based on Bible

principles, sir!" I said to Jerusalem's mayor as I handed him a copy of my book *Great Leaps in a Single Bound* at a reception.

"Does it have the answers to peace even in the Middle East, young lady?" he joked, smiling knowingly.

"Yes, of course!" I smiled, knowing he "knew" something about Bible principles and the Christian witness.

"So this is your personal spiritual pilgrimage," he said, reading the blurb on the front cover. "I'll definitely read it!" he affirmed as he planted a little kiss on my cheek.

Later that year I miraculously entered Lebanon.

"Three governments oppose you, Miss Witte," I was informed at the arduous border patrol interrogation. "Two are leading world powers—Israel and your own United States government."

After two days of questioning and investigating, I walked across the border into Lebanon. (I knew I would. I was called. I had a message to deliver to war-weary believers.)

"Your Christian brothers and sisters in America are praying for you and sending supplies," I assured the Lebanese believers.

"Thank you for what the American Christians have already done. Give them the message that we are growing in numbers and growing stronger in our commitment to Christ," an ambulance nurse in a field hospital told me.

I promised I would.

I have not only *believed* but have also *experienced* the reality of Paul's writing to the Galatians: "I was not called to be a missionary by any group or agency. My call is from Jesus Christ himself and from God the Father who raised him from the dead" (1:1-2 TLB).

AUGUST 18   **I NEED YOU**

Hey? Any strugglers out there?
Is there anybody in my journey—this pilgrimage? Followers of Christ?

Please take my hand.

I don't fit the formula writer-speaker-missionary.

How I've always wanted to.

That writer who writes in an office off her kitchen and has a husband who takes her to the airport. (The husband whom she calls from an Atlanta or Seattle hotel with "Hi, Honey, I got here safely.")

I'm still a little shaky at times.

No rock.

I doubt.

I don't give God time.

I cry. No, I mean bawl.

I ask, "Why, God," not "what God."

And "When, God."

Sometimes.

I sing "Victory in Jesus"
    but sometimes I can't hit the right notes and forget the
    words to the next line.

But I want to continue on the journey.

I want to be a great Christian.

More than anything else in the world.

Oh, yeah. I also say, "God, why couldn't I get a wonderful mate by the eleventh hour, like Ann Kiemel has?" She led us to believe that God would pull through for the faithful.

Those who "gave God time."

How I believed.

The eleventh hour passed.

I think.

"God, are you arranging wonderful plans for my life on this
    gray January Monday morning? Are you?" I pray.

There's the problem.

Now, what's the answer?

Trust.

Available for the shaky?

Yes.

"God, go ahead. Increase the risk. I invite you. But then you
   must pour on the power," I pray.
That sacred link between God and me: trust.
I'll trust. Further.
Will you?
With me?

AUGUST 19   **SURRENDER**

If I really believe there is a God, I will trust him to desire
for me that which is for my highest good, and to have
planned for its fulfillment.

It's incredible. But I chose to believe: God has a perfect
plan for Käaren Witte. That plan fits into his overall purpose
for the whole world.

You know what? I am grateful for every situation or
person who created pain and hurt for me. For in
abandonment, I had to choose withdrawal or entry into a
new oneness—healing and wholeness with God.

"God," I now pray, "take my will. My soul. I give it to you.
I yield. Gladly, now. Finally. So transform all I am—heart
and emotions—into your image to work out your awesome
plan."

I surrender all.

I need to be totally God's. I need to release anything I
clutch.

God chooses to use me or hide me. I ask no questions. No
"why God's." I surrender all rights to him, who desires the
ultimate best for me. The loud voice of common sense will no
longer lead me.

I want to be known for only one thing: loving. And to be

known as "one who has risked her life for the sake of our Lord Jesus Christ." (Acts 15:26) and to rejoice as those who "were counted worthy to suffer dishonor for the Name" (Acts 5:41).

Surrendering my rights and serving will be a far greater reward than receiving the world's approval or wealth, or succeeding in the world's estimation—and that means even the Christian world.

To stay in a place of danger after being advised to leave, and to stay sweet and quiet in the midst of humiliation, as I comfort and encourage others, are my goals. I center on sacrificing love.

And only in sacrificing does love speak.

AUGUST 20   **A NEW PERSON IN THE OLD CITY**

The cross. It's unchanging.

Two thousand years later I stood at the place of the cross. Though I lived in Jerusalem as a journalist, I stood not as a reporter or writer but simply as a believer. "So little has changed in two thousand years," I'd often think as I walked through the narrow streets, watching donkey carts and touching the stones that built the houses in Christ's time.

I was away from the rat race and Rolodexes. Trekking through the hills of Judea, I often thought about my own life. In the quietness God's spirit revealed sin. I faced it. Finally. Yes, I was forgiven. I would no longer be self-destructive through old resentments and wrong motives.

"It's hard for me to know someone who lived two thousand years ago," a fellow journalist's words replayed. "Is Jesus Christ who he said he was?"

At dawn on that memorable summer day, I had returned to Calvary, for I had memorized some Bible verses, and I wanted to say them out loud and let the wind carry them to God:

We despised him and rejected him;
  he endured suffering and pain.
No one would even look at him—
  we ignored him as if he were nothing.
But he endured the suffering
  that should have been ours,
  the pain we should have borne.
All the while we thought that his suffering
  was punishment sent by God.
But because of our sins he was wounded,
  beaten because of the evil we did.
We are healed by the punishment he suffered,
  made whole by the blows he received.
                        (Isaiah 53:3-5 GNB)

The cross is unchanging. It still changes us.

AUGUST 21   **ABRAHAM, ISAAC AND MY**
                        NEIGHBOR SOPHIE

"I was number 317-212 in Auschwitz," my Israeli
neighbor Sophie began. "I knew I had to turn to God.
Branded like cows, this number gave me a membership in a
death camp."

"I was twenty-three years old," she said, bursting into
sobs, "and to this day, I can't control my crying when I look
back. No one who has merely read about it can possibly
imagine the torment and torture. Our hair was cut off and we
were forced to walk naked in the streets while German
soldiers watched and laughed at us. I still smell the odor of
burning corpses. My mother, father, husband, and three
little children died in those fires.

"Käaren, darling, young woman with such a future," she
exhorted, "remember how our father Abraham believed
God. No, we don't see justice in our everyday life,
oftentimes. So many Jews have turned their backs on God

because of the Holocaust. But it also brought many of us back to God."

After her words, I knew I had to make a spiritual pilgrimage too. I walked to Mount Moriah, where Abraham had paved the way for believers like me thousands of years ago.

You see, I had my own "Isaacs." I needed to say, "Whatever you require, God—I want no other gods before you."

At Mount Moriah, a part of my Jerusalem neighbor, I touched the huge rock, the altar, with my hands.

My Isaacs? My gods? Success, recognition, marriage, attention were laid on the altar.

In that awesome setting and at that unforgettable hour, I prayed, "Thank you for Isaac, Abraham, and my neighbor Sophie. They helped me to unmask my relentless, insatiable gods."

It was a funny thing. No, a phenomenal thing. My loneliness, which so often had dogged my heels, lifted.

My loneliness had nothing to do with singleness after all. It had to do with sin.

AUGUST 22   **LONDON: BUS DEPOTS AND JUSTIFICATION FOR SINS**

Bus depots. Exhaust fumes. Tired humanity pushing boxes and lugging bags that cut into already weary shoulders. The late afternoon crush of people.

"Round trip ticket to Leeds," I said smilingly to the ticket seller at whose window I had queued. Before I returned to the United States from the Middle East, I had another special appointment, for which I had waited fifteen years: sharing the plan of salvation with a nonbelieving friend.

The angry, frustrated, overburdened ticket seller made an error on my ticket. He ripped it and shouted obscenities.

"Please!" I quaked, outraged.

He yelled more without looking me in the eye. I looked around. Nobody else heard him.

"Where is the manager?" I asked.

"Excuse me, but I don't ever remember being treated as rudely as I just was by the man at ticket counter 10. He used horrible vulgarities and obscenities even when I asked him, begged him, to stop! What a terrible, angry employee you have. You really must get him out of here." I pleaded my case with enough evidence to convict ticket seller 10.

The manager lowered his head, and his eyes left mine. He softly said, "I ask forgiveness for him."

What more could I say? Nothing further. The sins were paid for. Justification obtained for the man. Grievances satisfied.

I need to remember the analogy—always.

AUGUST 23 **THE SUPERNATURAL CONNECTION**

I love walking in the supernatural.

When I was a recent journalism graduate, one of my first assignments was to interview a Holocaust victim, a camp survivor. I arrived at her hotel room, and her secretary (combination nurse and traveling companion) greeted me. The "camp survivor" turned out to be the greatly admired author and speaker Corrie Ten Boom.

Nearly speechless with excitement, I asked her questions about the camps, hiding Jews, losing her sister in a concentration camp, her family, and her near marriage. When Corrie started to share, she encouraged me in my singleness and said God would meet my needs. She spoke with strength and trust in her voice.

"I believe God heard *her!*" I thought to myself. "She knows, *really knows,* God!"

Through the next fifteen years I followed dear Corrie Ten Boom's life through her books, tapes, speeches, and public appearances. On the day I read of her death, I cried and also thanked God for the rich experience he gave, through her, to a young woman like me.

Years later I returned to the United States from an overseas assignment and entered a Sunday school class at a local church. Not only did I recognize the beautiful blond woman who taught the class, but I had "followed" her life also. In a flash I remembered that first assignment. The woman was Corrie's traveling companion, Ellen Stamps. Once again, our lives intersected. No, make that meshed. For her family became mine. God had answered Corrie Ten Boom's prayer in many ways. My needs have been met. But just like Corrie, I am still single.

Once again Corrie's words proved true: "Jesus is Victor. No pit is so deep . . . he is not deeper still."

So often when I leave Ellen's home, she walks me to the car and says, "Corrie must be smiling that she was the cause of our friendship."

The supernatural connections that God arranges are far-reaching, aren't they?

AUGUST 24   **FRIENDS IN SPITE OF FRITOS**

"I hate living with you! I'm moving! You are so unorganized, plus I hate how you eat a whole bag of Fritos and leave crumbs. You're always late, and you never park right in the driveway." Julie, my friend and housemate of three years was upset.

"You're right," I confessed, slightly grinning. "I will try to mend my ways, eat fewer Fritos and more celery for fewer crumbs."

"You're not funny. Your jokes can't redeem you this time," she insisted.

"But Julie, we have been friends for years! You and I will always be friends. We have a history together. Plus you know all the bad things about me, and I know all the bad things about you, so we have no images to protect! We also know each other's wonderful virtues!" I wailed, realizing that *this time* she was serious.

"We became writers together, and we have gone through family tragedies and personal disasters. We have been open and transparent and have upheld each other. I felt healed many times when you said, 'I understand.' Sharing deep secrets, we were vulnerable and risked wildly. We have memories! With whom do you share history, openness, vulnerability, and memories in this life?" I continued. "Remember when our pet cat died? We cried. How we loved that little buddy! Look, you and I are always going to be friends. Our souls are meshed; our lives intersected because God arranged this friendship," I said.

"I'm ready to forgive you. Come over for dinner," Julie telephoned a year later. "I have so much to share with you. I know *you'll* understand!"

Loneliness is detested by our heavenly Father. That's why he gave us friends.

AUGUST 25   **PRAISE: FLUFF OR THE RIGHT STUFF**

I love a great compliment. I can soar for a week on one! (And maybe even a lifetime.)

"Käaren, I love your outfit! You radiate in red! You are always so stunning and gorgeous. You look like Elizabeth Taylor, only you're more beautiful and younger!" One lady exclaimed in an orgy of emotion every time she saw me.

Initially I commended her for her insightful judgment, remarkable discernment, and keen sense of observation.

However, as I jogged by her yard one day I not only questioned her judgment but a few other things too.

Seeing me, she waved and called me to her yard and motioned to a neighbor.

"I wanted you to meet this beautiful young woman! Isn't

Käären stunning?" She asked the neighbor. "Don't you think she is pretty?"

("Only if this guy's into gym clothes and sweat," I thought to myself.)

The neighbor indulged her and smiled.

I died inside.

The experience taught me that praise is good, but unthinking, prattling flattery may be destructive and counterproductive, even though flatterers may truly believe they are encouraging, loving, uplifting people.

Another friend compliments like this: "I want to compliment you on your lovely dress, but more so I want to compliment you on your character qualities—your hospitality and generosity." With this compliment I don't cringe, but rather I'm encouraged to do more good.

I recalled my clothes that the flattering lady exhalted. If we as humans really wanted to be praised and noticed for superficial things like dresses, we would carry them around on hangers. Then we wouldn't get spots on them. "Flattery is a trap" (Proverbs 29:5 TLB).

AUGUST 26 **THE CIRCLE TO CONTENTMENT**

I visited a friend two days before I was to be the speaker at a convention in Washington, D.C. She and her three beautiful children drove me to the palatial hotel where the committee had reserved a suite for me.

"Luci, you have everything in the world! A close family, a very nice, handsome husband, and a gorgeous home!" I rejoiced as we drove.

My words bounced off her. Tension and frustration painted her face as she barked scalding words to her children. Something was wrong, and I thought I knew what it was.

Once we were in the extravagant suite, I tried to minimize my good fortune. "Oh, this is rare. My days are usually spent at a typewriter or in tiny apartments on the other side of the world as a single journalist."

"Well, last time I met you at the airport, you were going to Rome," she retorted. She sounded bitter and somehow lonely.

"Luci!" I insisted, jarring her, "I'm grateful for my life's work, but we have been friends for twenty-five years—since we were small girls. We must remember the only thing we take out of this life is relationships. The only thing that matters is relationships. They last forever and never die."

Darkness had come over the city. A beginning smile met mine in the reflection of the window that glistened with the dazzling city skyline lights.

"I know how to live on almost nothing or with everything. I have learned the secret of contentment in every situation" (Philippians 4:12*a* TLB).

AUGUST 27   **HIS HANDS, EYES, AND SMILE**

I have never told some of the people who changed the course of my life. I figured these people had forgotten what I now know were fleeting but profound incidences.

Joan Stafford—our lives connected so briefly. Yet during that difficult, insecure time in my life, her eyes would meet mine across a church hall or vast congregation and say in a two- or three-second gaze, "I love you. I believe in you. I know what you're going through. I am older. I know you will do well. Keep going, Käaren!"

Elaine Townsend was a guest missionary one summer at my Bible camp. The tall, graceful lady lovingly smiled at me, an insignificant thirteen-year-old, for no apparent reason. I needed it at that precise moment in my young life.

I never saw her again.

Mrs. Moody wrote a little note to me when I was elected to the Honor Society in high school. I read and reread the note for years and kept it in my Bible, which I felt was a fitting place of honor for the words.

A doctor in northern Minnesota whom I only saw once allowed his waiting room to get clogged while he sat and used tissues to dab my tears for a half hour as he told me, "I think you're pretty, Käaren."

A teacher whose name I can't remember (we thought he was funny because he carried a big black lunch bucket) one day handed me a play book and said, "I want you to audition!" I yelped out loud and leaped inside; I really wanted to audition but felt too awkward and shy. How did he even know?

A life's work in media and drama lay ahead for me. How ever did he know?

"You are my eyes, my smiles, and my hands that wipe away young girls' tears and give scared little actresses the script." (I think Jesus said that.) "I have no other hands but yours." (He said that too, or something close to that.)

"No, I will not abandon you or leave you as orphans in the storm—I will come to you" (John 14:18 TLB).

AUGUST 28   **THE REAL PURPOSE OF A VILLA**

"What is the purpose of living? For what?" A former beauty queen who married well (as we used to say) questioned in frustration. We sat on the mountainside lawn of her villa overlooking the majestic French Riviera, gazing at the azure blue Mediterranean Sea.

"Do you want to know the truth?" she began. "We hope the specialty stores, the designers, the catalogs, the gourmet foods will create new, unique things for us to buy. So what's left? We spend twenty years accumulating houses, collecting art, and developing advantageous social circles. But it's all so much 'champagne wishes and caviar dreams.' Nobody knows but sometimes I feel so empty that I curl up, just hoping to stop the spasms of emptiness in my heart or soul or whatever you call the thing inside that feels so painful and big.

"But don't tell me about sin, because I have been a good person," she continued to confide reiterating how for many years she volunteered in community work and raised money for the arts.

In the lavish citadel of the rich, I contrasted our lives. One had purpose; the other longed for it.

"Elizabeth," I said, "the great apostle Paul wrote something in Acts 20 about the purpose in life—the purpose for the believer. Are you interested?"

She said she was.

From my little Bible in my purse, I read, "But life is worth nothing unless I use it for doing the work assigned me by the Lord Jesus—the work of telling others the Good News about God's mighty kindness and love" (Acts 20:24 TLB).

After a few seconds she lifted her lowered head.

"I could become a believer and then tell others the good news from the mountain tops!" she said.

I told her she could.

AUGUST 29 **HARVEST TIME**

So where does a seventy-one-year-old widowed woman who decides to change the world begn? Join the senior citizens for discussion on the social implications of needlepoint, pacemakers, meeting their Maker, and coronary bypasses? Does she debate in Scrabble circles the virtues of aspirin versus Ibuprofen for the treatment of arthritis?

Not Ruthe Lamb. She decided to tap into the singles' market. Among seniors? Au contraire. She advertised, went on television and radio, rented a lavish hotel hall (only linen tablecloths, thank you), and believed.

"Singles' groups only last on the average of two years; plus you need youth in leadership," they said. (She asked to speak to "they.")

Four years later we singles of Tulsa, Oklahoma, celebrated Ruthe's seventy-fifth birthday. We thought she looked like an angel. You must have seen the type: white hair, bright, loving eyes for all who meet them head on, the kind of smile people describe as dazzling.

"Singles must have their self-esteem restored. Many have been dumped and dumped on, burned and burned out. They've been left bloody by the side of the road. They need status, the same status as given to the most outstanding married couple who has succeeded in thirty years of marriage," she insists.

Status. That's what we get. Inoculations of it, in massive doses. Every weekend she plans positive speakers and pumps slogans into our hearts: "The best is barely good enough for you!"

I have come to believe it.

"As you know him better, he will give you, through his great power, everything you need for living a truly good life: He even shares his own glory and his own goodness with us!" (II Peter 1:3 TLB).

AUGUST 30   **OUR GREAT NEEDS**

I hate dances. People get left out, feel unloved and unaccepted—especially older ladies sometimes. (I know I'll be in "the older lady category" too, one day.)

Love. There's something all-consuming about it. It's my chief emotional occupation. I have difficulty being interested in other things.

That's why I hate dances. I just can't bear to see anyone left out, because I know how much I need love and acceptance.

I know about loneliness and not belonging. I wasn't invited to the senior prom and was always chosen last for the baseball team and any other team. I have walked down the streets of the world's great cities—teeming with people—

feeling such loneliness that I thought I was dead but standing up and moved along by the crowd.

Loneliness is a universal condition. However, it was loneliness that often brought me to the center of my faith and restored my sense of indebtedness to Christ.

Once, as I boarded a plane for the Far East on a writing assignment, a friend gave me a hand-written prayer. In every bathroom mirror I looked into for the next decade, that worn, water-stained little prayer met my face each morning:

> Dear God, you want my total heart focused on you. I often forget this as I try desperately to fill the gaping wounds and black holes of need for things and shallow relationships. Continue to remind me that you are my source and answer. You know my heart's desire to share my life with a mate and a good friend. Bring that person into my life. Until then I will wait knowing that this unknown person will be an overflow of you. Amen.

"Pray all the time. Ask God for anything in line with the Holy Spirit's wishes. Plead with him, reminding him of your needs" (Ephesians 6:18 TLB).

AUGUST 31   **THE HIGH COST (BUT WORTH IT)**

"I come from Romania," a defector now living in the United States tells me continually; "I have seen those who say they are followers of Jesus Christ go to labor camps, have their families threatened, and get demoted to humiliating jobs." That's the price they pay.

So what about the exacting demands of following Christ? Have we hidden them? Covered up the truth? What is the cost of being a Christian? It may be giving up your rights to a home, safety, comfort, and even a husband. Nothing less.

Jesus knew, however, about the deep core of need within every human heart. The great need for a cause, something in which to believe intensely. A cause to fight for, to die for. A flag to fly. A banner to wave.

Humans are—or could be—at their most noble, their most courageous, their most loyal, their most sacrificial, in the cause of Christ. For here the inner qualities, so desperately desiring a channel and vehicle, get pushed to new heights. That's what following the incredible Christ offers.

It's like what a friend told me in the Le Havre, France, harbor: "You are like that great ship. You could remain safe and soft in the harbor and not face the challenges of storms and destiny. But that's not what you're made for!"

The other requirements? People may not want to hear "For all have sinned, and come short of the glory of God" (Romans 3:23). Christ's teaching doesn't advocate the popular saying, "I'm okay, you're okay."

Well, if I'm okay and you're okay, then why the Christ on the cross?

Harvest and Wonder

RUTH C. IKERMAN

SEPTEMBER 1 **STARTING OVER**

As I was turning the calendar to the first, fresh page of September, the telephone rang. A friend was calling to see if we could "catch up with our catching up" after the summer months. When I told her I was writing down many activities on my September calendar, she said, "Yes, it is the month for starting over. I almost feel like saying Happy New Year to you."

School is beginning again not only for the children but also for adults, who will have endless opportunities to engage in part-time studies or pursue hobbies. There is fresh opportunity to renew the promises to ourselves to be more outgoing in entertaining or to feed the family more nutritious meals. New opportunities appear for service on church and civic committees.

The winds of change blow over the heart in September, even as the winds of fall are blowing away the hot summer days. This is a time when the calendar seems to remember the Bible's promise, "Behold, I make all things new" (Revelation 21:5).

So welcome September, friend, with a heart eager for new experiences and joys and with hands outstretched to help others in the family and within the circle of friends.

SEPTEMBER 2   **MOVING ON**

In the mail were two notes from family friends, now living in different parts of the country. We had shared poignant moments of farewell when they left our hometown in years past.

One note said, "Our son has won a scholarship and is going to the college of his choice, but we shall miss his presence." The other said, "My parents have decided to move into a retirement community, and we are helping them move out of their home, but the decisions are so hard to make."

Change is never easy because the familiar has a firm grip on our hearts. Whether the change is for the better or caused by distressing circumstances, emotions are close to the surface.

Real help is available in times of decision making if we remember the blessings inherent in the precious verse of Malachi 3:6: "For I am the Lord, I change not."

At a time when outer circumstances are changing due to a new location, job promotion, or health problems, it is wonderful to be able to rely on divine assurance of a changeless God.

With this inner knowledge, all earthly change becomes easier to contemplate. Remember to take God with you in any decision to stay where you are or to accept the opportunity to move on to new opportunities and responsibilities.

SEPTEMBER 3   **LABOR DAY**

On the first Monday of this month America observes the national holiday of Labor Day, in honor of its working force. Last year a little boy said to me, "I like Labor Day because both my mother and father are home and don't have to work."

His remark reminded me of how the labor force has grown to include many women as well as men. The little boy was glad he had both parents home on the same day, because their working schedules were not often the same. The father would take the child to school in the morning, and the mother would be the one to bring him home after school.

On this all-important Labor Day, the family could be together all day for happy family fellowship. As the working force increases, including many single parents, it is important to find time somehow for the family picnic, a game of ball, or reading a story together.

Some churches now have group picnics on Labor Day afternoon to welcome vacationers home and greet newcomers to the community. The Labor Day holiday gives a fine opportunity to remember that "we are laborers together with God" (I Corinthians 3:9).

This verse reminds us that we have the privilege of remembering our blessed heritage as children of God as we work together in our homes and churches on behalf of the kingdom.

SEPTEMBER 4   **EVERY PERFECT GIFT**

When I went to pick up a birthday cake for my mother's birthday, I told the clerk that it was for a party where all the guests would be more than eighty years old. She asked me to wait just a minute while she went to another part of the store.

Soon she returned with a brown paper bag in her hand and said, "I'm sorry there wasn't time to get this gift wrapped, but tell your mother it is wrapped with my love for her and all her friends."

The sack contained an artificial red geranium in a white plastic container, and mother flashed a beautiful smile as she opened the surprise package containing the bright flower.

The impulsive gift made by the clerk seemed to me a part of the great legacy of loving gifts described in James 1:17: "Every good gift and every perfect gift is from above, and cometh down from the Father of lights, with whom is no variableness, neither shadow of turning."

Any gift made in love brings blessings and extends God's goodness. A loving heart remembers to be grateful to God for his never-failing gift of life, available to all who accept his love through Christ. Such inner security leads to sharing blessings with others, adding to their happiness.

SCHOOL DAY MEMORIES

When the school year picks up its tempo as fall swings into action, it is time to think of the blessing of school day memories.

Recently a snapshot I was using as a bookmark fell out of a book as I was dusting the shelves. The picture showed the smiling face of a girlhood friend and classmate. On impulse I mailed her the picture and soon received a reply. "Thank you very much. I had forgotten all about the picture being taken. It brought back memories of a new dress I had made at school, and brand new suede shoes. Oh, how on top of the world I felt that day."

She added, "A lot of water has gone under the bridge since then, hasn't it?" Indeed it had, but we could still walk over the bridge of friendship.

Importantly, the picture had revealed my friend in a characteristic pose, with a big smile on her face. She had always been a good example of the words in Proverbs 15:13: "A merry heart maketh a cheerful countenance."

This positive attitude showed in the picture and was a testimony to her merry heart, which managed always to see the best in every situation. Learning to do this may be one of the most important lessons a school or Sunday school can teach.

SEPTEMBER 6 ## THE PLACE

My husband and I enjoy the friendship of a young couple who have an adorable little girl, who on one visit gave us a memorable experience The family had moved to our capital city, and when we visited they volunteered to take us sightseeing in their automobile.

The little girl at once said she wanted to go to "the place." The parents assumed she wanted to see the lights on the domes of the buildings. This proved a beautiful sight, but she urged them to go further.

After touring the business district, the father drove down a side street and parked in front of a small church with a steeple rising amid the trees. At this the girl clapped her hands and shouted in glee, "You found the place, you found the place!"

She began to sing us a song she had learned in her Sunday school class, making gestures to accompany the loving words. As I listened, I recalled a favorite verse from Psalm 119: "Thou art my hiding place and my shield."

The little girl's happiness at finding her favorite place in Washington, D.C., seemed an example of the happy heritage of religious freedom under our government. We resolved to remember to attend "the place," seeking God's help in being good citizens.

SEPTEMBER 7   **AN EXAMPLE**

A business man said to me recently, "There is nothing funnier than people. They so often turn out to be so different from what they seem to be before you get to know them."

We spoke of a friend who wears frivolous costumes, but who does so many substantial acts of kindness that she has become a sturdy symbol of support in many areas.

"I supposed she was as fluffy as she looked," said the acquaintance to me, "and I was so very, very wrong. I am going to try not to judge so quickly again."

He had seen this woman roll up her sleeves to wash communion cups in the church kitchen after a worship service. And he had enjoyed the homemade bread she had brought to his family at a time of illness.

He said to me, "She is like one of the men I work with who has been honored for his sturdy strength and the grace of his gentleness."

How wonderful when these two qualities can be combined in the same person and lead to Christian action! The Bible encourages us to perform even the humblest of acts well. Jesus said after washing the feet of his disciples, "For I have given you an example, that ye should do as I have done to you" (John 13:15). Many are the opportunities for service today.

SEPTEMBER 8   **THE CHEERFUL BOUQUET**

Waiting on the porch chair when I came home from the grocery store was a lovely bouquet of asters, traditional flower for the month of September. Their shades of pink, rose, lavender, purple, and white made a beautiful picture against the green chair in the golden sunshine of late afternoon.

Looking at the cheerful bouquet, I realized that an elderly neighbor had stopped by and remembered what she had told me about her garden. "I grow flowers so I can give them to my friends. I don't have much money now, but I love my friends, and flowers help me to tell them so."

With gratitude I accepted her gift, and while placing the flowers in a favorite vase, I searched my heart to see if I myself was truly sharing substance and self with others.

All of us have something to give, if only a smile or a cheery hello. Such gifts are magnified when they are pure, as we are reminded in II Corinthians 9:7: "Every man according as he purposeth in his heart, so let him give; not grudgingly, or of necessity: for God loveth a cheerful giver."

It is with a prayer in my heart to God that I may be a cheerful giver in small ways and large that I enjoy the lovely flowers grown and given by my friend.

SEPTEMBER 9   **UNFAILING HELP**

A family man who had retired from business because of a physical disability said to me in great discouragement, "There are so many things I want to do, but I can't find the strength to do them." He was lonely for old friends still at work.

His wife told me of the problems they were having in finding the proper direction for their retirement years. They began to draw on their inner spiritual resources when they realized the truth of the Bible promise in Psalm 73:26: "My flesh and my heart faileth; but God is the strength of my heart, and my portion for ever."

When the husband renewed his appreciation of God as his true strength and companion, he began to think about other people whom he might help with his limited energy. He started with a single telephone call to the son of an acquaintance whose family had been in a bad traffic accident. Soon the boy looked forward to talking each day to his older friend, and both benefited.

Once his mind was released from his own problems, my friend began to feel better physically. One sunshiny day he walked to the library where he found friends of former business days also browsing in the reading room.

He was strengthened in his heart through fellowship, which began with the daily reminder that in all circumstances God is always our strength and help.

SEPTEMBER 10   **TOWARD THE LIGHT**

Sometimes the coming of fall brings fresh impetus to decorate the home. On the morning when I picked out wallpaper for our kitchen, the paint merchant gave me a word of advice that helped me also in my spiritual growth.

Looking at my chosen pattern and its texture, he said, "Remember to lap your wallpaper toward the light, and never away from it." He said I would have a big, bulky seam showing where the two pieces joined unless I used this rule.

At work on the project, I remembered his words. If in lapping the paper I should face it toward the light, then certainly in the journey through life it would be best to learn to walk toward the light.

With so many problems confronting all families these days, we may stumble unless we are fully aware of the blessing of light. Romans 13:12 admonishes us, "Let us therefore cast off the works of darkness, and let us put on the armour of light."

If we fail in our endeavors, we can confess our shortcomings, which are covered by the light of God's love. I finished the wallpaper job with a prayer in my heart: "Father, give me light to see afresh how to solve daily problems and renovate my heart as well as the rooms of our home."

SEPTEMBER 11 —   **CUMBERED**

My grandmother used to sing hymns while she did household chores, and a favorite phrase was "cumbered with a load of care." As I listened, I was fascinated by the big word *cumbered*, and I asked grandmother what it meant.

She told me not to worry but to be happy playing with my dolls. Later I found in the Bible story about Mary and Martha and their friend Jesus that "Martha was cumbered about much serving" (Luke 10:40).

So I looked the word up in the big family dictionary and found that *cumbered* means "to be burdened or perplexed." Sometimes the burden may seem "unwieldy, unmanageable, or not easily borne or managed."

Yet grandmother amazingly always managed to carry her load of daily duties with seeming ease. I wondered what steps she had taken to become unencumbered.

I remember seeing her read her Bible as she sat in her easy chair by the window where the sunlight streamed in the most brightly. Sometimes her head would be bowed in prayer. Then she would get up and go into the kitchen to bake a pie for a family facing illness or sorrow.

Grandmother knew how to keep her heart from being cumbered by relying on help from God to sustain her as she tried to help others, and I am increasingly grateful for her example.

SEPTEMBER 12   **THE IMPORTANT NOW**

For over a year I had planned to send a book to a friend who had been kind to me when I was in the hospital. Somehow I never found the time to wrap a copy and put it into the mail.

One morning in the middle of housekeeping, I decided to stop my work and tend to the errand of love right then. I dropped the dustcloth, went into my office to autograph a copy, and got it ready for mailing. On my way to the grocery store I stopped at the post office.

Once the package left my hands, I felt an immediate sense of release and went about my other chores with a lighter heart.

Within a week I received a long-distance telephone call from my friend. "I have been housebound with illness and feeling quite forgotten. I thank you from my heart."

The experience reminded me that it is never too late to do what we have intended to do, if we take advantage of the all-important now of the present moment. It is so easy to put off doing love tasks in the rush of daily duties.

What loving chore of thankfulness do you need to complete today? Such an action for a friend or acquaintance is one way of thanking God, our Father, for the great gift of his healing love. The Bible tells us in II Corinthians 6:2, "Behold, now is the accepted time."

SEPTEMBER 13 **RAINY DAY BLESSINGS**

Often it is the month of September that brings the first rainy day of the season. When that happens I remember the joy of running home from school through the rain to find a big pot of vegetable soup simmering on the stove.

The fragrance of the vegetables mixed with a big soup bone would permeate the house, and mother would say, "I think I'll make you some cornbread to go with that soup for supper."

Now through the mist of years I can see clearly the faces of dear ones who have shared the joys and sorrows of the changing seasons. A rainy day seems to provide an opportunity to enjoy a quiet moment; nature seems to be urging us to relax our usually hectic schedules and consider our heritage.

Such a day is a blessing from God, as set forth in Job 5:10: "Who giveth rain upon the earth, and sendeth waters upon the fields."

Gray days have their advantages, for even as the rain sinks into the dusty earth, making possible better flowers in the seasons ahead, so our hearts' rainy days lead to spiritual crops of faith and love when we savor them wisely.

Indeed, we often find that what has seemed a dark memory of sorrow is now seen as positive, since it urged us forward to better action in the future. Life's rainy days bring blessings that cultivate virtues leading to valuable fruit.

SEPTEMBER 14 **SAYING GOOD-BYE**

At the close of the morning church service the pastor called to the altar a young couple who had been active in the church and the Sunday school. Their two small children were with them.

"We come to the moment of saying good-bye to our friends," said the pastor, "and we want to wish them

Godspeed in their new assignment. We shall hold them in our loving and sustaining prayers."

They were headed overseas to serve in a missionary enterprise involving airplane travel to remote areas. It was expected that they would not return home for the next three years. Friends and family inevitably felt sad at this separation.

They were the modern counterparts of the early missionaries described in the Bible passage about the apostle Paul, Acts 20:38: "Sorrowing most of all for the words which he spake, that they should see his face no more. And they accompanied him unto the ship."

Saying good-bye today is somewhat easier because of quick airplane travel and long-distance telephone calls. There is not the seeming inevitability of farewell as in the time of Paul. Yet saying good-bye is never easy, and it is good to be able to rely on the blessings of prayer. Each of us can ask God for courage and grace to accept separation in this earthly life, secure in the knowledge of our "eternal forever."

SEPTEMBER 15   **DECISIONS, DECISIONS**

It is the custom in our church for the pastor to invite all the children to join him at the front while he tells them a story. The adults also find this a profitable practice.

One morning a tiny voice in the pew behind me kept saying "No, no, no" when the mother would ask the little girl if she wanted to go down the aisle. Yet when the other children started down, the child began to cry. She got out of the pew and into the aisle, but then hung back timidly. At this the mother took her by the hand and helped her into the line.

Many of us are like the little girl. We live in a dismal land of indecision. But the Bible recognizes this very human trait and reassures us: "Multitudes, multitudes in the valley of decision: for the day of the Lord is near in the valley of decision" (Joel 3:14).

We may wish to serve, but we hang back for reasons best

known only to our inner selves. While we hesitate, opportunities for service or friendship slip away from us.

It may take the hand of a loving friend to lead us into the mainstream of life. The fall season gives us many opportunities to make fresh decisions to enjoy family and friends. We grow in spiritual grace when we forsake indecision.

SEPTEMBER 16 **CROWDED SCHEDULES**

I was shopping with a friend when she stopped suddenly beside a counter given over to athletic caps. "I should buy one of these for myself," she said, "because I seem to be acting as a chauffeur most of my days."

She mentioned the crowded schedule of taking her son to baseball practice, Scout meetings, and band practice. "Then my daughter needs to go to her music lessons, the rehearsal for the church pageant, and the library to return some books." Meanwhile, my friend looked at her long grocery list and sighed, "I don't know when I am supposed to find time to buy this food for the cupboards and freezer."

We looked at each other in loving understanding, knowing that somehow the time would be found in the crowded schedules. Increasingly, doctors are treating stress illnesses caused by the number of jobs that men and women have to juggle in these busy days of traffic problems to and from work, household tasks, and community service.

One way to stay on top of a crowded schedule is to first take time to ask for divine guidance by spending time in prayer. We have the loving invitation in Matthew 11:28: "Come unto me, all ye that labor and are heavy laden, and I will give you rest."

SEPTEMBER 17 **FOLLOW PEACE**

The irritations began when I spilled the milk on the kitchen floor while preparing breakfast. The mail was delayed, causing a hurried trip to town before the bank closed. Then at night a friend telephoned with a complaint about a committee of which I was a member.

Sinking into the easy chair, I said to my husband, "I hope tomorrow is not so full of irritations." Fortunately, it was a better day. I was thankful I had not lost my temper and "told off" the friend who called me while I was weary. In this instance I had remembered to act on one of my favorite Bible verses, Hebrews 12:14: "Follow peace with all men and holiness, without which no man shall see the Lord."

It is hard to be peaceful when the day is filled with trivialities that vex the spirit. If we remain peaceful, we are adding another stitch to the fabric of holiness. This garment of peace and holiness can be easily torn and soiled if we let the irritations of the day take precedence over peaceful thoughts.

A prayer I say to help myself in such situations is "Father, help me control my unpeaceful moods, that my heart may expand through peace to embrace others also in need of thy peace."

Prayer can help reduce the havoc caused by the accumulation of trivial irritations that disturb daily peace.

SEPTEMBER 18   **COVET NOT**

When I was a student attending college on a scholarship, I was well aware of the beautiful clothes of a girl in the poetry class. One morning I confided to my English teacher how much I longed for a blue suit like the one in the front row.

The teacher said, "Do I detect a note of envy in your voice? Please don't ever let me hear envious words from you, for the most unbecoming thing you can wear in this world is the cloak of covetousness."

In years since I have remembered that conversation when tempted to be envious of another for any reason whatever. The teacher's casual comment proved a wonderful lifetime lesson, which I prize as highly as the love of literature she gave me.

Recently I walked into a store to buy a new suit for a happy reunion, and I reflected again on the wisdom of my teacher. She knew that a heart and mind free from envy add a special radiance to life. This is a blessing open to all regardless of outer apparel.

How fortunate is the person who can say with Paul, "I have coveted no man's silver, or gold, or apparel" (Acts 20:33).

This verse is a reminder to ask God to help us keep covetousness out of our lives and to be grateful for daily blessings.

SEPTEMBER 19 **PRODUCTIVE WORK**

A young man who works in the poultry business chatted with me recently, and his remarks gave me refreshing insight. He remarked in passing, "It's not the hen that never lays an egg that takes the profit out of egg sales. You can spot her by her coloring and actions and take her out of the flock."

He said it is the hen that only occasionally produces an egg that steals the profit. Meanwhile, she is stuffing herself with expensive grain, so the owner keeps extensive records to identify and then remove her.

It occurred to me to wonder what would happen if some such record could be kept of the nonproducers in club and church circles. Perhaps what we all need is guidance for setting our priorities and goals, so that we may become more productive in our work for the kingdom.

The Bible tells us in Proverbs 16:3, "Commit thy works unto the Lord, and thy thoughts shall be established." With our thoughts fixed on God we can give to others out of the abundance of blessings that are ours.

Nourished by spiritual food from the Bible, we can improve our productivity as we work with Christians in our hometown churches for better local, national, and world conditions.

SEPTEMBER 20   **COMFORT AND COURAGE**

When the telephone rang, I took my hands out of the dishpan, dried them hastily on the kitchen towel, and picked up the receiver. I was surprised to hear the voice of a friend who had been in an automobile accident.

"Good, I have succeeded in dialing you correctly with the fingers of my left hand" she told me. "It is so hard to feed myself and get my clothes on while my right arm is in a cast."

She wanted to thank me for a get-well card I had sent. "It came on a day when I was deeply discouraged and in need of comfort and courage," she said.

As she concluded her call, she asked me, "Please keep on praying as your card promised." So I asked her to include me in her own prayers, for her call had come when I faced a puzzling problem of my own.

Returning to my tasks, I thought of the comfort of her call and went to my Bible concordance to find a favorite verse: "Blessed be God, even the Father of our Lord Jesus Christ, the Father of mercies and the God of all comfort" (II Corinthians 1:3).

To the God of comfort my friend and I were committed to raise our prayers, asking for fresh courage and comfort for crisis times and daily tasks.

SEPTEMBER 21   **HOLY SAFETY**

As we walked out of the church together, my husband remarked on what a beautiful sermon we had heard on brotherhood. Indeed, the choir had sung its best, and the red, white, and blue flowers on the altar had reminded us of patriotism and democracy. We would remember the short text from I Peter 2:17: "Honour all men. Love the brotherhood. Fear God. Honour the king."

Before we were off the parking lot, this mood had been broken. With skidding tires and a honking horn, the car to the right of us backed out in a hurry, narrowly missing a small child and scattering gravel onto the coat of an elderly woman.

We were glad there had been no accident, but the harsh looks exchanged because of the incident changed the lingering feeling of brotherhood to one of dismay and fear. We wished that the mood of holiness and brotherhood had extended to holy safety in driving, for surely there is a need for brotherhood among those behind the steering wheels of automobiles.

Women and men who drive belong to a great brotherhood of motorists, and each is deserving of respect and honor from persons in passing cars. Driving gives an opportunity to put Sunday sermon concepts into action for holy safety.

SEPTEMBER 22   **MONEY PICTURES**

The chore of balancing the checkbook is one that many dread. I was helped to see it in a different light, though, when an accountant said to me, "Money shows a record of living."

He said he could get a good picture of a family by just looking at its canceled checks. This prompted me to wonder what kind of picture our checkbook painted of our lives. Did it show us to be selfish or concerned also about the church and the community? Was I revising my giving to keep in step with inflation?

Such questions helped me recall the often-quoted Bible verse from I Timothy: "For the love of money is the root of all evil" (6:10). The accountant had shown me that the opposite is also true: The wise love of money can bring the growth of good.

Balancing the checkbook can also be a time of reckoning

spiritual accounts. If the checks show a picture of greed, then there is fresh opportunity to become more outgoing in giving. When the debits and credits have been accounted for, I get to my knees and thank God for the family funds and ask for wisdom in the month ahead to spend wisely and well.

SEPTEMBER 23 **ETERNAL FRIENDSHIP**

When I walked into her room in the convalescent home, the frail woman in the bed said to me, "It is so good to see an old friend again. Please give me every scrap of news you have about our mutual friends."

As I began to think of things to tell her, I was aware that the reason this woman was holding onto her friends was because she was interested in hearing about them. Had a child received a nice promotion at the bank? Was there a new grandchild in the daughter's home across the country?

This friend was confined to her room but was always willing to rejoice in the happiness of others. Constantly she turned attention away from her own aches and pains to the concerns of others, always hoping for the best.

This was a part of her Christian philosophy and of the type of friendship Jesus described in John 15:14: "Ye are my friends, if ye do whatsoever I command you."

My friend was limited in what she could do physically, but she was unlimited in her loving concern for others and in the expression of her Christian faith.

I always left her room heartened and strengthened for my own daily living. She had shown me the joy and blessings of eternal friendship with Jesus when we follow his commands and love others.

SEPTEMBER 24 **THE BOOK**

My first visit to a public library came when I was in elementary school and a favorite teacher took me there. I still remember what she told me: "Books are friends and should be treated as such." She said that each book has its own personality and that I need never feel alone as long as I have books around me to read. How proud I felt, carrying home the library card she had cosigned. Later she gave me a book to keep in my own room.

Looking at my bookcases now, I realize some books have power to guide us over the rough spots of life by offering examples of courage or inspiring us to use our own talents to better advantage. Others offer escape from the monotony of life by describing travel experiences or introducing living characters in a novel. A self-help or how-to book serves the useful purpose of encouraging growth.

But it is to the Bible that I turn when the need is the greatest. Daily it offers wise counsel. We always have authentic help available when we open the Bible and ask God's guidance in taking the holy words into our lives.

Thus the promise is fulfilled from John 5:39: "Search the scriptures; for in them ye think ye have eternal life: and they are they which testify of me."

SEPTEMBER 25   **THE CROSS**

One of the ways to keep life interesting is to always have a list of possible projects or places to visit. My husband and I had on our list the beautiful Crystal Cathedral church in Garden Grove, California.

When the time came when we could drive there, we almost missed the church because we did not know the proper freeway off-ramp. It was getting close to church time when we stopped at a service station to ask a truck driver for directions.

"Of course I can tell you," he said. "All you have to do is to follow the cross. It shows me the way home when I am returning from a trip."

He told us how to get to a nearby street that in turn would

lead us to the cathedral, but he reminded us to keep our eyes on the large cross atop the building. Guided by his graphic directions, we located the church and had a wonderful morning.

The truck driver knew the way because he followed the cross, keeping it in his vision.

We remember his words whenever we become confused and bewildered in our faith. Our search for the cross and the church reminds us of the important words in Galatians 16:14: "But God forbid that I should glory, save in the cross of our Lord Jesus Christ, by whom the world is crucified unto me, and I unto the world."

SEPTEMBER 26   **SUNSHINE AHEAD**

Where I live, a sure sign of approaching fall is early morning fog that obscures the sun. Sometimes this change of season can produce feelings of dimness in the spirit as well, and a sense of sadness at the swift passage of time.

When fog swoops down over our house, my husband will occasionally say to me, "Let's go find some sunshine today." This calls for a trip to the desert, for where the freeway goes through a little pass between the hills, invariably there will be a patch of sunlight.

This seems the embodiment of the vivid Bible verse in Ecclesiastes 11: "Truly the light is sweet, and a pleasant thing it is for the eyes to behold the sun" (verse 7).

On one occasion, as we drove slowly through the fog, it seemed impossible that we would reach sunlight, but then at the hilltop pass the first rays came into our automobile.

With the sun came a lifting of our spirits from troubled thoughts about the sorrow in the home of one friend, the illness of another, and the business problems of a third.

All of us need to find the sunlight in our lives. There is power and strength in remembering that no matter what the current spiritual weather, there is sunshine ahead when we reach for the light.

SEPTEMBER 27   **GOD'S SKIES**

"Come quickly," called my husband from the yard, urging me to hurry outside. He pointed to the sky above our home. There, in perfect formation, was a flock of birds winging their way southward before the impending fall and winter.

How beautiful they looked, flying in a large vee behind their leader. We wondered how this lead bird had been chosen. What instinct had caused the birds to gather behind the leader, once selected?

In awe we watched the beautiful picture, as the honkers flew onward, determined to reach their chosen destination. In silence we recalled what the Bible says about the changing seasons: "To every thing there is a season, and a time to every purpose under the heaven" (Ecclesiastes 3:1).

Leaving the yard to return to my kitchen duties, I thought of the changes ahead in my own life due to the problems of an aging relative. There were changes for our church also, with a new pastor. And young friends were beginning a business. All of these outer circumstances were evidence of the increasing need for a true sense of direction in my life. How could I find this with the unerring instinct of the birds we had just watched?

Humbly I turned to God in prayer, thanking him for the companionship and leadership of his Son Jesus, my Savior.

SEPTEMBER 28   **SUNSET'S MOMENT**

On one recent September evening our hilltop was entirely surrounded by rare pink, red, and golden clouds. To the north the sky was mauve over the tops of the nearby hills. To the south the pink glow made the trees gray etchings against the clouds.

I stepped to the kitchen phone and dialed an artist friend to be sure she did not miss the spectacle. She said, "I'm sitting here by the window, looking out at the sunset as we speak and wondering how I could possibly find the right colors to paint it accurately."

As we spoke of the sunset's moment of beauty, my friend said that she had been reminded vividly of a lovely phrase from the book of Psalms: "Let the beauty of the Lord our God be upon us" (Psalm 90:17).

How glad I was that I had taken time to make the call and that I had glimpsed the sunset. Its beauty startled me into staring silently as the bright colors faded to deeper hues and finally into the blues and grays of the descending nightfall.

The sunset's glory had created a moment of thankful worship, leading to serenity of heart. I offered a silent prayer of gratitude to God for the beauty he has given to his world for his children to enjoy daily.

SEPTEMBER 29   **HARVESTS**

As this month draws to its close and the first bright autumn leaves appear, it is time for the harvesting of fruits. Former neighbors now live on an apple orchard in the nearby hills, and the mother telephoned to say, "Come on up for a visit and enjoy our crop."

We had been there in springtime when the limbs were pink and white with blossoms and looked like frilly parasols. Now, the trees bore apples beautiful with red, green, or golden skins, which we admired as we picked them from the heavily laden branches. The Bible mentions apples in a beautiful verse in Proverbs: "A word fitly spoken is like apples of gold in pictures of silver" (25:11).

There was something about the time in the orchard that was conducive to conversation and confidences. And how good it was to share companionship with family members later at home, while paring the apples for a pan of bubbling applesauce to go with the evening meal. Good talk made the meal memorable.

Harvests are joyful occasions, and none is more enduring than the harvest of good traits of integrity, which come from kind words. They lead to the exercise of patience, the discipline of service, and the fulfillment of duties in accord with the understood will of God.

SEPTEMBER 30   **PLANTINGS**

Each September I try to plant a few daffodil bulbs in our garden. One year a little boy watched me and asked, "Are you putting them in the ground to sleep?" Since then I had always thought of the brown bulbs as dreaming of springtime, when their golden blossoms will make the garden a place of beauty.

Friends know of my fondness for daffodils and sometimes there will be a new bulb of pale pink or pistachio-green flower given me as a birthday present during this month. When I can marvel at the new developments in flower creations.

If there are to be blossoms in the garden, the bulbs must be planted ahead of springtime. Now is the time to seize the minute and plant favorite bulbs. Even one bulb in a flower pot is better than none at all.

But on the knees in the garden is a good time to resolve to plant also the seeds of goodness in the heart. Then the blossoms of kindness, compassion, tenderness, and gentleness may come alive, sturdy and abundant, in months ahead.

God is gracious in blessing all such plantings of the spirit and heart, for Psalm 31:23 says, "O Love the Lord, all ye his saints: for the Lord preserveth the faithful and plentifully rewardeth the proud doer."

A Growing Heart to Feed

JEAN BEAVEN ABERNETHY

OCTOBER 1 **LIFT US UP**

What a cacophony of song, dance, and offerings to our God is this! Lord, take my commuting day—traffic, jostling elbows, and elevators; eight hours of office computers and telephone; then errands on the way home, supper, dishes, television, and tumble in . . . Dear Lord, take my dusty African-road day—one child by the hand, one strapped to my back, another on the way; a jerry-can on my head for the water I fetch three times a day; drought threatening, crops failing, firewood scarce . . . Take my long day of stroke and immobility, O God, lying here in this nursing home, in this old, bedridden body, tubes to help the feeding . . . Dear Jesus, take my refugee-camp day, here near the Thai border. I can't attend regular school because we're not citizens; can't leave camp for the guards and barbed wire; lost my father crossing the river; my mother and I arrived here under fire. Nationals around this camp resent our presence. We've tried to emigrate but there are no openings.

O God of all, who knows each of us regardless of geography or age, gender or skin color, and who thyself has known our human condition, take our dailinesses, for this is where and who we are—racing around from stress to stress, bending under the weight of poverty, sleeping with our painkillers, longing to flee our confines. Give us thy vision of why we are here and who we are. Lift us up so we do not remain prisoners of our circumstances—so we may indeed experience that "more" about ourselves even as we know we are that "more" in your sight. Amen.

OCTOBER 2 **TO COME POOR IN SPIRIT**

Buried deep in each of us is this longing for relatedness, for meaning. It is the most human thing about us. So we call out to our God from our multiple days. But we need to examine how much time we take for this call and whether it ends up more monologue than dialogue.

We take time, but often only in fits and starts. Or we may interpret taking time as going through certain forms. Then one day we meet up with another whose whole personality immediately bespeaks a quiet center and an inner authority, and we realize wistfully that there must be depths and heights we've not yet tapped. Or we take time, find answers, and then have an unexpected kind of crisis in which our answers do not hold up, so we come away puzzled and "on hold."

Diverted, discouraged, sometimes disillusioned, we tend to let go the inner search, whereas perhaps what we need to let go is our limited concept of it. God's invitation is not to perform certain rituals, solve problems, or ask for favors. It is to go into one's closet poor in spirit, and to be quiet and "know" Presence. And the promise is that when we do this, we will discover resources within and horizons beyond that we had not even dreamed existed.

The cry, ancient and modern, is "Oh, that I knew where I might find thee!"

And the answer, "Know ye not you yourself are the temple? You already have everything you need for search, for finding."

Who? Me?

Yes, thee.

OCTOBER 3   **THE BREATH OF LIFE**

Have we within ourselves all that we need for our spiritual journey? Then can we be specific?

First must surely be this real and crucial but also intangible and taken-for-granted sense of "I." Who, what, is this who continues to feel an "I" even though it is constantly changing? And even though the body in which the "I" lives is completely new every six years? This "I" (of amazing uniqueness, unrepeatable, never before anyone exactly like it and never again) causes me to ask questions. How is this possible, given the vastness of time and of numbers? This "I" causes me to ponder, for what does it mean? Causes me, ultimately and in the quiet, to move into awe and reverence before Mystery.

We are unique; there is also a remarkable rhythm at the center of each of us—the basic rhythm of the universe, which beats in our veins as well as with each breath we draw. How did we know, infant born, to draw on it and take our first breath? Consider all our breathing does for us, throughout our bodies—going on for us even as we sleep. The breath of life, to which at any moment we can return to listen for its wonderful message: Leave your hectic pace and slow down to mine; become aware of each life-giving "in and out, in and out," of the air around and all about.

Indeed, become aware and draw near to the Giver of gifts, so generous continuity amid change, uniqueness or midst vast numbers, the breath of life whose rhythm is always there to remind us amid hectic life.

OCTOBER 4   **CLOSER THAN BREATHING**

"God gave us memory," James Barrie says in his book *Courage,* "so we . . . might have roses in December." Not only roses but thorns, though, for memory is also what makes possible the finding and reliving / relieving of the painful, the still festering, which we have long since hidden even from ourselves. Blessed-distance-from and the fact that "time heals" are both on memory's side. We can, if we will, enter the great room called forgiveness to explore its various quiet corners—the one called "my forgiveness of others," the room called "my forgiveness of myself."

Imagination, like memory, also extends the present, but in different ways than does memory. Let someone say "Once upon a time" (whether in novel, television series, or movie), and we moderns still gather round very much as did our ancestors around their bards and wandering minstrels, who told and retold great myths and wonderful tales. Symbols and images, as well as stories, are the tools of imagination, turning notes into music, paint and canvas into pictures, feelings into dance. Imagination is the spirit that helps us create. It roams land, sky, and sea for ideas and comes up with wheels, planes, and scuba gear.

It is our imagination that is stirred by all the little calls to the little beyonds. It is also that part of us most receptive to the Big Call of the Beyond Beyonds, which though beyond the power of words to describe and even imagination to conceive, can be experienced in more intimate ways than any human relation, is felt to be closer than the breath, nearer than hands or feet.

OCTOBER 5   **THE MIRROR OF MEMORY**

This "I" also has many selves, the most intriguing of them all perhaps being the one that Arthur Dyckman calls the Observing Self, in his book of the same title. It's the self who stands back and listens in on our stream of consciousness, the everflowing conversation we hold within ourselves. In some interesting way, then, we aren't just all the commotion and chitter-chatter going on inside of us. We're more than that. It's like having in the bosom of the family a good secretary who takes careful notes on all that's going on and, not only that, who stands ready to make it all available whenever needed. Through memory (and sometimes with professional assistance), then, we have something to draw on if we find it necessary to "see" ourselves in a new way—to see ourselves as others see us, as God sees us.

There are times, too, when this "observing self," still with its observing, detached stance, puts down in a daily journal, in all honesty, the "noise" the various selves are making, in order to go back regularly and reread what has been recorded. It does this not to rehash, but rather to look for any persistent trends, especially toward more anxiety and defensiveness. If such is found, this may be the moment when the record can be experienced as a kind of invitation. Having "seen" ourselves in such broad strokes over a period of time and under our own private auspices, we may decide to face a particular reality we've been avoiding. We may also be ready to take the whole matter into the quiet time and let it "be" in God's presence.

OCTOBER 6   **THE GIFT OF HUMOR**

The observing self has, one might say, a junior partner to help in this matter of putting distance between us and our foibles so that we're able to "see" them rather than being completely identified with them. That's the part of us able to laugh at ourselves. We do it when the pandemonium inside us gets to be too ridiculous, too much ado about nothing, or when, all dressed up and impressed with ourselves, we look in the mirror just before leaving for the party and note some flaw—a strand of hair that still won't obey spray, earrings not matching. Or, driving to the party, we use an old shoe to deal with the accelerator better, only to forget to change it back before going in. True, it's easier to laugh at ourselves before the party than to get there and be laughed *at*. But if the commentary on how ridiculous we can be is a collective one—through cartoons, for instance—we usually enjoy a good laugh at our own expense and come away refreshed for the spoofing.

Animals can't laugh at themselves. Whence comes our sense of humor? It's a gift, a godsend, which, like the Ancient Mariner's sleep, is "beloved from pole to pole." Except that laughter, unlike sleep, doesn't "slide into our soul." It bursts out spontaneously and under its own steam, carrying us with it, which is often exactly what we need since we don't always seem able to get there on our own.

OCTOBER 7   **BEAUTY HERE?**

Could we take this distinctively human ability to observe and to laugh at ourselves and some of our other distinctive assets, such as memory, imagination, and a sense of continuity in change and uniqueness, and use them to enrich our spiritual journey?

The poet Edna St. Vincent Millay once said,

> Beauty where beauty never stood,
> And sweet where no sweet lies
> I gather to my querulous need,
> Having a glowing heart to feed.
> ("My Heart, Being Hungry")

Could that give us a clue, and if so, how? Growing hearts to feed we have, and needs too, some querulous and chronic, others more serious and immediate. But Beauty where it never stood? In the unlikely? The unlikeable? The not-like-me situations? How is Beauty to be found here? Is it not so much that Beauty is facing us as that it might someday be reflected in our faces, were we to take a hand in creating it?

Or again, is Beauty in the familiar, the ordinary, the daily? Maybe it's not so much that we haven't found Beauty in our every-days—because, of course, we have—as that there might be a good deal more of it were we to take time and find eyes to "see" much that we've overlooked as we've hurried on.

This month we'll be talking about some possible initiatives we might want to try and suggesting some ways to get new perspectives on our society, our personal relationships, our spiritual tradition, and nature.

OCTOBER 8 **ALPHA AND OMEGA AND THE WAY**

Beauty? New eyes with which to see the familiar and the unlikely? Then let's begin with the most daily familiarity of all: the rat race. We're a mobile society—mobile homes, moving vans, all on the move toward what? Progress? Comparing the everyday world of mobility in our society with the biblical view of movement may help us gain perspective and "see" what a state we are in. Men and women in the Bible are also on the move.

In the modern world mobility is a subject for research and doctoral dissertations, with demographic charts and chapters dividing mobility into "physical" and "social," and social mobility divided in turn into "upward" and "downward," each with several stages. All this so we can understand causes and effects, predict trends, see where the problems are, decide whether development schemes and investments are worth it.

Movement as conceived by the people we read about in the Bible has a different outlook and vocabulary. God, the Author of all movement, is verb, noun, participle, and beyond grammar—Alpha and Omega as well as the Way. Here there are no charts and predictions, no markets to be watched for or cultivated. Rather, before time began, the spirit of God moved upon the face of the waters to bring order out of chaos. It was God, not some technological marvel, who breathed into this inert, motionless lump of clay, who gave this clay a name, a mind, an imagination and set it free to move across land, sea, and sky. Set it free for another kind of search too: "Ye shall know the Truth and the Truth will make you free" (John 8:32).

OCTOBER 9   **DON'T FORGET TO WONDER**

Who are the actors in modern mobility? Car-poolers, big business, tourists, the military, diplomats, and Number One. In the Bible they are pilgrims on a journey, the people of the Way, wanderers on the face of the earth. The equipment for movement also differs. Moderns have pills for jet lag, driver's licenses, credit cards, and contacts for contracts. In contrast, equipment in the Bible is of an intangible nature: faith in promises and potentials.

In modern mobility the unwritten assumption is that human progress is up to us alone—collectively, institutionally, but especially individually because, in this cutthroat setup, if I don't "get there" no one's going to do it for me. But perceiving all movement as being created by God means we're not free to exercise mobility in whatever manner dictated by the current scene. This does not mean we're not responsible for our movements, but the way we carry that responsibility has a different feel to it. There's a vast, dynamic movement of which we are integral parts; the ultimate lies in God's hands. The Christian even feels, at times, a kind of holy disregard (not flippancy) about geography and the details of time. Said Anne Hutchinson in Theda Kenyon's *Scarlett Anne,* when facing exile from the Bay Colony for her stand on freedom of conscience, "I know Who leads; it cannot matter where." And Henri Amiel's words, "From every point on this round earth, we are equally near to heaven" *(Amiel's Journal).*

OCTOBER 10   **IN BUT NOT OF**

We face a dilemma. We live in a mobile society; there is no escaping it. Moreover, we all make plenty of ego trips in our mobility, being the humans we are. But the Bible is also integral to Western culture and still, for all the competition, a best seller, so it is present in our thinking whether we take it, or deny it, as a reference point. Sometimes the tension between the modern and the biblical perspectives (if we decide to take both seriously) gets beyond our coping or puts us on an unproductive guilt-trip, or we find ourselves too busy to care.

But the Bible is a book of good news. Those who wrote it were no Pollyannas, unrealistic and naïve. It is full of people who deceived, stole, and committed adultery; who betrayed, denied, and gossiped even as moderns do; who for all their distance from us in time and culture still shared with us the task of surviving under threatening conditions. They struggled, we struggle, with the recurring human questions "Who? Where? How? Why me in all this?" Yet they were also people whose record is about a radical breaking through into their lives of a call, a promise, a Presence, and a sense of forgiveness and newness.

The Bible is full of rich imagery describing how the tension between being "in" but not completely "of this world" can become a creative one—how we can find growth in all our comings and goings, no matter what the time and place.

OCTOBER 11   **PLACE**

Let's begin our thinking about the creative relevance of the biblical perspective for our mobility by using the idea of "place" as the pivot point for all our comings and goings. Because we all need a place; if not a house with some grass, then at least a room of our own. Or, if things are crowded and we need to share that room, then at least a corner in it somewhere, so no one will mess the papers on our desks when we have to leave. Or, if not that, then, as one woman told her psychiatrist, "At least my bed is where I can be private enough to cry and dream."

Even Abraham, called by God to become sojourner and stranger in the land of the Hittites, needed a place, a plot of ground on which to bury his wife. Even Abraham? Even God! Though universal and nonlocalized, when God entered history, a place was needed: a manger, a hillside, a cave with a stone rolled in front.

No matter how much we all need place, though, we cannot stay in the same one all the time. And in the final analysis, we cannot take a place with us. So we come-back-to and go-away-from, with place, though crucial, pretty much as background.

OCTOBER 12 **THE OLD AND THE NEW**

Wonderful things can happen when we come-back-to and go-away-from. When we come-back-to, there's the comfort of the familiar. Tired at night, we return home, find the light switch in the dark, gravitate to our favorite chair, and sink down into it. There's the feel of the good fit. We belong.

More than familiarity, coming-back-to gives a sense of connectedness with what has gone before. Actually, it's easier to enter "Once upon a place" than "Once upon a time." The latter requires an exercise of the mind. To return to place, however, gives us something immediate, tangible, visible. We can reach out and touch the "it happened here" spots. Perhaps that is why pilgrims like to visit the Holy Land. Even though changed, as we walk around that ancient land we nevertheless know this is the place he walked, the river in which he stood, the olive grove in which he prayed. Somehow we feel closer.

The Bible is full of scenes of welcoming and invitations to come-back-to and rest: a robe for the prodigal, green pastures for lying down, a table spread, and the house of the Lord, a forever place.

Wonderful things can also happen when we go-away-from. For one thing, all is new, so we're free to try again without the millstone of "they knew us when" around our necks. We may even find we're talking to ourselves in a new way too, trying on for size "Maybe I just can, after all," as we take another look at old habits, begin to stretch tired muscles into fresh-start positions.

OCTOBER 13 **NEVER ALONE**

But what about those times *after* we've left and before we've arrived—the in-between times? No man's land. No woman's land, either. In any case, it's not a place. That's the whole point. It's the feeling of no place. So we panic.

Swinging from trapezes must offer this same giddy experience of inbetweenness. The art of letting go, however, involves more than disciplining muscles. It involves an attitude of mind *and* the feel of trust in our guts—the *whole* of us moving forward in faith and assent. Rites of passage in the human life cycle symbolize the need to let go of one stage of life in order to graduate into the next. But the passage is never neat and tidy, and for many of us there's pick-up work to do throughout life. Nevertheless, to the extent we can learn to live gracefully our in-between moments (or years), the more we're apt to feel in tune with some far-off rhythm at the heart of life.

Surely the time between Good Friday and Easter, for those who went through it, must have been one of the bleakest in-between experiences in history. Later, the two on the road to Emmaus were to walk another in-between: between total loss of hope and their experience around the table in the inn. Even our Lord himself was caught between earth and heaven, asking his agonized "Why?"

In-betweens are one of life's most poignant experiences. The good news of the Bible, however, is that we are never alone in our in-betweens. Jesus drew near and joined them on-the-way and draws near and joins us too.

OCTOBER 14 **A STORY TO GO BY**

Risk is also integral to the mobility and rapid change we know in our society. Risk is felt during that time when we are still safe, still only *facing* the moment of swinging on the trapeze, not out in the middle, halfway there.

In Martin Buber's collection of Hasidic tales from nineteenth-century Poland is the story of a woman who complained to her rabbi that she'd been married twelve years and had no son. "What are you willing to do about it?" he asked. She did not know. So the rabbi told the woman this story: "My mother was also aging and still had no child. When she heard that the traveling Baalshem was in town, she went and told him. 'What are you willing to do about it?' he asked. My mother answered, 'We are poor, but I do have a beautiful cape. I'll fetch it for you.' When she returned, however, the Baalshem was gone, so she had to walk many more miles. When she found the Baalshem, he took the cape, saying, 'It is well.' Then my mother walked the long way home. A year later I, her son, was born."

"Oh," cried the woman, "I, too. I'll fetch a cape for you so I may have a son like your mother."

"That won't work," replied the rabbi. "You've heard the story. My mother had no story to go by."

Christians do have a story to go by, but it is not a script to repeat by heart. Rather, it's one to be taken *to* heart by each of us and allowed to grow. Jesus did not teach formulas to be followed slavishly. He came not to make us "never-dares" but to show us the truth that alone can make us free.

OCTOBER 15   **LET US CELEBRATE**

Let us celebrate, then, our faith as a many splendored thing that can help us live creatively in a society of rat-race mobility. A faith that meets our strong need for roots and continuity, giving us a sense of place to come back to and offering us the thread of God's love to hold together the scattered pieces of our days. A sending-us-forth kind of faith, too, calling us to go out from a place whenever we begin to think our task is now mainly maintenance of whatever has been achieved so far, with no further need to stretch, discover, grow.

And let us celebrate the Divine Mystery, beyond space and time yet present tense and creating anew now. Beyond, too, our ability to put into words, seen only through a glass darkly, yet intimately known in the tested experience of human beings across the centuries.

"The Lord shall preserve thy going out and thy coming in from this time forth and even for evermore" (Psalm 121:8).

OCTOBER 16 **THE REAL ME**

Comings and goings? Yes. Yet for all this seeing of each other, how often we remain strangers—across our borders, in our housing complexes, even, at times, in our living rooms. In what specific ways, then, can this I-Thou dimension, which gives a sense of companionship to our lives, help us improve our you-me relations, especially when "you" is strange or a stranger? That depends in large measure on who we believe we are—not our *professed* belief but one rooted in the deepest feelings we have about ourselves.

The sociologist George Mead developed a theory about who we are, based on empirical evidence. He speaks of "the social self." The theory says that we take our sense of identity from the functions and roles taught us by "significant others" in the growing up process. That is why it is so difficult to say definitively and at any one point who the real me is, since I can be anyone of a number of roles—hurried shopper, tired parent, vocal baseball fan, traffic violator, weekender, white liar . . .

One more thing. The more I see you exclusively in terms of the functions and roles you perform (put crudely, your usefulness), the more I relativize you, make you replaceable. Why? Because anyone else can do as well, especially if you fail my expectations, get sick, grow old. There is something costly about one's identity being dependent on human beings who forget, move away, change their minds, and in any case die.

OCTOBER 17   **ONE BY ONE**

Mead's theory of human identity is obviously different from the Bible's. There, reality has a third dimension to it. It is God saying your identity and worth are greater than humans esteem them, whether humans in institutions or those "significant others" nearest and dearest to you. In the Bible God confronts human beings with a choice about their identities, except that God never "speaks" to aggregates—families, groups, societies—only to persons, one by one. Each of us, in our personhood (unrepeatable, irreplaceable, nonexchangeable), is asked to make an existential choice. The invitation is "I have called you by your name, you are mine" (Isaiah 43:1 RSV). You are free to choose. Who do *you* say you are?

It is also God saying to each human being, "The worth of *another* human being must be seen by you as it is seen by me, and that worth is infinite."

All this extends the height, depth, and breadth of reality for me. It makes me make room for concepts and definitions beyond my current ones. Now there are *real* depths in you not yet faced by me, real resources shared between us but not yet tapped. Even more challenging and difficult, I do not have to wait until you see Reality in this way in order for me to trust and act on it out of my own sense of commitment.

The truth of our identity from God is, of course, not available to us through empirical analysis. We can only affirm it (or, for that matter, deny it) in faith. But if affirmed, it too can be costly. History is full of that cost, especially when God's recognition has brought human beings into conflict with the recognition societies give.

OCTOBER 18   **ANOTHER LOOK**

There's something heartwarming about feeling oneself at the other end of a divine imperative like *agape*, which is defined as the creative cause that enables us to love ourselves and others. It is God, knowing all there is to know about us, including those unacceptable parts we've been hiding even from ourselves, yet affirming us nonetheless.

Experiencing the reality of *agape* love, however, is both costly and difficult. Paul Tillich says accepting our acceptance is the *most* difficult thing in the world. For if God is not estranged from me, knowing all there is to know, then I no longer have reason to be estranged from those repressed / avoided parts of myself. And as I respond, slowly and painfully, allowing those parts in me to "be" in God's presence, it may just be that I can also look in a new way at the stranger I've never liked—never liked because, possibly, the stranger has those very qualities I've never liked about myself? Or because the stranger has reminded me of unfinished business in myself?

OCTOBER 19   **WALKING IN ANOTHER'S SHOES**

Choosing to add a third dimension to our sense of identity is never a once and for all commitment, because we frequently lose sight of it. But it can often give us a readiness to experiment with ideas in our relationships that we've only theorized about before.

Take the Native American saying, "Never judge someone before you take off your moccasins and walk in his." Sometimes it takes a lapse of years for us to really be able to do this—like having to be parents of teenagers ourselves to fully appreciate what our parents went through with us. Sometimes it just takes plain courage. A couple goes to a marriage counselor, each primed to pour out his or her side to a listening ear. The therapist says to the wife, "Would you be willing to try something? If you were your husband, what do you think *he'd* be telling me about *you?*" Then the therapist says to the husband, "You're next."

The Yellow Wind is a powerful book written by David

Grossman, a young Israeli who, before the recent violence, went into Palestinian villages asking, in effect, "Tell me what it feels like to be you" and then recording what he heard. He went because, he said, he'd been bypassing the problem and felt he had to know.

Walking in another's shoes does not necessarily mean we end up agreeing with or excusing the other. It is not appeasement. But it has the potential of changing the dynamics, the atmosphere. It requires, however, discipline and, above all, faith, because it can be costly. God, who came to where we are and walked in human sandals on dusty roads, knows how costly it can be.

OCTOBER 20 **A CHALLENGE**

Challenging our own stereotypes may be another way not only to help us understand "strangers" better but also to learn how much they have to teach us.

Join my husband and me as we teach in an African school where they had never had Europeans before. We go for walks roundabout the school's mud huts, which have no windows, electricity, telephones, stoves, or refrigerators. There are no cars. Though we're called the teachers in school, this walk is *our* classroom, and we're learning plenty—for instance, that it's possible even in backbreaking poverty to enjoy life. No one lectures on the subject of joyousness. People just *are* joyous. We also discover that Europeans are called "those who suffer from hurry sickness" and "Mr. No-smile-when-you-meet." Yet the moment we smile, the welcome begins. "Come into our hut." We do. With sign language we "chat" and share what's cooking in the pot.

On another year in the Rift Valley, we make regular visits to twenty small churches and again experience that special quality. In spite of drought and dust, the people walk long distances to worship, dance, and celebrate together, carrying firewood, water, and food, leading the blind and the old.

Even when we helped in the Quaker Biafran Relief Program back in 1968, where war and famine, far more serious than drought, were everywhere, we still found that same capacity for joy. Long lines of thin mothers and children with swollen bellies, waiting for their food rations, still clapped, swayed, sang and laughed. All this is very different from the lines in our supermarkets where, bored and impatient, people wait for their food to be checked out.

Who is "rich"? Who "poor"?

OCTOBER 21   **BIG QUESTIONS**

What is it we are saying? Joie de vivre, mutual aid, generosity, and hospitality in poverty, drought, famine, and war? How does one who does not know poverty and has something of a stereotype of it respond? Of course one is interested in developments challenging poverty. They are crucial. But when you meet individuals who are trapped in it yet who don't let "poor" be the last word about who they are, it makes you want to learn their secret.

We might begin by asking ourselves some questions. How can we "rich" Westerners really help the "poor" in Africa until we can genuinely receive from them as well. And what is it they have to give us, whose premises are pretty much that possessions solve human problems and are the key to happiness? Perhaps they need to strip us of our illusion that we permanently possess our possessions; they see life as a fleeting reality to be entered into in joy but never taken for granted.

"Rural Africans who live out under the sky," said President Kenneth Kaunda of Zambia once, "have a spiritual dimension to their lives that makes them ask the Big Questions." Possibly they know the limits of the human condition more directly than do we, who live our days amid the products of technology. Do we perhaps need to "look up" by sitting quietly and looking inward? Big Questions are not only framed by geography.

OCTOBER 22 **PRECIOUS AND FLEETING**

Insulated as we may be by our technology from living out under the sky and pondering nature, there are moments, are there not, when our tendency to take life for granted is stripped away, and we too stand exposed to the Big Questions? At those times we are like the lad in Chaim Potok's book *My Name Is Asher Lev,* who didn't want to look at the dead bird he'd just come across, nor hear his father's explanation: "Everything that lives must die, Asher. . . . That's the way Ribbono Shel Olom made His world."

"Why?" asked Asher.

"So life would be precious, Asher. Something that is yours forever is never precious."

Once people really find each other on the common ground of our human condition, namely, that our days are mortal (and therefore, by that same token, precious), something amazing can happen. A kind of detribalization occurs, whether we are Masai, Kikuyu, or American middle class. Or put another way, the dynamic of our relations with others becomes one of *mutual* aid.

Of course, America is " rich" and Africa is "poor," and we need to help out of our abundance. But perhaps our greatest gift would be to offer Africans the chance to help us by bringing us into creative contact with our own poverty—the inner impoverishment we all know in our personal lives, as we hurry about, taking no time to smile at each other or to ponder under the sky.

OCTOBER 23 **ABOUT LONELINESS**

Walking in each others' shoes and challenging our stereotypes are two possible ways to help us move from estrangement to some kind of genuine sense of relationship. But what about loneliness? This is not a matter of getting along with others but of getting along with a stubborn reality about ourselves—the inevitable fact of our separateness, our aloneness. And if I can't openly and fully deal with this "inevitable," then my relationships with others may well be manipulated to help me avoid this reality.

Is loneliness inevitable? It has always been, of course, but surely it is exacerbated today by the impersonality of modern life, with its canned voices, ID cards, and lonely crowds. We cannot give our aloneness away, nor can any human being relieve us of it. Yet here is something interesting. One of the most outstanding things we human beings have *in common* is our *separateness*.

If we take seriously the dimension God gives to our lives, then we must see both our loneliness/separateness and what we have together in common not as unwelcome givens but as gifts. Is there a clue in this that neither loneliness nor togetherness has the last word about who we are? Each has something to give us for our growth; each is different yet not antagonistic. The images of mutual loneliness and togetherness in solitude can help us to respect and love the reality of each. As does Rilke's definition, for example, of a good marriage, which he said was "not a tearing down of boundaries" but each appointing the other guardian of his or her solitude.

OCTOBER 24   **CREATIVE SOLITUDE**

To read a book about prison experiences helps us realize how some Christians have had the capacity to deal with stark loneliness in yet another way—by turning it into creative solitude.

Here, for example, is a POW in Vietnam in solitary confinement. Cut off from all human companionship, he yet draws on it through memory and imagination—picturing and following family and friends back home, though he is not allowed mail; recalling heroes and martyrs in his spiritual tradition who have also endured suffering; remembering daily in his prayers the men in the cells around him.

If one reads the testimonies of those who have been able to turn loneliness into creative solitude, however, we know that this capacity comes, above all, from experiencing the presence of One who himself knew loneliness in all its nuances—One who was alone in a garden while others slept, alone in a trial while a trusted follower denied, alone on a cross, in agony yet still able to reach out to the two on either side and identify with their loneliness.

Christ never spared himself, nor does he spare us. "Do not cling," now that you know my risen Presence. "Pick up your bed and walk," now that you are healed. "I am your Companion on the way, but you too must walk with me as I with you." "For God hath not given us a spirit of fear; but of power and of love and of a sound mind" (II Timothy 1:7).

OCTOBER 25   **NEW EYES**

We need new eyes to see our mobility, our relationships, and our aloneness, yes. What about new eyes also for seeing afresh aspects of our spiritual tradition? How often our Christian heritage—for many of us internalized since childhood—becomes habit, its rituals rote. This can easily happen to prayer.

Marvin Hiles writes in *Jacob's Letter* (Spring 1988) that from his childhood he'd inherited the idea that when the minister announced, "Let us pray," this meant "We are now going to try very hard to *do* something" (*Jacob's Letter* no. 4). He writes it has taken him many adult years to move from this "aggressive, hard-work kind of prayer" to prayer as "response" as he tries to maintain a posture of attentiveness and waiting on the Lord.

Alan Paton also hints at what can happen when we let go

of habitual words and forms as the primary feature of prayer and discover something, out of its own authority, arising spontaneously and from deep within us. He was writing years later about how he'd handled his grief after his wife died. He'd done what he was supposed to do in praying to God and putting his grief away, only to have it suddenly return. "But now," he writes, "it will not return again. Something within me is waking. I am full of thanks for life. I have not told myself to be thankful—I just am so" *(For You, Departed—A Memoir)*.

OCTOBER 26   **THE IMPORTANCE OF RITUAL**

Gratitude and grief, joy and loneliness—we know them all. And there are, of course, wonderful liturgies for such times, which our spiritual tradition encourages us to follow. It is good this is so.

But if we find our minds continually wandering or our hearts too often elsewhere as we go through some of the familiar motions, it may be helpful to try a fresh approach. We can create our own rituals to enhance those moments when we *are* fully attentive and our hearts *are* in it.

The quiet time for meditation offers us an opportunity to explore just such new rituals, to sit in the darkness, for example, and recall a dark ordeal we've been through and conquered and then light a candle, or to ask ourselves what were our "green pasture moments" during this day and then compose our own psalms, with images of dance and cymbals, as we bring offerings to an altar of our own making, or to chant our own chant and beat our own drum for the slow, pounding heaviness within us when grief overwhelms us.

Ritual is often thought of as a once-and-for-all, a given from the past. It can, however, be a new and creative venture as well.

OCTOBER 27   **INTO ALL THE WORLD**

New eyes, too, for the way we may be conceptualizing our spiritual tradition. We are witnessing in this century a transition from a predominantly Western church to a worldwide church of enormous variety and vitality. For example, African Christianity is currently the fastest growing sector of Christianity, and this is occurring mostly under African leadership. Trends are similar in Asia and South America. Scholars predict that by the year 2000 the church will have shifted its center of gravity to the Third World.

Here is Koyama, a Japanese theologian working in Thailand and writing a book entitled *Water Buffalo Theology*. Here is Masao Takenaka, collecting works of Asian artists on what the Bible means to Christians in the context of Asian suffering and hope. Open its pages, and one finds a dark Madonna on an Indian batik, a representation of Pentecost in a Japanese flower arrangement. Or stand before the Murang'a Cathedral murals, painted by the East African artist Elimo Njau, and see, for instance, the story of Christ's life against the background of Kenya's suffering in achieving independence.

For those of us brought up on Christmas cards of Italianate Madonnas and Easter cards of the Crucifixion in the Flemish style, it is an important and stretching experience to see Njau's portrayal of the Last Supper, in which the participants leave African walking sticks at the door and the wine is served in calabashes rather than the goblets of medieval Europe.

Today the Incarnation is being heard, experienced, and expressed by all God's children in new and exciting ways, and our image of our spiritual tradition needs to keep up with this fact.

OCTOBER 28   **WATER**

And lastly, what about new eyes with which to see the world of nature in which we live?

Our earliest, most primal memories are of water in the mother's womb. Then we are born, bathed, given water to drink, and the lifelong thirst in us begins.

We bathe our bodies, wash our garments, irrigate our fields. Water rains down on the just and the unjust, splashes in puddles to our children's delight, carries our ships. We watch fearfully as it whirlpools, floods, sucks up in undertow. We read about its absence in drought and are moved to compassion. We revel in its beauty, swim in its cool, stand on the seashore fascinated by the spectacle of water become waves.

Water can just "be there," channeled and stored to come out of our faucets or harnessed for our energy—taken for granted as long as it functions usefully, a nuisance when it interrupts our picnics, a problem when its scarcity threatens our way of life.

Do we really "see" water? Do we care enough to learn how to preserve it? Care enough to share it?

OCTOBER 29   **FUNCTION OR GIFT?**

The most ordinary of happenings. We buy some potatoes, come home and dump them in the sink to wash off the dirt. Dirt. Look at it before washing it away, because it can't tell us all it does for us; we're the ones who're going to have to stop, look, and listen if we're going to hear.

Not only do we wash it away as soon as it "dirties" us, we add insult to injury: "He treated me like the dirt beneath his feet." Yet take a chunk of potato with an eye in it and put it in that same "dirt beneath his feet" and see what happens.

Take a new look at dirt? At water? Yes. Yet for all their power and potential, where would they be without the sky overhead—warmth and light from above, the air around, wind to carry the seeds?

If our identity is a question for each of us to answer—Am I valued for my usefulness only or am I also valued as a person in my own unique right—why cannot we ask the same question about earth, sky, and sea? Do they exist only to be useful to us? Or are they gifts from the Creator and therefore possessed of intrinsic value that we need to remember, respect, revere?

OCTOBER 30   **HOMESICKNESS**

The world in which we live is not only *our* home but the home of our *faith* as well. On its mountain tops, in its valleys, wildernesses, and baptismal waters, our spiritual tradition was born and nourished. Earth, sky, and sea gave it its first great images, questions, and answers. "As the hart panteth after the water brooks, so panteth my soul after thee" (Psalm 42:1). When I consider the heavens, who am I that Thou art mindful of me? (Psalm 8:3). Let the dry land appear, and let it bring forth. . . . (Genesis 1:9). And it came to pass, God walked in a garden and called out, and the first man and the first woman heard the Voice and answered.

The world *our* home and *also* home to our spiritual tradition? Yet there's still this haunting sense of homesickness in all of us that will not go away. What is it, and where does it come from? Could we not speak of it as a longing for wholeness—for a city whose builder and maker is, ultimately, God?

"Blessed are the homesick" does not come from the Bible but from the pages of Carl Jung. But it is biblical nonetheless. We could paraphrase it to read, "Let there be no place I may go on this round sphere where I'll not feel I'm known and belong." And if this is homesickness in the ultimate sense for me, can it not also be for all God's children? Each of us, therefore, has a part to play in making others feel they are known and belong in this highly mobile world we all call home for a while.

OCTOBER 31 **THE HEART GROWS**

I rise after a night's sleep and begin by looking out the window for sign of day. I turn on the tap and water comes. I walk or drive over the ground that furnishes us with life-giving crops and fuel, as once more I move into my fast-paced day, rubbing elbows with all kinds of people.

Do I remember, as companions on the way, the commuter next door? The poor and starving I see on television? The shut-in elderly I hear about? Refugees and the homeless here and abroad? Walking in one another's shoes? Challenging our stereotypes? Loneliness in a crowd? Creative solitude? My own resources for exploring anew? New eyes for seeing my spiritual tradition in my surroundings—in the coins I use, the history books in my libraries, art and music, and, it may be, internalized in me in ways I may not even recognize?

Find that quiet corner. Discover your own call to worship. Find your own best posture to use to maintain awareness. Then keep the tryst, wonder, ponder, praise, and wait, learning to "be" in the Presence.

Presence? Alpha and Omega, crowned with gem and diadem, beyond human words to define or human minds to describe, who yet came to us in manger straw, "a small and little thing."

With Gratitude

ALICE JOYCE DAVIDSON

NOVEMBER 1   **MEDITATING**

When daily pressures build inside,
To put my mind at ease,
I close my eyes and meditate
On blessings such as these.
I picture nature's wonders,
And all my favorite places,
I think about my loved ones,
Happy times and smiling faces.
I let my mind go wandering,
Then softly as a breeze
My pressures seem to lessen,
And I feel much more at ease.

Dear God, thank you for quiet moments and blessed memories.

NOVEMBER 2   **CLOTHED IN BEAUTY**

Clothe me, Lord, in beauty—
   not in silks, brocades, or lace;
      but clothe me in the happy glow
         of golden deeds I've done!

Robe me, Lord, in splendor—
   not in velvet trimmed with mink;
      but robe me, Lord, in joy that comes
         with causes I have won!

Crown me, Lord, in riches—
   not encrusted in fine jewels;
      but crown me with eternity
         when life on earth is done!

Dear God, thank you for your guidance. Help me become a better person, starting with today.

NOVEMBER 3   **THE GIFT OF FRIENDSHIP**

What good fortune it is to have a dear friend
To share with, to care with and treasure,
Someone who's there for your happiest times
And whose presence helps double the pleasure.

What a comfort it is to have a dear friend
Who's there to help shoulder a load
When your burdens and troubles are heavy,
Or you're lost on a bend in life's road.

What a blessing it is to have a dear friend
To scheme with, to dream with and love—
Of all of life's treasure a friend truly is
A gift from our Father above!

Dear God, thank you for the friendships that round out my life.

NOVEMBER 4   **WALKING WITH GOD**

Keep me on the straight and narrow.
Hold me back when I would stray
Down a pleasure path or roadway
That brings selfish joys my way.

Keep me, too, from winding trails
Of prejudice and spite,
Maliciousness, and bitterness,
Which cloud your holy light.

Nerve my will against temptations,
So wherever I may be,
I will walk the straight and narrow
Staying close, dear God, to thee!

Thank you, Lord, for showing me what paths to take, what diversions to avoid.

NOVEMBER 5   **A PRAYER FOR TOMORROW**

Be with me, Lord, tomorrow.
Help me keep my courage high.
Let me see the silver linings
In the clouds that fill my sky.

Be with me, Lord, tomorrow.
Give me confidence and calm.
Let my trust become a stepping-stone,
My faith become a balm.

Even though my heart is aching and my hands are trembling, I feel you near. Thank you, Lord, for being close.

NOVEMBER 6 **SILVER LININGS**

Have you ever watched a rainstorm
When dark clouds dim your view,
Then suddenly a burst of sun
Makes silver rays come through?

We all have had our dreary days
When troubles pour . . . and then
Our faith bursts through like sunshine
and hope grows bright again!

Dear Lord, thank you for seeing me through the cloudy
days and bringing sunshine to my heart.

NOVEMBER 7 **WORTHY GOAL**

The richest man is one who lays
A storehouse of kind deeds;
His spoils are rewarding days
From filling other's needs.

The greatest man is one who knows
Not glory or applause,
But quietly his effort goes
To help a worthy cause.

The richest and the greatest man
Is one who has a goal
Of doing all the good he can
With all his heart and soul!

Thank you, God, for giving me a husband with such a rich
and noble heart.

GLOW

As we've gone together
Down life's long and winding road,
We've met all kinds of weather,
And we've shared each other's load.

The sparkling love we started with
Has turned into a glow
That warms our family and our friends
And everyone we know.

For each day we're together,
We thank the Lord above
For the beauty of our marriage
And our life that glows with love!

I'm grateful, dear Lord, for so many years of sharing, of caring, of love.

FINDING MYSELF

Save me, Lord, from wallowing
In too much self-concern,
From finding fault with petty things
Everywhere I turn.

Let me see beyond myself
And comforts that surround me,
Open up my vistas
To the big world all around me.

The world is filled with people
With hardships to endure—
The handicapped, the aged,
The hungry, and the poor.

Let me lose myself in service,
In a cause or worthy deed.
Let me reach a little farther, Lord,
To fill somebody's need.

For only when I've gone beyond
The little world I know,
Will I begin to find myself—
Will I begin to grow!

Dear God, thank you for the opportunity to grow. Be with me and guide me today.

FAITH

Through times filled with uncertainty
When thickest fog envelops me,
Something keeps me going.

Through days that dawn and end with dread
When every burden's made of lead,
Something keeps me going.

Through times when I've so much to bear
I'm almost drowning in despair,
I look within and find faith there—
It's faith that keeps me going.

Thank you, dear God, for planting faith in my heart.

QUEST FOR PEACE

Why must there be war?
Why must there be hate?
What is this beastly, evil thing
within the heart of man
that makes him lust for greatness
and prove his country's best,
and then use blood and battlegrounds
as the arena for his test?

Just like Cain and Abel,
through every generation
mankind keeps competing,
and brothers slay each other
to make a mighty nation,
and history keeps repeating on and on and on.

Dear God, why must there be wars?
Why must there be hate?
Please help us find the answer
before it is too late!

Dear Lord, thank you for hearing my supplication. Make
me a channel, an instrument of peace.

NOVEMBER 12   **CHANGE OF MOOD**

We are our own worst enemy
When troubles or bad news
Affect our moods and bring about
Depression and the blues.
But before you're down and under,
Before the blues have won,
Think how much you're needed
And the work that should be done.
Concern yourself with others,
Get a helpful attitude,
And once you're set in motion
You'll have a change of mood!

I'm grateful, Lord, for being needed, for being loved—for
your help in the ups-and-downs of my life.

NOVEMBER 13   **OLD MOLLY**

Sitting in a corner
   rocking to and fro,
Her skin has lost its luster,
   her eyes their eager glow.

Alone, alone, all alone,
   not needed any more,
Back and forth she rocks and rocks,
   staring at the floor.

Unwanted and not needed,
   she waits for death to call,
And when she goes, she won't be missed
   by anyone at all!

Dear God, thank you for opening my eyes when I visited
the nursing home. Let me remember to open my heart and
give a poor lonely old lady a hug the next time I visit there.

NOVEMBER 14 **WHO INVENTED LOVE**

Dear God,
it's unbelievable!
I just met an unbeliever
who believes in unbelief!
SCIENCE IS THE ANSWER!
But can science tell us
where the energy came from
to make the atom,
to make the stars,
to call all life to being?
Where did the soul,
the mind, come from,
and miracles beyond
all seeing?
Who planned the rhythm
of the earth,
the tides,
the moon above?
Who gave us seasons
of our lives,
and who invented
    LOVE?

Thank you, Lord, for always being there for me. I know you will be there when you're needed by believers and unbelievers alike.

NOVEMBER 15   **GOD IS REAL**

This I believe: There is a God
Who rules the sky, the sea, and sod,
Who made the mountain and the plain,
And brings both sunshine and the rain.
Even on the darkest night
I have felt his holy light.
His goodness and his gifts surround me.
He lives within me and all around me.
Yes, I believe that God is real,
As real as all his love I feel!

Thank you, Dear God, for being part of my life, my heart,
and my soul.

NOVEMBER 16   **QUEST**

I search within myself and ask
What am I doing here on earth?
What is my designated task,
Some way in which to prove my worth?

Is life a dream that fades away,
A dream for which I've no control?
Or do I dare to live each day?
Can I afford to pay the toll?

I search still deeper, and I find
It matters not which paths I take,
Which purpose that I have in mind,
Or contribution that I make.

I do not seek to make a name
To satisfy my inner quest—
I'll trade the shallowness of fame
For knowing that I've done my best!

Thank you, Lord, for challenges, and the energy and zeal
to meet them.

WELCOME VISITOR

Contentment came to visit me.
She didn't stay too long,
For I began to pout about
Some things that had gone wrong.
I courted her with promises.
She came to call once more,
But when Impatience greeted her,
She stopped outside the door.

I'm trying to be more at peace,
To learn to love myself,
To put my cares and worries
And my troubles on the shelf,
So when Contentment comes again,
And sees my happy smile,
She'll feel so welcome in my heart
She'll stay a nice long while!

Thank you, God, for all your blessings. May I remember to
count them all today!

NOVEMBER 18 **YESTERDAY AND TOMORROW**

We can't relive
our yesterdays
for they are gone,
forever gone,
and life moves on . . .
and we move on.

We cannot live
tomorrow's days,
which may or may not hold
our plans, our schemes,
our precious dreams,
waiting to unfold.

We can only live
our life-span
day by day by day,
growing stronger . . . wiser . . . better
from whatever
comes our way!

Dear Lord, thank you for this new day. May I live it to the fullest.

NOVEMBER 19   **THE BLESSING OF LOVE**

What is love?
It's a blessing from our Father;
It's a seed within our soul;
It's the substance of our being;
It's the thing that makes us whole.

It's a gift we get from giving;
It's a wonderful reward
From following the pathway
And examples of our Lord!

Thank you, Lord, for your awesome gift of love!

NOVEMBER 20   **THE FAITH OF A CHILD**

Children's faith is wonderful
For in each tender heart
Is nothing but pure innocence
Where true love has its start.

Nothing is impossible,
For all their hopes and dreams
Are real to them the moment
They're imagined—so it seems.

Children's faith is beautiful,
And with it they may go
Down the paths that lead to God,
Who loves his children so!

Thank you, Lord, for my beautiful pair of blessings!

NOVEMBER 21   **ANOTHER CROSSROAD**

I want to learn and broaden
from this opportunity.
I want the chance to grow . . . and yet
continue being me.

I love my home, but still I want
to find my own small space.
I want to do my share to make
the world a better place.

Even though I'm happy
as a mother and a wife,
I yearn to have more purpose—
more fulfillment in my life.

Dear God, I'm grateful for this new door you have
opened. May I live up to your expectations.

NOVEMBER 22   **MASTER GARDENER**

God sows his seeds of wisdom,
but they cannot, will not, grow
in souls that lie beneath a crust
of hard red clay and rock.

But God's a master gardener,
and so he takes a hoe
and breaks through crusts
of selfishness, of evil ways, of sin—
for in the smallest crevices, his good seeds
can come in!

Dear God, thank you for being there with your hoe. Let
me know your ways so that my life may become a garden of
faith.

THANKFUL HEART

I am thankful today
for your world all around me,
for nature's array of colors
and the generous gifts from her earth.

I am thankful today
for the people in my world,
my loved ones, family, friends,
teachers, co-workers, preachers,
and everyone who touches my life.

I am thankful today
for this country of freedom,
freedom to speak, to think, to worship as I please,
freedom to work, to play, to rest in peace.

I am thankful today
for all that you planted within me,
feelings of ambition, drive, fervor, faith,
feelings of affection, sympathy, passion, and life.

But most of all, Lord,
I am thankful today for my soul,
for my kinship with you,
our partnership in life . . .
and life beyond!

Thank you, God, for everything!

NOVEMBER 24 **THANKSGIVING GRACE**

We thank you, Lord,
for bringing us
the bounty of the season,
and pray that there will come a time
when hunger is no more.

We thank you, Lord,
for giving us
this great land of the free,
and pray that people everywhere
will live in freedom, too.

We thank you, Lord,
for families,
for friendship and for love,
and pray your love will light the world
and someday we'll know peace.

Dear Lord, divine giver, thank you for everything you give, everything you do—everything you are!

NOVEMBER 25 **SLOWING DOWN**

I might not go as quickly
As I did in years gone by,
But I plant my feet more firmly
And I choose my paths with care.

I might not see nor hear as well
As I did years ago,
But my feelings are much deeper
And I've lots more love to share.

I might be getting older,
But I've finally reached the stage
Where life's so very precious,
I just don't mind my age!

Thank you, God, for every year, every day, every hour!

NOVEMBER 26 **WINTERTIME**

Bent from winds
and heavy storms
its gnarled branches bare,
the tree endures the winter's chill
and waits for spring to come.

And like that old
and weathered tree,
when sorrow chills my soul,
I go to God, who holds me close
till wintertime is done.

Thank you, God, for being there when I need you, for holding me in your loving arms and soothing me with your promises.

NOVEMBER 27 **SUCCESS**

Thank you, Lord, for this success.
I set, then reached, a goal,
And though I'm filled with happiness,
I know deep in my soul
I couldn't have done it all alone—
I've faith you were beside me
To help me through each step I took,
To lift me and to guide me.
So thank you, Lord, for this success,
It feels so good inside.
I pray that you are happy, too,
And also share my pride!

Thank you, God, for another step forward.

EDIFICE

Dear God, I'm truly puzzled
By your worshipers who claim
They need to build an edifice
In honor of your name—
Stained glass, brocades, and velvets,
And crystal chandeliers,
Dig deep and write a bigger check
To cover the arrears.

The money flows, the building grows.
How beautiful! How fine!
But does this lovely edifice
Fit into your design,
When elsewhere in the world, God,
In a place that's not so nice
Swollen-bellied starvelings
Stand waiting for some rice?

Dear Lord, thank you for hearing me. In my heart I feel
that any place is a place of prayer, and from your teaching I
know you value charity beyond stained-glass windows!

NOVEMBER 29   **RESPITE**

> There is a solitude,
> a quietness,
> to wintertime—
> long cozy nights
> made for meditation
> and prayer.
>
> I used to wonder
> why the new year
> didn't begin
> in the springtime,
> when all things
> are fresh and new.
>
> Perhaps it's the Lord's way
> to remind us
> that before a burst of newness
> comes a time of contemplation
> and prayer.

Dear Lord, thank you for this quiet, cozy winter day!

NOVEMBER 30   **THE HEART OF HAPPINESS**

> Happiness comes when we are close
> To those we cherish and hold dear.
> Happiness comes from memories
> Of joy-filled times of yesteryear.
> Happiness comes from dreaming dreams,
> From reaching for the stars above,
> From burning faith, from golden hope—
> Happiness comes from knowing love.

Thank you, loving God, for every happy thing, for every blessed memory, and for every golden dream.

Come, Lord Jesus

MARTHA WHITMORE HICKMAN

DECEMBER 1   **BEGINNING**

I begin this month of meditations with something of the same combination of dread and excitement that seems to adhere to the Christmas season. The wonder of Christmas—its gift—is constant and unshakable, though always a surprise. But will I be so preoccupied I'll miss it? Will I "get it right"? It's God who "gets it right," but will I be able to hear it, much less write it down for others to hear?

There is no time of year, I suppose, when one has to struggle harder to pay attention to God, to what is going on in the life of the spirit. All the commercialism, the pressure to buy, buy—expensive electronic gifts, toys, jewelry, extravagant clothing. Often things we don't need, can't use, and that might break before the day is over.

On the other hand, it is a gracious feeling to be thinking of one's special loves and of what could add joy to their lives. And people do seem more generously inclined toward the needy, and though these seasonal efforts are no substitute for working toward a more just society, still, burdens are lightened, hearts are made glad, at least for a little while.

And maybe the "little whiles" accumulate, for us as well as for the unfortunate, and maybe we get a sense of what it could be like if we really loved one another, not by our power (hopeless, in some cases!) but by the power that sent love into the world in the form of a child and sends love to us now. Even so, come Lord Jesus.

DECEMBER 2   **GIFT GIVING**

The matter of gift giving within our immediate family has been so much simpler for us—more sane, more in keeping with the season—since we agreed a few years ago, in our family of three sons and three daughters-in-law, to draw lots and buy one handsome present for one person, instead of trying to spread our resources and powers of decision and shopping time over so many people. We do each buy something for our spouses. And the children chose to pitch in on gifts for their grandparents—whom we also remember—and a special aunt.

It began the Christmas we were going to have sixteen people at our house. The thought of 240 presents being chosen, paid for, wrapped, unwrapped, and assimilated into households was too dizzying to contemplate. Even if we'd reduced it by giving gifts as couples, to couples, there would still have been close to 75 items purchased, exclaimed over, and stored in living spaces already well furnished.

So now we're doing it differently, and there's none of that panic of getting the right thing, of equalizing costs, of handling the sheer array of gifts. The season seems so much more generous, the smells in the kitchen more savory, the songs to waft onto a clearer air.

When we have grandchildren, perhaps that will change. Children change everything. As did the Holy Child.

DECEMBER 3   **PREPARING THE WAY**

The song from "Godspell" keeps going through my mind: "Pre-e-e-pare ye the way of the Lord, Pre-e-e-pare ye the way of the Lord." In the musical it's a Holy Week song, not an Advent song, but it works for now, too. Only perhaps it's stretching it a bit to think in Advent of Jesus in those swinging, marching words of welcome along the highway leading into Jerusalem. More appropriate to think in terms of "Away in a manger . . . the little Lord Jesus lay down his sweet head." We like to focus on that baby, the arrival of God in the world in the appealing form of an infant. No one can resist a baby. The joy of that baby is part of the rationale for the lights and the tinsel, the celebrations all over our streets, in our schools, in our public places.

Whom do we leave out? For whom is there no room in the spectacle of Christmas? For the poor, the homeless? For those of other faiths who must feel on the outside as a kind of civic faith takes over, blares itself all over the public consciousness? I have been aware of this for a long time but am perhaps more sensitive to it now that I have a Jewish daughter-in-law and know how painful some of her experiences of being on the outside have been.

In that kind of often mindlessly excluding climate, perhaps the Babe would again be found outside the gates of the city.

DECEMBER 4   **ADVENT SUNDAY**

We'll light the second candle in our Advent wreath. We always did it when the children were small. But the first Christmas after our daughter's death I felt I couldn't—any more than I could hang up the stockings with hers not there. The hope in Christmas? The Christian story of Jesus' life, death, and Resurrection? Oh, yes, that was what sustained us. But some of those symbols of family warmth—I couldn't re-enact them that year.

And having skipped the Advent wreath once, we let it go. Until a few years ago when, around Christmas time, a young friend who'd been a friend of our daughter's was staying with us. Her marriage had hit some rough spots, and she'd left home suddenly and driven a long distance to come to us. We'd had many long talks; she'd talked a number of times on the phone with her husband. They were going to try again to work out their differences. He was coming to see her at our house, and in the evening she set out for the airport to meet him.

While she was gone, we got out the Advent wreath for the first time, and with glad hearts at last, we lit the Advent candles, and then we got all the other candles from their musty drawers and put them all around the house. So that when this young couple drove into the driveway, there was a candle in every window and on the tables and the sideboard—every candle we had, a sign of Advent hope, to welcome them home.

DECEMBER 5   **CHRISTMAS LETTERS**

Less than three weeks now until Christmas Day. We are writing the last notes on our Christmas letters. Despite all the parodies, we still do a Christmas letter to duplicate and send to faraway friends and family. Even that mass produced effort seems to consume all our time and energy for at least a week in the rare and precious time of the Christmas season. Yet each name on our list brings its own warmth and memory—a kind of inner surge of love and care toward that person or family. I suppose it is a form of praying, this holding each person in the light of the season's love.

We love to receive the letters in return, to feel again the bonds of community and common life and love that hold us close to people we may not have seen for years but who continue to be important points of light in the constellation of our own particular night sky. Here are a distant cousin, an aging uncle, a young woman from a youth group of years past, a stranger we met at a conference who became an important friend, fellow pastors' families, and other professional colleagues who have become close friends. In gratitude for their lives and their presence in ours, in gratitude for the message of Christmas—of God with us, in commemoration of which we gladly lay aside the usual patterns of our lives and write these letters—we tender to them the joy of the season, the joy of the Lord.

DECEMBER 6 — **MORE ABOUT CHRISTMAS LETTERS**

I am thinking more about the Christmas letters we send and receive, and how they have changed over the years. When the children were young, we watched all year for a special accomplishment, an apt quote, that reflected that particular child, so that it became a family joke that if a child said something particularly noteworthy, one of the others would chime in, "Put it in the Christmas letter!"

Then the paragraphs about children became more a matter of school activities or music lessons or emerging vocational interests. And then acknowledgments of passages through high school and into college, and jobs and marriages.

We still cherish the opportunity to give at least a one-sentence account of what each of them is doing, as well as of our own activities, and perhaps a word on aging parents for those who have known and loved our families of origin, then an account of travels and family gatherings over the year.

And then, at last, an acknowledgment of the ancient mystery and wonder of God's gift to us in Jesus. It seems a small proportion of our letter in which to celebrate the event that gives our life so much of its meaning. And yet it is in the dailiness of our human lives that God's love comes to us—as in the so-human event of giving birth it came to Mary and Joseph in that stable of Bethlehem.

DECEMBER 7 — **PEARL HARBOR**

It's the anniversary of Pearl Harbor, and I think again of how changeable are the faces of our supposed national enemies. When a major Japanese presence was about to come to this southern state, the newspaper welcomed our new residents, the Art Center put on a Japanese tea ceremony at which there was an SRO crowd, and the opera company did a splendid performance of *Madama Butterfly*. We seemed to have bridged the chasm of our old anger.

Yet, I remember being on a boat touring Pearl Harbor. On board were large numbers of Japanese and Americans. The tour narration came over the loudspeaker in English and again in Japanese. A group of us, church people from the United States, wondered among ourselves whether we were getting the same message as that being given to the Japanese tourists. All felt a certain self-consciousness, looking stalwartly ahead as the descriptions and locations of damaged craft were given. We were all very polite. What would we say to one another if we spoke a common language?

There are times when the Tower of Babel, with its assurance of nonunderstanding, may be a convenience—if we can't speak with you, we can keep our distance. And yet at Pentecost, when many also spoke in different languages, the strength of the Gospel transcended the differences. I think of it on this anniversary, as we look toward the universal language of birth and hope and infinite love, which is Christmas.

DECEMBER 8   **UNUSED CALENDARS**

Cleaning out a desk drawer today, I came upon two unused calendars, one for this year, one for last. They are of a type we've often used and enjoyed; each month has a variety of quotations. My husband refers to them as "a smooth blend of the Bible and Benjamin Franklin." I have often found comfort and insight in the exhortations of the months as they pass.

But here, for two years, I've let them go by, unused. I felt sad, as though I had let the two years themselves go unheeded. I took time to read through each of them before I threw them away and still felt impoverished, as though I had shortchanged the equation of my life by not letting these insights speak to me month by month.

It isn't really that I am throwing time away. But it does

remind me—the passing relevance of calendars—of the poignant passing of time.

As we enter the deepest winter and look toward the turn of the year, the shadow of lost time and, ultimately, of death, hovers, sometimes uncomfortably close. In another calendar—one I *have* used—I came upon a quotation to the effect that death gives meaning to our love—that knowing life is passing, we continue to risk loving what we cannot keep.

This would be the case, whether or not I used every calendar I received. But it brought home to me how much I need my faith in a God who promises to be with us, in unfathomable love, forever.

DECEMBER 9   **MY BIRTHDAY**

I have mixed feelings about birthdays now—about being another year older and all that that implies.

But I think back to my childhood years and how the day loomed ahead, full of excitement, the unknown. I didn't mind at all having a December birthday. The intensity of the month, which came to include our wedding anniversary and the birthday of our first child, spread its magic over everything. Everything seemed heightened and luminous.

A childhood memory surfaces from the plumbline of birthdays. There came a year, somewhere in middle childhood, when the number of gifts (toys, trivia, etc.) went down. I was disappointed, though I felt guilty for even noticing. Looking for some redeeming aspect, I made mental calculations and realized that the monetary value of individual gifts was greater than usual. I said to my mother—probably trying to share my discomfort and its possible redeeming resolution—"Everything I got this year cost more than a dollar" (which bought a lot more than it does now). A look of displeasure crossed her face. She said, "Oh, don't be like that." I was ashamed of my mercenariness, disheartened by my mother's disapproval, and I regretted ever harboring such a thought.

I think of that exchange when I hear the term "original sin." It may not be what a theologian thinks of in terms of our egotism and its effects, but it says something to me.

DECEMBER 10   **ANOTHER BIRTHDAY GIFT**

One year on my birthday I received Andrew Lang's *Blue Fairy Book*. I have it still. On the cover the butterfly-winged fairy extends her hand to the kneeling prince in his rust-colored tunic. It contains magic enough for a lifetime of writing, and when I hold it in my hands, so do I.

When I think about why I became a writer instead of, for instance, a teacher or a social worker (both of which I considered for a "second vocation" after my children were launched), I think of this book and others of special significance that my parents gave me over the years. Books that appealed to the imagination. Books like the study on poetry they gave me at a time I didn't know I particularly cared for poetry. They could have misfired, if I'd felt pressured to be what I wasn't, or if the book was too wide of the mark. Books that said to me, "Maybe we know something fine about you that you don't even know yourself."

I like to think of gifts like these as little nudges from God, moderated through those who love us, into whose care we have been entrusted. They say, "See how I have loved you. See what you have the possibility to become." The affirmation in it swells the heart. And if we listen, the world is changed for us.

It is one of the better gifts we can give our children, or anyone, at Christmastime or on a birthday or at any time of the year.

DECEMBER 11   **ANOTHER ADVENT CANDLE**

In church today we lit the third candle of the Advent wreath.

A child always lights the new candle. (The pastor lights the first two; it would be too much for a six-year-old to light three candles on one match.) The chosen child comes forward with her teacher, who tells us who it is who is lighting the candle this morning.

I love to watch. The church is small. I can see the child's parents' faces, too. Such loving anxiety, such concentration as they sit on the edges of their chairs, hoping the child won't flub it, won't set herself on fire, drop the match, do something to embarrass herself or them—hoping she'll *succeed*. Maybe hoping, too, that the wonder and suspense, the participation, the *ownership* of this moment will imprint the child with faith, with wonder.

The match is struck, awkwardly handed to the eager child. The flame moves toward the candle, the congregation holds its breath, the teacher and pastor lean forward.

The wick catches, holds the flame. The child blows out the match (fortunately not blowing out the candle at the same time), turns shy and proud, and returns to her chair.

We all sit back, relaxed. We have weathered another crisis. The candle is lit. The warmth of Advent, of the child—and of the Child—has gladdened our hearts again. We are God's people. We have witnessed a wonder.

DECEMBER 12   **MY CHRISTMAS CRÈCHE**

Today I put up my Christmas crèche. I received it on my ninth birthday. I remember unwrapping the pieces one by one—Mary in her scarlet dress and blue cape, Joseph in his purple garment, the baby Jesus modeled in delicately painted wax, a golden paper halo affixed to his head. There are shepherds, the wise men, the camel, the pasteboard manger, the sheep resting on a fringe of hay.

The years jump ahead. One summer night, while all but my father were away from home, our house was struck by lightning. The damages spooked us all: a hole in the ceiling

above my bed, a heavy iron grate that fell on the floor at my father's feet as he ate a snack in the kitchen. The next day's paper carried a picture of our house, showing pieces of the roof scattered on the lawn.

One of the consequences of the lightning strike was that a fragment of roof timber pierced the box in which I stored my crèche and gouged the camel's side. So now I always place the camel facing left, so the wound won't show.

My children, respectful of my crèche, are skeptical that lightning really struck the camel. "Sure," they say, their voices verging on ridicule. I am staunch in my insistence. It is part of my own Christmas story, the long history of my crèche—the narrow escape from danger, the forces of nature scathing us in that way. My need to sensationalize? Or another way of saying Christmas is an astonishing story? Implausible things happen. Believe!

DECEMBER 13   **THE TIDDLYWINKS**

The tiddlywinks were another birthday gift, years ago, and they were a gift in more ways than one.

I was never a very athletic child. But I was very good at small-motor coordination. So I was good at tiddlywinks—press down the disc, shoot it into the cup. I cherished them for that reason. I cherished them also as precursor of things to come. I knew there were grander gifts to follow.

When, later in life, I learned the meaning of the word "penultimate"—almost ultimate, next-to-ultimate—I began to search in my writer's/believer's mind for analogies. And I thought of the tiddlywinks—the penultimate gift.

Then I thought, in one of those grand leaps that are sometimes crazy but may have a grain of truth in them nonetheless, that for a Christian, life itself may be the penultimate gift.

At its best moments, can we imagine anything more wonderful than this? I recall the writer Camus speaking of

the delights of life—the smell of flowers, the passion of lovers—and saying, "What is eternity to me?" Yet this is our claim: that beyond death are greater gifts of love, of God's presence, and it is that truth that Christmas, with its music, its hushed moments, its mystery and intimate wonder, foreshadows for us all.

DECEMBER 14   **DISINTERESTED IN GOD?**

There are days when I feel quite disinterested in God. Not hostile or denying, just, in terms of attending to or enthusiasm for, no particular interest. I continue to go through the motions—morning and evening prayers, the pause of silence before meals.

Sometimes that doesn't trouble me at all. But sometimes I miss the intensity, the sense of God's vitality, and wonder what I can do to make that more of a constant in my life. Like Brother Lawrence saying he could be as attuned to God while doing his kitchen work or yard work or whatever else as while on his knees at the blessed sacrament.

In taking one of the recurring "personality inventory tests," I learned I may be addicted to intensity! Always wanting conversations to be significant, relationships to be moved forward in profound ways. I never say, "It's a nice day, isn't it?" It's always "Tell me, how is your Life?"

Maybe I've been wanting the same of God. No run-of-the-mill ordinary days (especially during Christmas?). All days heightened with cosmic awareness.

Forget it! Sometimes I'm not particularly interested in my husband, either; I want to be left alone to pursue my own agenda, as he does his. But I know he's always there for me—for comfort, for presence. Is it the same with God? I need constant Being from God, but I don't need constant Attention. Maybe God feels the same way?

DECEMBER 15   **DIFFERENT PARTS OF THE DAY**

I am impressed again with the different quality of different parts of the day. For me, mornings are the time for innovation, for creative work, for feelings of adventure and that anything can happen. It is, in some ways, harder to pray in the morning; there is such an urge to move on into the day's work that to stop for meditation, to listen and absorb a presence, seems like foot-dragging.

But if it goes right, if I find a new freshness in some quiet moments, if a reading from the Bible or some other seminal work touches some creative nerve in my own consciousness, then it heightens that adventure of prayer too, and I find myself galloping along with some thought or awareness, some bubbling, holy delight. In prayer as in work, I have a sense that anything may happen. I'm prepared for a surprise!

In the afternoon or evening, when my own nature has quieted down and is beginning to grow tired, it's easier in some ways to pay attention to the Spirit. But my attention is thinner, less energetic. If there are surprises now, they will probably come from outside, not from within.

Maybe it's like going to school when I was a child: in the morning, the adventures all ahead, unknown; returning in the afternoon to security and rest, to the haven of home. So God can be the starter for the race or the quiet haven where, with encompassing love, the day is blest.

DECEMBER 16   **OUR WEDDING ANNIVERSARY**

How the years have accumulated! And what different groundswells and configurations they have had! Our first years—everything was new. We lived in a huge parsonage with two other divinity students and the wife and baby of one of them. It was a lot of relationships to manage at once.

Then we moved to our half-quonset hut and had the luxury of space to ourselves. There we brought our firstborn son home; life forever changed with that event.

Other children came. We moved around. The children

grew into adolescence. I had more time for writing but already dreaded their growing up and leaving us.

Then, of course, they did. And we were alone again. What a delight that has been, a surprise, almost—that life could be so good when that for which I had given much of the energy of body and mind and spirit for so many years had gone. And gone far. None of this everybody home for Sunday dinner every week. Of course, we're in close touch; we see each other as often as we can.

I relish the freedom to pursue my own work, and the time the two of us have together. Gracious developments—and I was fearful of how it would be.

I still miss the children; I long sometimes for the days when they were home all the time. But I may be longing for my own youth, for extra time to be alive, as much as for the daily presence of family.

DECEMBER 17   **THINGS I NEVER MANAGED**

There are so many things I'd like to have done and didn't. So many things to feel guilty about. Every Christmas season when the children were small, I thought how nice it would be to take each one on a separate shopping expedition, to savor the excitement of the sidewalks and the stores and then to come home. I never managed it.

Now I am berating myself for not taking time enough for meditation and prayer.

There is always some guilt handy to inflict on ourselves: regrets for past good ideas not followed up on, or for present ones that we're not doing better with. Justified recriminations? Perhaps. But probably not. Most of us do the best we can. Certainly this kind of wandering guilt isn't productive. It's also very egotistical—that somehow the world would have gone much better had we performed this or that a little more ably.

I was thinking of that today and how I would like to allow

myself freedom from this siege mentality. There is always so much to do.

Then I looked out the window, and it was snowing. Huge flakes drifted down slowly, settling on the pavement, softening the spiky branches of evergreens, rounding all the sharp corners, seeming to drop a stillness down.

It was its own prayer of peace and gentle quiet.

Thanks. Amen.

DECEMBER 18   **THE FOURTH CANDLE**

Sunday. We lit our fourth Advent candle. One more week to go.

Now that I've had to put writing on hold until after Christmas, I've been thinking of writing as gift.

In some ways it is a gift to the self—an indulgence, to pay that much attention to what one sees, to one's particular way of experiencing the world.

In another way, though, writing, particularly imaginative writing, is a complete surrender of the self. Defensive barriers must be dropped one by one, peeled back like the skin of an onion. All must be available to the muse, to the Other; nothing may be withheld.

The rich young ruler who went away sorrowing because he had great possessions is akin to the writer who wants to cap her wells of experience and creativity, saying, "Not there. Not available." But that is often where the richest (and riskiest) material lies. In one's heart one knows this—hence the going away sorrowful. It took me a long time to realize this.

It isn't peculiar to writers, of course. Anyone who tries to put his or her deepest resources into the service of God but holds back on what is most deeply cherished is experiencing the same thing.

The good news is that in giving it away, we are able to be

recipients of the gift we give to others—or to God, which is the same thing viewed through a different lens.

DECEMBER 19 **COPING WITH THE BAD NEWS**

The news in the paper is terrible. There are not only ongoing international crises, to which we sometimes become inured, but local tragedies too: a domestic fight ending in murder, a young doctor father found guilty of abusing his children, a family dispossessed just before Christmas for nonpayment of rent (though if the parents were divorced, public assistance would be readily available).

One is tempted to wonder how we dare tell the Christmas story in a world where there is so much suffering and injustice.

Leafing through the psalms, I came to Psalm 136, in which accounts of violence and injustice (attributed to God!) are alternated with the assertion, "His love is eternal."

Was the writer trying, on God's behalf, to produce a monumental piece of self-justification? Or is it a reminder that even in the midst of terror and disaster, God's love goes on and on and, equally scandalous, is available to us even as the world that God has made seems to find ever more ingenious ways to demean its children.

In spite of all this, in acknowledgment and defiance, we dare to continue to tell the story of the Nativity, about a family of travelers for whom there was no room in the established hospitality of the state or town. We hope the blessing we claim for this story, this family, can be ours as well.

DECEMBER 20 **A TIME FOR EXTRAVAGANCE**

The season accelerates. It is important to take time to steady myself, to find the Center, against the frazzle of the day.

And then, maybe, to forget. To just give in to the rhythm of the day, or its chaos, even.

In a way, Christmas is the time for extravagance. We can so easily go astray on this and get caught up in materialism, consumerism.

But the extravagance of love, of God's love for us—making such an all-out effort on our behalf, sending us the Babe, waiting for all the developmental stages to take their measured time—is an extravagance of a different kind. There was to be no quick, fully-arrived Christ. Instead, God slowly, patiently, probably anxiously stood by while the child grew to manhood. Did God ever wonder, "Is it worth it, this risk? What if he doesn't turn out right after all? All these years, all this energy, this power to accept or repudiate that I've given him—what if it was all a bad gamble?"

Why didn't God do some kind of quick magic act—pull some divine rabbit out of the hat—to show us the way? Because then we wouldn't have seen any continuity between Christ and ourselves. Because we wouldn't have seen him to be one of us. So that we could be one with him.

DECEMBER 21 **FAMILY ARRIVING**

The family is beginning to arrive. Waiting at the airport, I watch others greet their loved ones: the elderly, requiring wheelchairs; young people coming home to middle-aged parents; babies, passed to eager grandparents. I wonder about their stories. I pray that their visits will strengthen the bonds of love and custom that bring them here. That they will not find, as some do, that home is the hardest place to be at Christmastime, either because the year has brought losses unbearably painful or because the stress of being with family is so costly.

There is a special graciousness afloat here, too—a gift of the season, a contagion of love. Passengers waiting for luggage seem more relaxed, strangers nod as they brush past one another, the smiles bestowed on traveling children seem a little warmer than usual.

Last year our airline pilot son had to fly on Christmas Day. He told us on the phone that night that the chief pilot's wife had fixed a Christmas stocking for each crew member, filling it with tiny packages of toothpaste, Scotch tape, boxes of raisins and candy, all laboriously wrapped, to make it less painful to be away from family and home. And that the hotel where they stayed had fixed them a special festive meal.

It lightened our hearts, hearing him tell about these good people, manifesting the Spirit, honing in on God.

DECEMBER 22   **PUTTING UP THE TREE**

Today we put up our Christmas tree and all the old ornaments: the silver star my parents gave us for our wedding anniversary, the boys' plywood cutouts with their pictures pasted on the front that they made in Cub Scouts, the single ornament I brought from my childhood home.

We have friends whose home was totally destroyed by fire, and part of the loss of all that was, of course, the loss of just such "sacred objects" as old Christmas ornaments.

I know the dangers of idolatry and trust that I could, as these friends have done, rebuild a life without the things that have such symbolic meaning for me: the *Blue Fairy Book,* the family photos, a coffee mug my daughter bought for me the year before she died. A revered professor, talking of this attachment to things, said, "We try to sit loose to our possessions." And we do. I admire the grace with which my husband's parents moved from their large home of forty-five years to a small apartment, with never a complaint. It may be so for us, too, one day. Surely our need for things and the space needed to keep them in will condense as we get older.

But in the meantime, as the title of the poem puts it, "Love Calls Us to the Things of This World." If matter didn't matter, if spirit were all, what need of the Incarnation, of

God made flesh? The Christmas trees, the candles, the clumsy honored Christmas ornaments made by our children carry their special grace.

DECEMBER 23   **PETER'S BIRTHDAY**

Our son will be here by evening, flying in with his wife. We will have his gifts, piled on his chair. We'll have his favorite dinner, then his cake, decorated around the outside as always with stick figures, mini-panoramas of significant events in his life this past year.

We began this custom years ago, when I was sole cook and cake decorator. Now others give suggestions and his geologist brother wields the cake decorator, drawing the symbols: a picture of an airplane, a new house, a diminutive woman with long hair—his wife. What else? Garden tools, a fisherman seated on a bank with swarms of fish lining up to be caught. And always, since the year we ran out of ideas and turned suddenly corny, an ascending staircase with a figure climbing from the first rung to the second: "the stairway of life." Everyone is always on the first step, no matter how old he or she is. It is our mutual joke but also an acknowledgment that our love is eternal.

At the table after the song is sung and the birthday candles are blown out, the honoree slowly turns the cake, guessing what each of the symbols means while the rest of us watch in rapt attention. It is one of our family's most cherished rituals, holy to us, overlain with years of saying in this way to one another, "I know you. I honor who you are. I am grateful for your life."

DECEMBER 24   **CHRISTMAS EVE**

There are only a few things left to be done. Such a change from those years when we'd get the children to bed and, already tired, do our work of wrapping and putting things under the tree and filling the stockings.

It's no wonder Christmas is a hard time for some people—a built-in invitation to nostalgia and regret. I've never felt we did Christmas Eve as well as the occasion called for. I've heard of families who, in assembled tranquility, gather in candlelight to hear the reading of the Christmas story and, in some kind of holy hush, experience the truest meaning of Christmas. We seemed always to be too busy for that.

Or families who, though they may never go at other times, betake themselves to church or cathedral and at midnight join in the ethereal songs heralding the Savior's birth. We never did that either. The children were too small, or their father had responsibilities at our own church that took him away.

Now that we are freer, could do what we want, it seems too late to adopt those customs. Someone always has last-minute wrapping to do. We may sing a few carols around the piano. But mostly we perform our small tasks and enjoy one another's company. I am a bit regretful, though it may not be a bad way, this going on with the dailiness of life, to celebrate God's coming into human life in human likeness.

DECEMBER 25   **CHRISTMAS DAY**

Holy God, it is Christmas Day. A long-awaited day, this particular Arrival of you, in mystery and heralding.

My mind drops back. The baby, the story always speak of early securities, of primal experience.

There is the Christmas I was recovering from a long illness and had a little tree by my bed; my father carried me downstairs so I could be on the couch for a while, with the others. There is the Christmas my sister and I received my mother's legendary childhood dolls, each outfitted with a wardrobe of beautiful new clothes she had made for us.

There is the Christmas we delayed opening our gifts until my grandmother came, and I crouched by my bed rereading the most exciting book I had, to try and make the wait bearable.

The children we were grew up. We learned to moderate our expectations, learned a more measured appreciation of the season, and that there are sometimes aspects of Christmas that lie heavy on our hearts.

But maybe the children were closer to the truth—the astonishment of a Christmas tree where there used to be a table or a chair; gifts unmeasurable, poured out and running together; festivity reaching to the edge of all the universe we know.

In the words from Charles Dickens, "Merry Christmas! . . . May God bless us every one!"

DECEMBER 26   **THE DAY AFTER**

The first flush of Christmas has passed. Today it is good to rest in all of what has been done, to rest in the presence of the family, to read the new books, to try on the new clothes, to put back the pieces of tinsel that have been jostled onto the carpet.

The paper today makes reference to that parade of misery that used to be an annual event of Christmas journalism: accounts of "the 100 neediest cases." Growing up, I read some of them with a mixture of voyeurism and compassion. I don't think we ever made extra gifts on behalf of any of these unfortunate people, though we certainly contributed regularly to church and charity.

It is always a high-wire balancing act, deciding how much to engage in the abundance of the world's pain and when it has become unnerving enough to make us ineffective in those our tasks.

How much of an environment that sustains us is it legitimate to surround ourselves with, when there are so many in need? I think of that with the house full of food and laughter and love. The gift of Christmas is ambiguous; it implies responsibilities both intimate and global to the self and to the world.

But today feels like a time for rest and regathering, for savoring, after all the hurry of the season, the blessings of *this* day.

DECEMBER 27   **A MESSAGE FROM AUDEN**

For years Hoyt and I read aloud to each other, in preparation for Christmas Day, W. H. Auden's long poem, "A Christmas Oratorio." We've not done it lately; perhaps we wore out the custom. The last section is much quoted. The poet speaks of our realization that we have overindulged, expected too much of ourselves, that we are now faced with the uneasy anticipation of Lent and Good Friday. Good cautionary words.

But there is another section I remember with gratitude each year, to the effect that the Christmas message beams its good news to all—to the powerless as well as the powerful, to betrayed lovers, to the aged about to die. In all situations, Christmas makes possible rejoicing, a laughing in the face of any despair.

It is not a denial of responsibility, any more than Jesus' appreciation of the woman who poured perfume over his feet and washed them with her hair is a denial of responsibility for caring for the needy. But there are moments of disclosure and joy that transcend logic and make a reasoned morality a dull, secondary consideration. Like the blind man shouting, "I was blind, and now I see!" Or like Henri Nouwen going to Central America to "help" and finding himself caught up anew in the joy of life.

In the legends, even the animals broke forth in song.

DECEMBER 28   **THE WISE MEN**

It was such a surprise to find that the wise men didn't arrive at the manger on Christmas Eve, along with the shepherds and the angels! In the pictures and tableaux, in the crêches, they were all there, standing around, offering their gifts and songs, their adoration.

But no, according to the ancient stories, they traveled for twelve days and got there on January 6. In the crêches of some cultures the figures representing the wise men progress through the house during the twelve days after Christmas, finally arriving at the manger. By Twelfth Night, I suppose, the holy family was used to the baby and ready for company.

Or they were ready to travel to avoid the slaughter ordered by Herod, so fearful for his throne that he ordered all male infants killed. It is another scandal of history that we often gloss over—until we hear in our imaginations the voice of Rachel, weeping for her children.

Already the supreme gift of God-became-flesh, become one of us, was escalating in cost. And we know what terror lies ahead before the joy of Easter morning.

It was probably well for Mary and Joseph that they didn't know, as it is probably well for us not to know what the future holds. We only need to know that in all circumstances the gift of Christmas will hold true, will redeem all circumstances with its promise of ultimate joy.

DECEMBER 29   **EVALUATING OUR WORK**

Incorporating the new Christmas books into the bookshelves, I think back to my own writing projects this past year. Some haven't succeeded, at least so far. Yet I felt called to them and continue to work at them.

What to do with that? When to quit revising, querying new editors, trying to sell what I have done? And if I can't sell it, what is its value to me?

Recently I talked with a friend about a project I had taken on with mixed feelings and recently completed. He listened carefully, was quiet a minute, and then he said, "Well, was it a blessing? Or not?"

It came to me, along with gratitude for his loving attention, that that really was the question. As Thoreau said, that no one is ever misled by a calling if it refreshes his or her life. Given the underlying assumptions that we will not choose something destructive of life and that economic necessity doesn't overrule our choice, subjective reasons are what validate a vocation, finally. As they must have for Jesus, wondering whether to jump down from that temple, wondering whether to turn stones to bread.

Something in the educationed intuition tells us.

"Was it a blessing? Or not?" my friend asked.

"Yes," I said, "it was."

DECEMBER 30   **THE CHILDREN LEAVING**

Of course I'm feeling sad, let down.

I always wonder how many more times will they be here, these children who grew up under our daily care and now return to our roof, our beds, our table, perhaps once a year. We see them other places—in their own homes, at vacation spots where we gather for family reunions.

But it has a different meaning, having them come home—though home has been many houses for them. Will they come perhaps fifteen more times, twenty even? Maybe a month's worth of days and nights when it used to be all the days and nights of the year we were together.

One of them spoke of it. "It surprises me, how we come here each year, and the years go by, and we all get older."

The passing of time. The passing of people, as grandparents grow frail and die. Worse than that, for many, including us. Our daughter, their sister, was killed on a summer's ride. The first Christmas afterward was almost unbearable, so we went away. The second was not much better. The grief remained unspoken until late on Christmas Eve, we gathered in the living room with our arms around one another and cried, acknowledging our grief. "Now maybe we can enjoy Christmas," one of her brothers said.

The deepest, most sustaining gift of Christmas is surely our hope of being together again, of eternal life in God. It is that which makes our temporal separations less painful, too. How many years left? How many times? Always.

DECEMBER 31 **NEW YEAR'S EVE**

The turning of the year. Growing up. I wrote in my diary my annual parade of adolescent thoughts on relinquishing the old year and beginning the new. I now use more sophisticated language, but I have the same feelings still. What will the year bring? What should I be doing with my life?

Last summer at a retreat in the country, I walked very early one morning to a lake at the top of the hill. As I approached I saw it was covered with early morning mist; the whole thing was obscured by vapory clouds.

But as I got closer I saw that while most of the lake was hidden, the section directly in front of me was not. The mist had lifted right here. The water was clear. I saw weeds and grasses, saw tiny fish swim beneath the surface.

I left this patch of mist-free shore and walked around to the other side of the lake, where the mist was still settled against the curving shoreline. But as I approached I saw the same thing was true—the water directly in front of me was clear. It was the distant surface that always lay under cloud.

So maybe the year ahead will be like that—the distant places will be unclear, shrouded in mist, but in front of me, where the next steps are to be taken, it will perhaps be quite clear. I will take one step at a time.

Who knows, if I am faithful enough, perhaps I can even walk on this water!